recipes simple

ravioli poultry

vegetables bak

fillets roastec

sauces wine

stir-fries on

drizzle purée

quick

sauces appetizer

greens sear toss

cutlets whisk

no-hassle sauce

How to
Cook
Without a
Book

basics skillet

hearty drizzle

soothing

deglaze fresh

pan sauces

stir-fries wine

simmer quick roast

chutney relish

vinaigrette

cutlets spreads

turnover bake

How to Cook Without a Book

Recipes and Techniques Every Cook Should Know by Heart

PAM ANDERSON

Broadway Books   New York

BROADWAY

Broadway Books titles may be purchased for business or promotional use or for special sales. For information, please write to: Special Markets Department, Random House, Inc., 1540 Broadway, New York, NY 10036.

BROADWAY BOOKS and its logo, a letter B bisected on the diagonal, are trademarks of Broadway Books, a division of Random House, Inc.

Visit our website at www.broadwaybooks.com

Library of Congress Cataloging-in-Publication Data

Anderson, Pam, 1957–
How to cook without a book : recipes and techniques every cook should know by heart /
Pam Anderson.—1st ed.
p.   cm.
ISBN 0-7679-0279-3
1. Quick and easy cookery.   I. Title.
TX833.5.A46 2000
641.5'55—dc21   99-043776

FIRST EDITION

Designed by Lee Fukui

01   02   03   04   10   9   8

To Gabrielle and Melissa,

who sassed up this book and

spiced up my life.

crispy creamy
pan sauce deglaze
relish roast

ACKNOWLEDGMENTS

Thanks to:

Harriet Bell, who got it, loved it, and bought it.

Sarah Jane Freymann, who always knows the way.

Amy Root, who came up with the perfect title for this book.

Roberto de Vicq de Cumptich, whose jacket design perfectly captures the tone and feel of this book.

Rebecca Holland and Ralph Fowler, whose editorial and design direction took it up a notch.

Michael Anderson, who took the time to improve each rhyme.

Serge and Betty Beccari, who showed me that eating well doesn't have to be difficult.

Jane and Jim Faraco, who taught me how to make ravioli out of wonton wrappers.

To all the food people in my community who help me eat and drink well every day:

Brian McCabe at Coté and Co.

Kate Hannan and John Arntz at House of Coffee

Dick Phillips and George Garrison at Phillips Fine Wines

Greg Heller and Scott Espenshade at Heller's Seafood

Micky Flood, Bob Seminack, Lena George, Vince Mirack, Jack Ennis, Mike D'Ambrosia, George Brundage, and Paul Comuso at the Delray Thriftway.

And to David, Maggie, and Sharon, with whom I am privileged to break bread almost every day.

CONTENTS

crispy creamy
pan sauce deglaze
relish roast

big bowl vegetables herbs spices hearty fresh

How to
Cook
Without a
Book

INTRODUCTION

I grew up eating good food. My mother and father, grandmother and aunts were all great Southern cooks. As a child I'd watch my grandmother make biscuits and pies by sight and feel. I don't think she owned a measuring cup or spoon; she certainly didn't own a cookbook.

I'd spend hours in the kitchen with my mother and aunts as they prepared for big family dinners—barbecue pork, coleslaw, turkey with cornbread dressing, banana pudding, peach cobbler. I never saw anyone open a cookbook. Everybody knew how to make what was on the menu. And, by God, everybody did it the same way.

Pretty soon I became an apprentice. One of my early jobs was making potato salad. My aunt handed me the ingredients, a large bowl, and a paring knife. She expected and trusted me to do the job. No cookbook. She tasted the salad and told me to stir in a little more mustard or give it another round of salt.

The menu was pretty simple back then. Vegetables were cooked one way: seasoned with a chunk of fatback and simmered for hours. Fish and chicken were mostly fried, and cornbread was our baguette. We had one kind of lettuce, two kinds of pasta—macaroni and spaghetti—and lunch meat meant bologna. Mushrooms, spinach, green peas, and black olives came from a can.

1

The limited ingredients and techniques made cooking very simple. My grandmother didn't need a cookbook. Every recipe was in her head and hands. Only when their memories failed would my mother and her sisters pull out *The Auburn Cookbook* (a product of the Auburn University home economics department) to remind them of their formula for divinity candy, 1-2-3-4 cake, and pecan pie.

Clearly, times have changed. Unlike our ancestors, we can buy or mail-order almost any ingredient we want from anywhere in the world. We also have much choice in how we prepare and cook these ingredients. Rather than incorporating all the new ingredients and techniques into our repertoire, however, we seem confused by it all. Bewildered by a world of choice, we seem to have lost our way.

Unlike my mother with her single preparation for green beans, I have many options. Should I snap them as she did, French them, leave them whole, or opt for haricots verts? Should I cook them for hours the way Mom did? Or should I steam, blanch, grill, broil, braise, roast, or even stir-fry them? Should I serve them hot, at room temperature, or even chilled with a dressing? Should I serve them unadorned or infuse them with flavors from the Far East, Far West, or someplace in between?

My mother bought green cabbage. I can buy green, red, Napa, Savoy, and even bok choy. I still buy the occasional can of California black olives, but I'm more inclined to buy kalamatas, picholines, niçoise, or those that have been cured in oil. I can't count the number of pasta shapes I can buy at my local grocery store.

Unlike my grandparents and parents, I own a roomful of cookbooks. I have cookbooks not only of remote and distant countries, but of specific regions within those countries.

Yet with a glut of cookbooks and an abundance of available ingredients, no one seems to know how or what to cook. For many, dinner means opening up a take-out carton, and "from scratch" means heating up a jar of spaghetti sauce.

What we grew up with doesn't work anymore, yet a new way of cooking is not clear. With our broadened palates, available ingredients, yet busier schedules, we need to discover one. Like our parents and grandparents, we need to learn how to cook without recipes.

Learning to Cook Without a Book

My learning to cook without a book was a slow process, one I'm still learning. I write about food for a living, and I cook a lot, but I'm no culinary purist, nor a glutton for punishment. Although I think dinner is important, and our family eats very well, I don't spend hours a day in preparation. Like the rest of the work force, I usually turn my attention to dinner each night at the last moment. I take shortcuts whenever I can, and rarely have much more than thirty minutes for weeknight dinner preparation.

There was a time when my family knew every cheap restaurant in town. We'd dine in or take out almost as many nights as we'd cook. It wasn't that we loved eating out so much, and it wasn't that I didn't know how to cook (I could fry chicken and braise a pot roast with the best), I just hadn't figured out a simple way of getting dinner on the table, night after night.

Typically, we'd come home from work with no idea what to have for dinner. I'd open the refrigerator door and stare. I saw individual ingredients—not dinner potentials. I knew a few recipes, but I didn't know how to make something out of whatever we had. If figuring out dinner required going to the grocery store or paging through a cookbook at that hour, we'd head for Chi Chi's or order Chinese every time.

Over the years we tried solving our weeknight dinner problems by following cookbook advice. Some suggested we prepare stews, casseroles, and soups for the coming week. Although this approach worked some of the time, we often found ourselves as busy on the weekends as we were during the week (or sick of chili by Thursday). We also tried the bake and freeze approach. As with weekend cooking, we weren't consistently organized enough for this style of cooking to work.

Other cookbooks offered recipes based on minimal time or ingredients. Some recipes worked. Many, however, felt contrived or extravagant, or relied heavily on processed ingredients. All of these Band-Aid approaches worked some of the time, but we needed help getting dinner on the table with whatever time and ingredients we had on hand.

Ultimately I realized that we didn't need more recipes; we needed to learn to cook without them. With a decently stocked pantry and the grasp of a few basic techniques, we found that eating well could be very simple.

Over the years, we began to develop our own way of cooking without recipes, internalizing basic cooking techniques and memorizing simple formulas that worked for the way we ate during the week. Now, if we've got a few ingredients in the refrigerator or pantry, chances are we've got a technique that will help us turn those ingredients into dinner.

On those bone-weary nights when following the cooking instructions on the back of a box (much less a full-blown recipe) feels like too much, dinner's got to come from just knowing what to do. You've got to be able to fire up a skillet and go with what you've got. The last thing you need on a night like that is following a recipe. The words simply get in the way of what you need to do.

How to Cook Without a Book addresses the problem we all face three times a day: how to feed ourselves and those we love. This book teaches you how to prepare a meal based on available ingredients, limited time, and a simple cooking technique, not on a recipe you need to look up calling for ingredients you don't have.

Give a man a recipe,
he eats a meal.
Teach a man to cook,
he eats for a lifetime.

There may be millions of recipes, but there are only a handful of cooking techniques. You don't need to memorize recipes to cook without a book, you just need to learn a few techniques.

Five years ago if someone had asked me to make seared sea scallops with a lemon parsley sauce, I'd have said, "Give me the recipe." Since then I have learned not only how to sear, but also that the technique is virtually the same regardless of what I'm searing. I have also developed a two-minute pan sauce. Now, without cracking a book, I can make that scallop dish, or sear a New York strip steak with a horseradish pan sauce, or sear pork tenderloin medallions with an apple cider pan sauce.

I have learned a technique for stir-fry and have internalized a formula for making quick soup using whatever meat and vegetables I have around. And if I've got eggs, we've got supper now that I know how to make a big omelet or frittata for four.

When making pasta with vegetables, I know there are two kinds of vegetables— firm ones that cook with the pasta and soft ones that sauté with the garlic. With that kind of knowledge I no longer need a different recipe for spaghetti with broccoli and red pepper flakes or penne with bell peppers and capers. One formula works for both, or for any other vegetable I may have. The same is true for pasta with tomato sauce. With a 28-ounce can of crushed tomatoes, a few tablespoons of fat, and an onion or a couple of garlic cloves, you have the foundation for scores of different tomato sauces. You don't need one recipe for tomato sauce with sausage and peppers and another for tomato sauce with tuna and olives.

If I've got a baguette, I can make toast rounds, and chances are I have something in the refrigerator or pantry to make a spur-of-the-moment hors d'oeuvre. With a sheet of puff pastry, a bar of chocolate, and a jar of jam, I've got turnovers for dessert without ever peeking at a recipe.

And you can too. *How to Cook Without a Book* teaches quick, easy-to-grasp techniques—ones that will get you through the week and help you entertain with ease.

How to Cook Without a Book is simple to understand and easy to use. Chapters are divided into individual techniques and formulas. Taking them one at a time—divide-and-conquer style—makes them easy to master.

In *How to Cook Without a Book,* each chapter consists of five components:

- A mnemonic rhyme
- A step-by-step narrative of how the technique works
- A recipe, presenting the technique in its simplest form
- Simple variations, exemplifying how the technique works
- The key points of each technique at-a-glance

Each chapter begins with a playful rhyme capturing the technique's essence in verse. Not only is the rhyme a nutshell introduction to the chapter, it becomes the culinary cue card once the technique is mastered. For example, after reading the sauté chapter, the following verse may be all you need to remember the technique:

Heat butter and oil, swirling them around,
Add meat, seasoned and coated, and cook until beautifully browned.

The rhyme is followed by a step-by-step explanation of the technique. In this walk-through, you learn everything you need to know about the technique or formula to ensure success—the right ingredients, the right size pan and how to heat it, pitfalls, and formula variations. After reading the step-by-step, you will be confident enough to get in the kitchen and give it a whirl.

To reinforce what you've read, key points are highlighted as a reminder. For the novice cook, the technique or formula is written in detailed recipe form, but after following it once or twice, you may need only to review the highlighted points to make the dish.

Technique and formula variations follow the recipe. You may follow them or use them for inspiration, but they are in no way exhaustive. After trying a few of them, you will be ready to spread your culinary wings and create your own variations.

I love to cook and entertain, but cooking every night is a commitment. You do it whether you feel like it or not. As with any discipline, you may not love every minute of the process, but you appreciate the results.

We still go out for a cheap midweek supper now and again, but with a decently stocked pantry and refrigerator coupled with techniques and formulas I know by heart, it's a whole lot easier to say, "Set the table. We're eating dinner at home tonight."

The Right Stuff Stocking
the Refrigerator, Freezer, and Pantry

Cooking without a book starts with a well-stocked refrigerator and pantry. One of the signs of a successful businessperson is how few times she handles the same piece of mail. To me, one of the signs of a successful working cook is how few times she shops for food.

For want of any meal planning, many cooks end up repeatedly running to the store. Since most American family schedules are erratic and unpredictable, long-term meal planning can be frustrating, but running to the grocery store every day or two also takes time and energy that most people just don't have.

On vacation, I shop every day because I enjoy it. When I work, however, I try to stock up once a week, running back maybe once more if I'm entertaining or I've left something off the list. Every few weeks I go to my gourmet store for olives, cheese, oil, vinegar, and other pantry items. I also stop at a good bakery for French and Italian bread, which I freeze.

I take time to shop because if I find myself with an empty refrigerator at 6:00 on Wednesday night, I'm more likely to grab the family and head for a restaurant. Surrounding yourself with good food is the first step in effortless cooking.

In stocking my freezer, refrigerator, and pantry, I'm neither frugal nor extravagant. Sometimes I get hit with sticker shock at the checkout, but when I think of what I would

7

have spent if our family had gone out for dinner even once during the week, I quickly realize that food shopping is a bargain.

The following pantry, refrigerator, and freezer lists may look long. Although many of the items are necessities (e.g. canned tomatoes, chicken stock, salt, onions, garlic, oil, vinegar), others are not. Simply pick and choose from each list what looks good and makes sense for you. Besides, you probably have many of the ingredients in your kitchen now. And, once you're stocked, it's just a matter of replenishing the supply now and again. As time goes on, you will internalize the list and automatically know what's missing from week to week.

Poultry, Meat, and Fish

Depending on your preferences, keep the following in your refrigerator or freezer. Unless you plan to use it within a day or two of purchase, freeze all meat, poultry, and fish. They can be defrosted in the refrigerator or microwaved to room temperature at the last minute.

Poultry

- Boneless skinless chicken breasts (or thighs)
- Whole chickens
- Chicken wings
- Turkey cutlets (or boneless skinless turkey breast that can easily be sliced into cutlets)
- Ground turkey
- Turkey or chicken sausages
- Duck breasts

Beef

- Boneless New York strip steaks
- Boneless rib-eye steaks
- Filet mignons
- Ground chuck

Pork

- Thick-cut boneless pork chops or boneless rib-end pork loin roast for cutting into chops
- Pork tenderloin for cutting into medallions
- Raw and cooked sausage (Italian, chorizo, andouille, or kielbasa)
- Bacon
- A hunk of deli-style baked ham (or turkey). After letting package after package of sliced-to-order deli meat spoil within a few days of purchase, I've started buying larger pieces of these meats. This way the meat lasts much longer, and I can cut it the way I want—slices for sandwiches, julienne for salads, small dice for omelets, and large dice for soup. If you can't use what you've bought within a week, divide it and freeze one half.

Fish and Shellfish

- Shrimp
- Any fish fillet, such as thick flounder, catfish, snapper, tilapia, grouper, or other thin, white-fleshed fish
- Any fish steak, such as tuna, swordfish, or salmon
- Jumbo dry scallops
- Littleneck, top neck, or small cherrystone clams, eaten within a day or two of purchase
- Mussels, eaten within a day or two of purchase

Food for the Freezer

- Frozen green peas, spinach (two 10-ounce packages of spinach serve four people), and corn. On the nights when the vegetable bin is low or you need an instant vegetable, it's nice to look in the freezer and find something. It's also good to have corn on hand for soups and chowders, and for freshening up quick polenta.
- Good-quality bread. Well-made bread can turn a good meal into a great one. I shop for bread once every couple of weeks. I buy and freeze at least four baguettes, some crusty rolls for soup, and often a loaf of raisin bread or challah for breakfast.

- A quart of premium vanilla ice cream. Having a quart of vanilla ice cream in the freezer is like having a little black dress in the closet. Adorned or not, it's the ultimate quick dessert.

- Two packages of frozen fruit such as strawberries, blackberries, or blueberries. With frozen fruit on hand you can have a cobbler in the oven in ten minutes. They're also handy for baking a batch of muffins on the weekend.

- Frozen puff pastry. This is one of my favorite convenience products. If I've got a sheet of puff pastry, I can whip out turnovers, tarts, and quick cookies with very little effort and no recipe.

Food for the Refrigerator

- Buy fresh seasonal vegetables and fruits that keep well, then store them properly.

- In addition to seasonal fruits and vegetables, I almost always have the following on hand:

Carrots	Cucumbers
Celery	Red or yellow peppers
Parsley and other fresh	Cabbage
herbs on occasion	Lemons
Romaine hearts and	Limes
other lettuces	

- Although the following vegetables are not stored in the refrigerator, they are included in this section. For extended life, keep them in a cool, dark place.

Baking potatoes	At least one red onion
Red boiling potatoes	A couple of heads of garlic
A bag of yellow onions	Gingerroot

Besides low-fat milk, I keep the following dairy items in the refrigerator:

- Milk

- Eggs

- Butter

- Buttermilk. Since it has a relatively long shelf life, I use it for pancakes, muffins, biscuits, and corn muffins

- Heavy cream. Like buttermilk, heavy cream has a long shelf life and it's great to have around for impromptu entertaining and simple pan sauces

- Three or four cheeses of your choice. A good sharp cheddar, some sort of blue or goat cheese, a chunk of Parmigiano-Reggiano, and a bar of cream cheese are my favorites.

- Low-fat plain yogurt for making yogurt cheese and desserts. If not used for those purposes, it can always be sweetened and eaten for breakfast.

Food for the Pantry

General Pantry

• large and small cans of low-sodium chicken broth • bottled clam juice • cans of crushed and whole tomatoes packed in purée • canned tuna • canned clams • anchovies or anchovy paste • evaporated milk • peanut butter • honey • jam and/or jelly • dried mushrooms • oils: olive, sesame, and vegetable • 1 jar roasted red peppers • pastas: spaghetti, macaroni, egg noodles, and couscous • grains: long-grain white rice, instant polenta • Dijon mustard • capers • vinegars: red and white wine, balsamic, and rice wine • ketchup • barbecue sauce • bottled horseradish • soy sauce • Asian fish sauce • marinated artichokes • canned beans: black, white, and chickpeas • mayonnaise • dried breadcrumbs • dried fruit: raisins or currants and cranberries • 1 jar each: piquant black olives such as kalamata and green olives

Baking

• all-purpose flour • salt • cornmeal • granulated sugar • light or dark brown sugar • baking powder • baking soda • unsweetened and bittersweet chocolate • chocolate chips • unsweetened cocoa powder • vanilla extract

Herbs and Spices

• basil • bay leaves • ground black pepper • ground cinnamon • ground cloves • ground cumin • curry powder • herbes de Provence • ground nutmeg or whole nutmeg for grating fresh • oregano • hot red pepper flakes • sage leaves • dried thyme leaves

In addition to keeping a well-stocked freezer, refrigerator, and pantry, I try to keep a few cooked ingredients on hand as well.

- Cooked potatoes, pasta, or rice. I often cook twice as much as I need. Later in the week, I'll make hash browns, fried rice, or lo mein with the leftovers.
- Boiled eggs. As with potatoes, I boil more than I need. I'll use them over the course of the week for salads and appetizers.
- Tomato sauce. This is an easy recipe to double. Changing the flavoring ingredients, I often serve it twice during the week—once as a pasta sauce, then as pizza sauce or over polenta.
- Little bits of leftover cooked meat and fish. These can be used to beef up first-course salads and egg dishes, and, of course, are perfect candidates for hors d'oeuvres.
- Toasted nuts (walnuts or pecans and almonds). They always taste better toasted than raw, so I regularly toast a cup or two of walnuts and almonds and use them for tossing into salads as well as cooked rice and couscous.

Whack and Toss Salads

Drizzle salad with oil, salt, and pepper, then toss until just slick.
Sprinkle in some vinegar to give it a little kick.

I like to eat seasonally, but up to a point. I don't eat tomatoes and corn on the cob in January, and I try to wait until spring to eat asparagus and artichokes. Lettuce is where I draw the line. Our family loves salad, and we eat it year-round. Rather than serving the same salad spring, summer, winter, and fall, I combine lettuce with other seasonal ingredients—pears in fall, apples in winter—so there is no mistaking a winter salad for one I'd serve in the summer.

Lettuce and Other Salad Greens

I buy a variety of salad greens, but I always have a package or two of romaine hearts in the refrigerator. Unlike the packaged salad mixes that taste like a bad salad bar, romaine hearts are wonderfully convenient and fresh.

For weeknight salads, figure about $1\frac{1}{2}$ cups of lettuce per person. When using romaine hearts, you don't need to measure, knowing that each heart yields about 4 cups. Halve the hearts lengthwise. Any unused hearts should be left attached to the cores—they stay fresher that way.

Working with one half at a time, whack off the core and discard it. Leaving the heart intact, cut it lengthwise three or four times, then crosswise into bite-size pieces. Toss the cut lettuce into a salad spinner, rinse, spin, then transfer it to a serving bowl.

I cut other long-leaf lettuces, like red and green leaf lettuce and whole romaine, the same way with two exceptions. I remove some of the thicker ribs at the base. To ensure that the broader leaves near the top are bite-size, I also make a few extra lengthwise cuts as I chop.

Round heads of lettuce are easy to chop, too. For iceberg, rap the head, core side down, on the counter top to loosen the core and make it easy to pull out. Halve the cored lettuce, chopping each half lengthwise and crosswise into bite-size pieces. I chop Boston lettuce as I do iceberg, but the core can be easily removed without rapping on the counter.

Although my kids are not wild about salads made exclusively with bitter greens, they will eat Belgian endive, radicchio, watercress, and arugula when mixed with milder lettuces. Very often, I mix one romaine heart with two to three cups of the bitter greens.

When I want a nicer looking salad for a special dinner, I take a little more time with the lettuce, removing the ribs and tearing the leaves, but for week nights, I cut it up quickly and get it in the bowl.

Salad Servings

Here's how much lettuce to expect from an average size head of each of the lettuces and bitter greens. Unless you're serving small children, figure about 1½ cups of lettuce per person.

- 1 head Belgian endive equals a scant 2 cups chopped
- 1 medium head radicchio equals about 4 cups torn or chopped leaves
- 1 medium head iceberg equals about 8 cups chopped
- 1 medium head romaine equals about 12 cups, chopped or torn
- 1 medium head red or green leaf equals about 8 cups, chopped or torn
- 1 head Boston equals about 5 cups chopped or torn
- Watercress and arugula—packaging varies

Salad Extras

Unless the lettuce is garden fresh and tossed with real vinaigrette—an emulsified dressing made of olive oil, vinegar, minced garlic or shallot, and Dijon mustard—eating plain lettuce is as boring as eating two slices of bread instead of a sandwich. It's the extras that keep my family eating salad day after day. And it's the extras that make them seasonally appropriate. To minimize preparation, I don't usually add more than three. The following ingredients show up regularly in my salads:

Cheese

Salads dressed with oil and vinegar are clean and simple. If I want to boost flavor quickly, I add a little cheese, favoring assertively flavored ones like feta, blue, Parmesan, and mild or aged goat. For blue, feta, and goat cheese, break off a chunk and crumble it right into the salad. For Parmesan, shave it right off the block with a vegetable peeler. If using pre-grated Parmesan cheese (preferably not the kind in the green can), just sprinkle it in.

Figuring about 1 tablespoon of cheese per person, add one of the following optional cheeses to the salad greens:

- Blue cheese, crumbled
- Feta cheese, crumbled
- Fresh or aged goat cheese, crumbled
- Parmesan, shaved or grated

Fruit

In winter, when salad vegetables are high priced and often poor quality, I switch to fruits. Apples, pears, oranges, grapefruits, and certain dried fruits pair nicely with salad greens. And who doesn't have a lone apple or a pair of oranges hanging out in the fruit basket?

Add one of the following optional fresh or dried fruits to salad greens:

- Apples. Quarter, core, and slice thin. Don't bother to peel them. The skin color, especially of red apples, contrasts nicely with the salad greens. Figure about one apple for a salad for four.

- Dried cranberries and cherries. Of all the dried fruits, I like cranberries and cherries best with salad greens. Obviously there's no preparation—just snip the bag and pour. You will use about 1 tablespoon per person.

- Grapefruit. Like the orange, peel and section. Figure one grapefruit for a salad for four.

- Oranges. Peel and section. You'll need two oranges for a salad for four.

- Pears. Quarter, core, and slice thin. Don't bother to peel them either. Figure about one pear for a salad for four.

Nuts

Nuts and fruit are perfect salad bowl partners. Toasted nuts taste better than raw ones. So that I have them on hand, I toast a whole bag at once rather than a half a cup here and there. To toast any variety of nuts, place them in a single layer on a pie plate or rimmed cookie sheet just large enough to hold them. If the pan is too large, the nuts around the edges tend to overbrown. Toast in a 300 to 325 degree oven until fragrant and golden, about 10 minutes. You can also toast small quantities of nuts in a skillet over medium heat, stirring them frequently to ensure even browning.

Figuring about 1 tablespoon per person, add one of the following optional nuts to the salad greens.

- Toasted slivered or sliced almonds
- Hazelnuts, toasted, skins rubbed off and discarded, nuts chopped coarse
- Toasted pine nuts. Because of their high oil content, they burn quickly. So get them off the hot cookie sheet or skillet as soon as they are toasted.
- Toasted pistachios, shelled
- Toasted walnuts or pecans, chopped coarse

Ingredients from a Jar or Can

Like assertive cheeses, many canned and jarred ingredients add depth of flavor to a salad.

- Artichoke hearts. Cut into quarters.
- Sliced canned beets. Drain.
- Chickpeas. Drain and rinse.
- Olives. Pitted, if desired (or at least make sure everyone knows that they're not). Any olive—green or black, dry-cured, wet-cured, or packed in brine—makes a wonderful salad ingredient. I like kalamatas because they're big, meaty, and flavorful. Buy them pitted if you can. Figure about 1 tablespoon of pitted olives per person.
- Roasted peppers. Cut into thin strips. Figure about one whole bell pepper for every four salads.
- Sun-dried tomatoes, packed in oil. Cut into thin strips.

Vegetables

Vegetables are the most obvious of the salad extras. Add seasonal vegetables only when they're at their peak. Combine the ones available year round with ingredients in other categories. After washing them, prepare vegetables in the following way:

- Avocados (fruit, yes, but they taste like a vegetable), halved, pitted, and flesh cut into chunks or strips and scooped out of the skin with a spoon

- Bell peppers. Cut about 1/2 inch off base and stem end, removing stem from top slice. Remove core, make a slit down one side of the pepper, and open it up so that pepper lies flat. Cut into 1/4-inch strips. Thin-slice base and stem as well.

- Celery, sliced thin

- Cucumbers, peeled or partially peeled, quartered lengthwise, and cut crosswise 1/2 inch thick

- Fennel. Trim bulb of fronds and stalks. Halve, core, and cut each fennel half crosswise into thin slices.

- Mushrooms, sliced thin

- Red onions, halved, peeled, and sliced thin

- Radishes, tops removed and sliced thin

- Scallions, sliced thin

- Tomatoes (fruit, yes, but they taste like a vegetable). Whole tomatoes cut into large chunks, cherry tomatoes, halved

Cooked Ingredients

It's always a treat to look in the refrigerator and find an extra boiled egg or a couple of strips of bacon for salad. Don't make a special point of boiling eggs or frying bacon for salads. But when you do boil eggs, add a few extra to the pot. And if you fry bacon on a jelly-roll pan in the oven rather than in a skillet on top of the stove, there's always room for a few extra strips.

- Fried bacon. Figure about 1 strip of crumbled bacon per person.

- Boiled eggs. Figure 1 to 2 eggs for a salad for four. I like to dice the eggs on an egg slicer so that they're easily incorporated into the salad when tossed.

Croutons

Unfortunately there's not a single brand of croutons at my grocery store that is not artificially flavored. Instead of croutons, I buy plain bagel chips or melba toast. They offer crunch without the extra flavorings. Break them up by hand over the salad and toss.

The Dressing

With the lettuce chopped and the extras in the bowl, it's time to toss the hodgepodge ingredients into a unified salad. I quick-dress salads in one of two ways.

The simplest way to dress a tossed salad is Italian style, with extra-virgin olive oil, salt, pepper, and vinegar. The key to this oil and vinegar salad is to be generous with the oil and stingy with the vinegar.

Eyeballing about 1 tablespoon for each portion of salad, drizzle extra-virgin olive oil over the salad ingredients, sprinkle generously with salt and pepper, then toss. (I like spring-action tongs for tossing.) If, after a thorough tossing, the salad ingredients aren't lightly coated with oil, drizzle in a little more, toss again, then taste. At this point the salad ingredients should be lightly coated but not dripping with oil and should taste properly salted and peppered.

Depending on the extra ingredients, the salad may need very little, if any, acidity. Oranges, grapefruit, beets, and juicy in-season tomatoes may offer just the right amount of piquancy. If not, carefully drizzle on a couple of teaspoons of balsamic, red, or white wine vinegar, or squeeze a little juice from a lemon half, then toss and taste.

The vinegar should be subtle and in balance with the oil. If it's not acidic enough, add another couple of drops. If the vinegar bottle doesn't have a spout or plastic top that controls flow, stick your index finger in the bottle as you pour so that the vinegar sprinkles rather than pours. If watching fat, you can cut back on the oil and use a little more of one of the lower-acid vinegars, such as rice wine or balsamic vinegar or lemon juice.

Our family likes creamy dressed salads too. Unfortunately, most of those on the grocery store shelves are filled with artificial flavorings and coloring. I much prefer the creamy salad dressings in the refrigerated case. Marie's brand of buttermilk dressing is one of our favorites. Since it's thick, we use it as a vegetable dip, but I turn it into a creamy salad dressing by thinning it with a little milk or buttermilk, drizzling it over the salad to toss and serve. I also make a quick blue cheese dressing or mock Caesar from scratch (see page 263).

The Simple Tossed Salad

6 cups salad greens from 1½ heads romaine hearts, or from any other lettuce (see page 14), cut into bite-size pieces

2 or 3 salad additions (see previous list or suggested combinations below)

Extra-virgin olive oil

Salt and ground black pepper

Red or white wine vinegar, rice wine vinegar, balsamic vinegar, or lemon juice

Combine lettuce and salad ingredients in a large bowl. Drizzle about ¼ cup olive oil over salad ingredients, then sprinkle generously with salt and pepper; toss to coat. Taste salad ingredients, making sure they are lightly coated with oil and well seasoned. Sprinkle salad with 1 tablespoon vinegar or lemon juice; toss again, then taste. Adjust seasonings, adding additional vinegar or lemon juice, salt, or pepper, if necessary.

Add any of the following to the salad before tossing.

Blue Cheese and Red Onion

I particularly like this salad drizzled with balsamic vinegar. Regardless of your vinegar choice, slice the onion and sprinkle it with the vinegar while making the salad. Add onion along with the vinegar when giving the salad a final toss.

SALAD ADDITIONS:

¼ cup crumbled blue cheese

¼ medium red onion, sliced thin

Blue Cheese and Celery

As with blue cheese and red onion, this salad is also particularly nice when tossed with balsamic vinegar.

SALAD ADDITIONS:

½ cup thin-sliced celery

¼ cup crumbled blue cheese

Blue Cheese and Pear or Apple

Try this salad made with part or all watercress. With the sweet pear or apple, use a squeeze of lemon juice. Toasted walnuts can also be added.

SALAD ADDITIONS:

¼ cup crumbled blue cheese

1 medium pear or apple, cored and sliced thin

Blue Cheese and Walnuts

Bitter lettuces are the perfect foil for the rich nuts and cheese. If you're serving an adult crowd, make the salad with a mix of radicchio and Belgian endive and toss with balsamic vinegar.

SALAD ADDITIONS:

¼ cup crumbled blue cheese

¼ cup coarse-chopped toasted walnuts

Goat Cheese and Dried Cranberries

Balsamic vinegar nicely complements the tart cranberries. As with the blue cheese and apple salad, toasted almonds or walnuts make another nice addition.

SALAD ADDITIONS:

¼ cup crumbled fresh goat cheese

¼ cup dried cranberries

Goat Cheese and Beet

A salad made with all or part watercress nicely complements the goat cheese and beets.

SALAD ADDITIONS:

¼ cup crumbled fresh or aged goat cheese

½ (15-ounce) can sliced beets, cut into strips

Shaved Parmesan and Artichoke Hearts

With the piquant artichokes and nutty Parmesan, use a squeeze of fresh lemon.

SALAD ADDITIONS:

¼ cup shaved Parmesan cheese

8 canned artichokes, cut into quarters

Shaved Parmesan and Oranges

Squeeze a little lemon juice over this salad to complement the orange juice.

SALAD ADDITIONS:

2 medium oranges, sectioned

¼ cup shaved Parmesan cheese

Egg and Artichoke

Mild, buttery-leaved Boston or Bibb lettuce is especially nice with the egg-artichoke combination. Squeeze on fresh lemon juice.

SALAD ADDITIONS:

2 boiled eggs, cut into small dice

8 canned artichoke hearts, quartered

Orange and Pistachio

Fruit/nut combinations work well in a salad of all or partial bitter greens. This one is no exception.

SALAD ADDITIONS:

2 medium oranges, sectioned   ¼ cup chopped pistachios

Grapefruit and Red Onion

Try tossing this mix of grapefruit and red onion with arugula. Drizzle with either balsamic or red wine vinegar.

SALAD ADDITIONS:

1 grapefruit, sectioned   ¼ red onion, sliced thin

Red Onion, Black Olive, and Orange

Peppery arugula and red wine vinegar stand up to the piquant, fruity flavors of this salad. Toss the red onion in the vinegar while you prepare the rest of the salad ingredients.

SALAD ADDITIONS:

2 medium oranges, sectioned   ¼ cup pitted black olives

¼ medium red onion, sliced thin

Feta, Black Olive, and Roasted Pepper

Red wine vinegar pairs well with assertively flavored black olives and feta cheese.

SALAD ADDITIONS:

¼ cup crumbled feta cheese   1 jarred roasted red pepper, cut
                                     into thin strips
¼ cup pitted black olives

Chickpeas, Red Onion, and Feta

To remove the onion's bite, drizzle it with vinegar and let it stand while preparing the salad.

SALAD ADDITIONS:

¼ cup crumbled feta cheese

¼ cup drained canned chickpeas

¼ medium red onion, sliced thin

Avocado, Orange, and Red Onion

SALAD ADDITIONS:

1 avocado, halved, pitted, and cut into large dice

¼ red onion, sliced thin

2 oranges, sectioned

Avocado, Bacon, and Tomato

Red wine vinegar cuts through the rich avocado and bacon.

SALAD ADDITIONS:

1 avocado, halved, pitted, and cut into large dice

4 slices crisp cooked bacon, crumbled

8 cherry tomatoes, halved

2 scallions, sliced thin

Mushroom, Bacon, Tomato, and Blue Cheese

Spinach partners well with these ingredients. Other cheeses that would work well include goat cheese, Parmesan, and feta.

SALAD ADDITIONS:

8 mushrooms, sliced thin

1 medium tomato, cut into wedges

4 slices, crisp cooked bacon, crumbled

¼ cup crumbled blue cheese

Greek-style Dinner Salad

Although this salad contains more than my usual limit of three salad additions, it is a favorite of ours. I usually sprinkle a little dried oregano over this salad before tossing it.

SALAD ADDITIONS:

¼ cup crumbled feta cheese

¼ red onion, sliced thin

¼ cup pitted olives

8 cherry tomatoes, halved

¼ medium cucumber, peeled, quartered lengthwise, and cut into bite-size chunks

at-a-glance

THE SIMPLE TOSSED SALAD

- Figuring about 1½ cups of lettuce per person, core the lettuce, then chop, rinse, and dry it.
- Transfer the lettuce to a bowl and add two or three additional ingredients from the cheese, fruit, nut, vegetable, crouton, or cooked, jarred and canned ingredients categories.
- Drizzle salad ingredients with extra-virgin olive oil (about 1 tablespoon per portion) and sprinkle generously with salt and pepper; toss to coat. Taste. Adjust seasonings.
- Sprinkle salad with vinegar or lemon juice (about a scant teaspoon per portion); toss again. Taste, adjust seasonings, and serve.

salt and pepper mushrooms and
oil and parmesan and
vinegar tomato
red onion

Paired Salads Hold the Lettuce

Like the simple tossed salad, paired salads are easy to make.

Just drizzle with oil, salt, pepper, and vinegar. You can't make a mistake.

I can never resist those oversized baskets of dead ripe tomatoes at the farmer's market, and I welcome excess offerings from neighbors' gardens like those who take in stray animals. I'm always drawn to the "bruised and reduced" section of any produce department. I feel almost a duty to find purpose for unwanted and less-than-perfect fruits and vegetables. So when I find myself with large quantities of one fruit or vegetable or another, I can't afford to serve it up daintily, one-a-day style. I've got to move it fast by making a paired fruit or vegetable salad. Like The Simple Tossed Salad, the following vegetable and fruit pairings can be dressed with olive oil and vinegar or lemon juice.

Instructions for Paired Salads

- Place fruit and/or vegetables in a medium bowl.
- Figuring about 1 tablespoon per person, drizzle with olive oil, then sprinkle with salt and pepper; toss to coat.
- Drizzle with a few drops of vinegar or lemon juice; toss again, and serve.

25

Tomato and Cucumber Salad

Serves 4

Red wine vinegar is the acid of choice in this salad. Crumbled feta cheese and a few shakes of dried oregano are both welcome additions to this classic Greek pairing.

2 medium tomatoes, halved and cut into thin wedges

1 cucumber, peeled, halved, seeded, and sliced ½ inch thick

Follow the instructions for Paired Salads (page 25).

Tomato and Red Onion Salad

Serves 4

2 medium tomatoes, cut into thin wedges

½ red onion, sliced thin

Follow the instructions for Paired Salads (page 25).

Fennel and Orange Salad

Serves 4

Section the oranges over the salad bowl. They may release enough juice so that just a few drops of lemon juice may be all that is needed to heighten flavor.

1 fennel bulb, halved, cored, and cut into thin wedges

2 medium oranges, peeled and sectioned

Follow the instructions for Paired Salads (page 25).

Mushroom and Parmesan Salad

Serves 4

Use presliced mushrooms for this salad if you like, and sprinkle with lemon juice rather than vinegar.

8 ounces white mushrooms, sliced

¼ cup shaved Parmesan

3 tablespoons minced fresh parsley

Follow the instructions for Paired Salads (page 25).

Tomato and Mozzarella Salad

Serves 4

If the tomatoes are juicy and ripe, you probably don't need vinegar. If they are not, drizzle with a little balsamic vinegar. Unlike the other salads in this section, this one is arranged, not tossed.

2 medium tomatoes, sliced thin

10 to 12 ounces fresh mozzarella, sliced thin

Olive oil

Salt and ground black pepper

Balsamic vinegar (optional)

Alternating tomato and mozzarella slices, arrange a portion on each of four salad plates. Drizzle with oil, then sprinkle with salt and pepper. Let stand, if possible, until the tomato juices start to release, about 10 minutes. Drizzle with droplets of vinegar, if desired.

Iceberg Wedges with Thousand Island (or Blue Cheese) Dressing

Serves 4 to 6

Although this salad and the recipe that follows don't quite fit the paired salad format, they are both weeknight regulars at our house. Make a Thousand Island dressing by mixing ½ cup mayonnaise, 1 tablespoon ketchup, 1 tablespoon sweet pickle relish (or chopped sweet pickle) along with 1 tablespoon pickle juice. A chopped boiled egg makes the dressing taste even better. Don't forget a few grinds of pepper. If the group you're serving prefers blue cheese, follow the recipe on page 263.

1 small head iceberg lettuce, core left intact, halved and cut into 4 to 6 wedges, depending on lettuce size	½ cup quick Thousand Island (or blue cheese dressing

Set a lettuce wedge on each salad plate. Spoon dressing over lettuce and serve.

Quick Coleslaw

Serves 6

I don't like packaged salad mixes, but I do like coleslaw mixes. Like iceberg wedges, coleslaw isn't tossed with vinaigrette, but it's a salad that requires a special dressing. With preshredded cabbage, coleslaw is just a toss away.

1 package (16 ounces) coleslaw mix	½ cup mayonnaise
½ small onion, cut into small dice	1 tablespoon rice wine vinegar

Mix all ingredients in a medium bowl. Serve.

Vinaigrette The Single
Vegetable's Best Bet

Consider single vegetables for salads when you shop.
Steamed asparagus, for example, with vinaigrette on top.

Tossed salad is our knee-jerk solution to dinner most nights. We do break free of our monotonous pattern occasionally and prepare single-vegetable salads. These salads are a way to feature seasonal vegetables (artichokes and asparagus) or eat vegetables we might not otherwise (leeks and celery hearts) enjoy.

The one thing about single-vegetable salads is that except for avocados and radishes, most of them need to be cooked first. The good news about these vegetables is that most of them steam in less than twelve minutes.

Vinaigrette by Heart

While a tossed salad is delicious with just oil and vinegar, most single vegetable salads beg for vinaigrette. Being able to make good vinaigrette by heart is like knowing how to dance. You may not do it often, but it's sure nice to know how when it counts.

If you understand the formula, making vinaigrette is not hard. Start by mincing one or two cloves of garlic or a shallot and putting them in a small heavy bowl. Since making vinaigrette eventually requires the use of both hands—one to add the oil, the other to whisk—it's best to have a bowl that doesn't move around. Measure 3 tablespoons of vinegar (your choice) into the bowl, then season with salt and pepper. Be generous, knowing that it should be enough to season the salad (for me, it's a couple of big pinches of kosher salt and five or six grinds of pepper).

Dip a small whisk into a jar of Dijon mustard, picking up a couple of teaspoons on the tip, then whisk the mustard into the vinegar. Measure out $1/2$ cup of olive oil and whisk it in, first in droplets, then in a thin steady stream as the dressing starts to come together and emulsify.

This vinaigrette may look like a list of ingredients and a set of instructions, but it is merely the classic vinaigrette proportions of three parts oil to one part vinegar—with one slight change. Because I like the slight edge and bite of vinaigrette made with less oil, I use only 8 tablespoons of oil (rather than 9) to 3 tablespoons of vinegar. If you can remember $1/2$ cup of oil and 3 tablespoons of vinegar, the rest is easy—a couple of minced garlic cloves for flavor, a small whisk tip of Dijon mustard to aid emulsification, and salt and pepper to taste.

Making vinaigrette and steaming the vegetables takes a little more time than a simple tossed salad, but for me it serves as both salad and vegetable. On the nights we start with a steamed vegetable with vinaigrette, I follow with a very simple vegetable-less meal.

All-Purpose Vinaigrette

Makes a generous 1/2 cup

After making this dressing a few times, the only ingredient you'll need to measure is the oil. Don't try to spoon mustard out of the jar with a measuring spoon. Simply dip a small whisk into the jar to pull out what you need.

2 garlic cloves, or 1 shallot, minced

2 teaspoons Dijon mustard

3 tablespoons vinegar (balsamic, red or white wine vinegar—including tarragon and raspberry)

Salt and ground black pepper

1/2 cup olive oil

Whisk together the garlic or shallot, mustard, and vinegar along with a generous sprinkling of salt and ground black pepper in a heavy-bottomed bowl. Gradually whisk in olive oil in a slow steady stream to form a smooth, creamy emulsified sauce. (This can be stored in an airtight container for 1 week. Shake before using.)

Steamed Green Beans with Vinaigrette

Serves 4

If you like, serve this green bean salad with a garnish of fresh tomato wedges. Make sure to salt the tomatoes and drizzle them with a little vinaigrette as well.

1 pound green beans, stem ends trimmed

1/2 teaspoon salt

1/2 recipe All-Purpose Vinaigrette

1 shallot or scallion, minced

Bring the green beans, 1/2 cup of water, and 1/2 teaspoon of salt to a boil in a large saucepan or Dutch oven. Cover and cook over medium-high heat until the beans are just tender when pierced with a thin-bladed knife, 5 to 6 minutes, depending on desired tenderness. Drain the beans, divide among four plates, and let cool slightly. Drizzle a tablespoon or so of vinaigrette over each portion, sprinkle with shallot or scallion, and serve.

Artichokes with Vinaigrette

Serves 4

Because of the steaming time, I don't usually serve artichokes for supper, but they make a simple first course for a special dinner.

4 artichokes, stems trimmed and leaves clipped if prickly

1 recipe All-Purpose Vinaigrette (page 31)

Set the artichokes stem side up in about ½ inch of salted water in a Dutch oven or soup kettle. Cover and bring to a boil over medium-high heat. Reduce the heat and simmer until the stems are just tender when pierced with a thin-bladed knife, 30 to 40 minutes, depending on size. Remove from the kettle and cool slightly. Remove the chokes, fill the openings with vinaigrette, and serve.

Steamed Asparagus with Vinaigrette

Serves 4

Asparagus should be trimmed one of two ways depending on thickness. Thin to medium asparagus are usually bound with one or two rubber bands. Leaving the asparagus bundled, whack off the bottom 1½ to 2 inches. Thicker asparagus spears are woodier and should be snapped individually. Holding the tip end of an asparagus in one hand, bend the spear. It will break naturally at the tender part. Diced boiled egg can be sprinkled over the steamed asparagus.

1 pound thin to medium-stalked asparagus, trimmed (see note above)

½ teaspoon salt

½ recipe All-Purpose Vinaigrette (page 31)

Bring the asparagus, ½ cup of water, and salt to a boil in a deep skillet. Cover and cook over medium-high heat until the stalks are just tender when pierced with a knife, 3 to 5 minutes, depending on thickness. Divide the asparagus evenly among four plates and let cool slightly. Drizzle a tablespoon of vinaigrette over each portion. Serve.

Radish-Parsley Salad with Vinaigrette

Serves 4

For this salad, try not to make the boiled eggs optional.

8 ounces radishes, sliced thin (about 2 cups)

½ cup chopped fresh parsley

2 boiled eggs, chopped (optional)

½ recipe All-Purpose Vinaigrette (page 31)

Place radishes and parsley in a medium bowl. Add the eggs, if using, and toss with vinaigrette. Serve.

Braised Leeks with Vinaigrette

Serves 4

To prepare leeks for steaming, trim off the tough dark green tops and discard. Leaving enough of the root intact so that the leek holds together, trim the frilly root end. Quarter the leek lengthwise without cutting through the base. Rinse leeks well under cool running water, separating the leaves to expose hidden dirt. Diced boiled egg can be sprinkled over the braised hearts.

4 medium leeks, trimmed and cleaned (see note above)

1 cup chicken broth

½ recipe All-Purpose Vinaigrette (page 31)

Minced fresh parsley (optional)

Bring the leeks and chicken broth to a boil over medium-high heat in a deep skillet. Cover, reduce the heat, and simmer until leeks are just tender when pierced with a thin-bladed knife, 10 to 12 minutes, depending on size. Transfer the leeks to each of four plates and let cool slightly. Drizzle a tablespoon or so of vinaigrette over each leek. Sprinkle with parsley if desired and serve.

Braised Celery Hearts with Vinaigrette

Serves 4

To trim a celery heart for braising, shave off a thin layer from the base without causing any of the stalks to become unattached. Trim off half an inch or so from the top as well. In addition to the olives, diced boiled egg can be sprinkled over the braised hearts.

1 large or 2 small celery hearts, trimmed (see note above), quartered if large and halved if small

1 cup chicken broth

½ recipe All-Purpose Vinaigrette (page 31)

¼ cup chopped green olives

Bring the celery and chicken broth to a boil over medium-high heat in a deep skillet. Cover, reduce the heat, and simmer until the celery is just tender when pierced with a thin-bladed knife, 10 to 12 minutes, depending on thickness. Transfer the celery to each of four plates and let cool slightly. Drizzle a tablespoon or so of vinaigrette over each portion of celery heart, sprinkle with chopped olives, and serve.

Avocados with Vinaigrette

Serves 4

½ recipe All-Purpose Vinaigrette (page 31)

2 avocados, halved and pits removed

Place an avocado half on each salad plate. Put a spoonful of vinaigrette in each cavity. Serve.

One Easy Formula, Many Supper Soups

Sauté an onion, then add vegetables, starch, and meat.

Cook it in a quart of broth for a meal that can't be beat.

Commercial soups come in many forms—canned, refrigerated, frozen, even dehydrated. I never mistake store-bought for homemade, and other than the occasional can of clam chowder or tomato soup, they're just not worth the sacrifice in taste and flavor.

On the other hand, homemade chicken or beef soup is at best a two-hour investment—not the kind of time most people can spare on weeknights. Since my family loves hearty soup for supper, I've developed quick soups that look and taste like our long-simmered favorites, but can be made in about half an hour.

The formula is simple—1 pound of meat, 1 pound of vegetables, 1 quart of chicken broth, 1 onion, 1 cup of canned tomatoes, a starch such as potatoes, rice, or pasta, and herbs and/or spices. The technique is simple too—sauté the onion until softened, add the remaining ingredients, bring to a simmer, and cook for about twenty minutes. There are, of course, a few exceptions, but it's easier to know a formula and remember the exceptions than not to know a formula at all.

A Pound of Meat or Fish

When making quick supper soups, avoid meats that need long-simmering like whole chickens, beef shanks, and ham hocks. Instead, buy cuts that cook quickly. Boneless, skinless chicken thighs (because they're more flavorful than chicken breasts), pork tenderloin, boneless ham, Italian and kielbasa-style sausage, shrimp, and firm-fleshed fish are perfect candidates.

Although I use the same amount of meat for my quick soups (1 pound), the preparation and cooking vary slightly according to the type of meat. Fully cooked smoked meats like ham and kielbasa require no special treatment. Slice them into bite-size pieces and add them with the rest of the ingredients.

Fresh pork like sausage and tenderloin need browning before they are added to the soup. If you're in a hurry, brown them in a separate skillet while the onion sautés. If not, brown them right in the soup kettle before sautéing the onion. It is not necessary to fully cook these meats since they continue to cook in the soup. Add the browned and sliced sausage to the kettle with the remaining ingredients. Since the pork tenderloin overcooks and dries out so quickly, add it during the last five minutes of cooking.

Shredded chicken and flaked fish give the soup a from-scratch quality. Rather than add raw chunks, drop in whole boneless chicken thighs and fish fillets. After they simmer for a few minutes, pull them from the kettle, shred or flake them when they're cool enough to handle, then return them to the simmering soup.

Shrimp, like pork tenderloin, are an exception to the formula. Since they cook so quickly, add them to the soup during the last five minutes of cooking. Shrimp shells can wonderfully flavor a broth. If you have time, simmer the shells in part of the canned chicken broth to boost flavor, straining them out before adding the broth to the kettle.

Eat Your Vegetables

How do you know which vegetables to toss into the soup kettle? I look for the loners—that solitary zucchini in the vegetable drawer or the cabbage quarter on the bottom shelf. Do certain vegetables go with certain meats? Although some combinations are better than others—sausage with cabbage and potatoes or chicken with carrots and peas—I can't think of a single vegetable that clashes with any of the suggested soup meats or fish.

In addition to the pound of vegetables, add an onion for depth of flavor. While it sautés, prepare the rest of the vegetables, adding them along with the other soup ingredients. If the vegetables aren't prepared by the time the onion has softened, add the chicken broth to stop the sautéing and get a head start on simmering.

Obviously the broth for this quick soup is store-bought, not homemade. It lacks the body of from-scratch stock, but it is flavorful and convenient. Instead of the canned brands, I've come to like Swanson's chicken broth in the waxed one-quart box. Although you need the full quart for this particular recipe, many times you won't. Since the box is resealable, use what you need and refrigerate the rest.

Regardless of the soup you're making, use chicken broth. Commercial beef broths are generally inferior. And although bottled clam juice is fine in small quantities, it's not good enough to make an entire pot of soup.

Since the soup simmers for just twenty minutes, there's not much time for deep flavor to develop. A small quantity of canned tomatoes, like the onion, adds a subtle flavor dimension the soup often needs.

Unlike the rest of the recipe, the quantity of potatoes, beans, rice, or pasta is not neat and tidy. Except for the 1 pound of potatoes (the same as the meat and vegetable quantities), the quantities differ—2 cans of drained beans or hominy, 1/2 cup of white rice, or 4 ounces (2 cups) of egg noodles. Whatever you choose, add it along with the other soup ingredients once the onion has been sautéed. The rice and potatoes need the full cooking time to get tender. The canned beans are neither helped nor hurt by the simmering. And although you might think the pasta would be overcooked and bloated after twenty minutes, it isn't. If you prefer your soup noodles a little al dente, add them halfway through cooking.

Supper Soup

Clearly, the soup will not be affected with a little more or less of anything, so don't worry about the precise weight of the vegetables.

2 tablespoons vegetable or olive oil

1 medium onion, chopped

1 pound vegetables, cut into bite-size pieces (see individual recipes)

1 pound meat (boneless, skinless chicken thighs, Italian sausage in the casing, kielbasa sausage, ham, medium shrimp, or firm-fleshed fish)

1 pound potatoes, cut into medium dice, *or* 2 cans (16 ounces each) beans (white, black, or chickpeas) or hominy, *or* 4 ounces wide or extra-wide egg noodles *or* 1/2 cup long-grain white rice

1 cup canned crushed tomatoes (can be optional)

2 cans (16 ounces each) *or* 1 carton (32 ounces) low-sodium canned chicken broth

Herbs, spice, or flavoring of choice

Salt and ground black pepper

Heat the oil in a Dutch oven or soup kettle. Add the onions; sauté to soften slightly, about 2 minutes. Add remaining vegetables, meat of choice (shrimp and pork tenderloin are the exceptions—add them only during the last 5 minutes of cooking), starch of choice, tomatoes, chicken broth, and dried herb or spice of choice. Partially cover and simmer until vegetables are tender and flavors have blended, about 20 minutes. Add fresh herbs, season with salt and ground black pepper to taste. Serve.

Ham and Potato Soup with Leeks and Peas

MEAT:

1-pound chunk of ham, shredded into bite-size pieces or cut into cubes

VEGETABLES:

2 small leeks (about 8 ounces), dark green leaves trimmed off and discarded, leeks halved lengthwise, sliced thin, and rinsed thoroughly

2 small carrots (about 6 ounces total), peeled and cut into medium dice

3/4 cup frozen green peas

STARCH:

1 pound red potatoes (2 large), cut into medium dice, or 4 ounces pasta

HERB:

1 teaspoon dried thyme leaves

Follow the Supper Soup recipe, omitting tomatoes.

White Bean Soup with Ham and Escarole

Italian or kielbasa sausage is equally good in this soup.

MEAT:

1-pound chunk of ham (preferably bone-in), shredded into bite-size pieces or cut into cubes

VEGETABLES:

8 ounces (about 1/2 medium head) escarole, rough-chopped

2 medium carrots (about 8 ounces total), peeled and cut into 1/2-inch rounds

STARCH:

2 cans (16 ounces each) white beans, such as cannellini, drained and rinsed

HERB:

2 teaspoons minced fresh rosemary

Follow the Supper Soup recipe.

White Bean Soup with Sausage, Peppers, and Kale

If using a lean sausage, add a couple of teaspoons of vegetable or olive oil along with the water, to help the sausage brown. Chorizo or andouille sausage can be substituted for the Italian sausage if you like.

MEAT:

1 pound mild or hot Italian sausage in the casing

VEGETABLES:

½ pound kale, stemmed and rough-chopped

1 large red or yellow bell pepper (about 8 ounces), cut into medium dice

STARCH:

2 cans (16 ounces each) white beans, such as cannellini, drained and rinsed

HERB:

2 teaspoons minced fresh rosemary

Bring the sausage and ¼ cup water (and oil; see note above) to a simmer in the Dutch oven or soup kettle for making soup. Cover and cook over medium heat until the sausage loses its raw color, about 8 minutes. Uncover the pan and cook the sausage until the liquid evaporates, 1 to 2 minutes longer. Fry the sausage, turning it once, until it browns on both sides. Remove from the pot; cut into ½-inch slices.

Follow the Supper Soup recipe (page 38).

Sausage Soup with Mushrooms, Zucchini, and Chickpeas

Chorizo or andouille can be substituted for the Italian sausage if you like. If using a lean sausage, add a couple of teaspoons vegetable or olive oil along with the water, to help the sausage brown.

MEAT:

1 pound mild or hot Italian sausage in the casing

VEGETABLES:

½ pound domestic white mushrooms, sliced thin

1 medium (8 ounces) zucchini, cut into medium dice

STARCH:

2 cans (16 ounces each) chickpeas, drained and rinsed

SPICE:

1 teaspoon ground cumin

Bring the sausage and ¼ cup water (and oil; see note above) to a simmer in the Dutch oven or soup kettle for making soup. Cover and cook over medium heat until the sausage loses its raw color, about 8 minutes. Uncover the pan and cook the sausage until the liquid evaporates, 1 to 2 minutes longer. Fry the sausage, turning it once, until it browns on both sides. Remove from the pot; slice ½ inch thick.

Follow the Supper Soup recipe (page 38), sautéing mushrooms along with the onions.

Sausage Soup with Spinach, Cauliflower, and Noodles

As with the other sausage-based soups, if using a lean variety, add a couple teaspoons of vegetable or olive oil along with the water, to help the sausage brown.

MEAT:

1 pound mild or hot Italian sausage in the casing

VEGETABLES:

½ pound cauliflower, cut into bite-size florets

½ pound spinach, stemmed and washed

STARCH:

4 ounces bite-size pasta, such as macaroni or bow ties

Bring the sausage and ¼ cup of water (and oil; see note above) to a simmer in the Dutch oven or soup kettle for making soup. Cover and cook over medium heat until the sausage loses its raw color, about 8 minutes. Uncover the pan and cook the sausage until the liquid evaporates, 1 to 2 minutes longer. Fry the sausage, turning it once, until it browns on both sides. Remove from the pot; slice ½ inch thick.

Follow the Supper Soup recipe (page 38).

Pork Soup with Hominy and Peppers

Serve this soup with a squeeze of lime, tortilla chips, and The Simplest Guacamole (page 253). If you don't have leeks, simply substitute another yellow onion.

MEAT:

1 pork tenderloin (¾ to 1 pound)

VEGETABLES:

2 small leeks (8 ounces each), dark green leaves trimmed and discarded from leeks, halved lengthwise, sliced thin, and washed thoroughly

1 large bell pepper (about 8 ounces), cut into medium dice

STARCH:

2 cans (16 ounces each) hominy, drained and rinsed

HERB:

1 tablespoon minced fresh cilantro leaves

Heat a medium skillet over medium-high heat. Add the tenderloin; cook, turning frequently, until brown on all sides, about 8 minutes. Transfer to a cutting board; slice thin.

Follow the Supper Soup recipe (page 38), adding the pork and cilantro about 5 minutes before soup is done.

Chicken Vegetable Soup with Wide Noodles

MEAT:

1 pound boneless, skinless chicken thighs (about 6)

VEGETABLES:

2 medium carrots, peeled and cut into medium dice (about 8 ounces)

2 medium celery stalks, cut into medium dice (4 to 5 ounces)

¾ cup frozen green peas

STARCH:

4 ounces wide egg noodles (2 heaping cups)

HERB:

1 teaspoon dried thyme leaves

Follow the Supper Soup recipe (page 38), removing chicken thighs after 10 minutes of simmering. When cool enough to handle, shred into bite-size pieces and return to soup.

Chicken Spinach Soup with Rice and Lemon

For a thicker soup, whisk a cup or so of the hot soup into 2 beaten egg yolks, then stir the warm egg mixture back into the soup. Heat gently until the soup thickens. Be careful—if it boils, it will curdle.

MEAT:

1 pound boneless, skinless chicken thighs (about 6)

VEGETABLES:

1 bag (10 ounces) prewashed spinach, stemmed as needed

1 medium zucchini (6 ounces), cut into medium dice

STARCH:

½ cup long- or medium-grain white rice

FLAVORING:

3 tablespoons juice from a medium lemon

Follow the Supper Soup recipe (page 38), removing chicken thighs after 10 minutes of simmering. When cool enough to handle, shred into bite-size pieces and return to soup. Add lemon juice to the finished soup.

Curried Chicken Soup with Potatoes and Zucchini

Here, I use half chickpeas and half potatoes to exemplify how two starches can work in the same soup. If you don't have one or the other, simply double the amount of the one you've got.

MEAT:

1 pound boneless, skinless chicken thighs (about 6)

VEGETABLES:

1 medium-large zucchini, cut into medium dice (about 8 ounces), or 8 ounces cauliflower, cut into bite-size florets

2 medium carrots, peeled and cut into medium dice (about 8 ounces)

STARCH:

1 large red potato (8 ounces), cut into medium dice *and* 1 can (16 ounces) chickpeas, rinsed and drained

SPICE:

1 tablespoon curry powder

Follow the Supper Soup recipe (page 38), removing chicken thighs after 10 minutes of simmering. When cool enough to handle, shred into bite-size pieces and return to soup.

Saffron Chicken Vegetable Soup

MEAT:

1 pound boneless, skinless chicken thighs (about 6)

VEGETABLES:

1 medium-large zucchini, cut into medium dice (about 8 ounces)

2 medium turnips (about 8 ounces), cut into medium dice

STARCH:

1 each red boiling potato and sweet potato (16 ounces total), cut into medium dice

SPICE:

1 firm-packed $1/4$ teaspoon saffron threads

Follow the Supper Soup recipe (page 38), removing chicken thighs after 10 minutes of simmering. When cool enough to handle, cut into bite-size pieces and return to soup.

Fish Soup with Cabbage and Potatoes

If you prefer, substitute 1 pound of kielbasa or ham for the fish.

MEAT:

1 pound firm-fleshed white fish, such as halibut, cod, scrod, or haddock

VEGETABLES:

¼ medium cabbage (about 8 ounces), cut into thick shreds

2 medium celery stalks or 1 fennel bulb (about 8 ounces), cut into medium dice

STARCH:

1 pound red potatoes (2 large), cut into medium dice

HERBS:

2 bay leaves and 1 tablespoon minced fresh parsley leaves

Follow the Supper Soup recipe (page 38), removing the fish after 5 minutes of simmering. When cool enough to handle, flake it into large chunks and return, along with the parsley, to the simmering soup.

Gumbo-style Shrimp Soup

I prefer this soup made with half shrimp and half kielbasa (8 ounces each).

MEAT:

1 pound medium shrimp, peeled and deveined, shells reserved

VEGETABLES:

1 bell pepper, cut into a medium dice

2 celery stalks

STARCH:

½ cup long- or medium-grain white rice, rinsed

HERBS:

2 bay leaves and 1 tablespoon minced fresh parsley leaves

If you have time, bring the shrimp shells and 2 cups of broth to a simmer in a medium skillet. Cover, remove from the heat, and let stand 5 minutes. Strain the broth into the soup along with the remaining broth at the appropriate time; discard shells.

Follow the Supper Soup recipe (page 38), adding shrimp, along with parsley, a couple of minutes before the soup is done.

at-a-glance

SUPPER SOUP

- Know the formula—1 onion, 1 pound of vegetables, 1 pound of meat, 1 quart of chicken broth, 1 cup of tomatoes, plus starch and seasoning.

- Know the technique—sauté the onion, add the remaining ingredients, and simmer for twenty minutes. (Shrimp and pork tenderloin, the exceptions, are added for the last five minutes of cooking.)

- Prepare the meat and vegetables.

- Choose a quick-cooking starch—white rice, potatoes, egg noodles, canned beans or hominy.

- Simmer the soup in store-bought chicken broth until the vegetable and starch are tender, about 20 minutes.

Quick in a Cup,
Puréed Vegetable Soups

Simmer vegetables in broth until tender,

Add a little milk, then purée in the blender.

Hearty main-course soups are great when you need a complete meal in one bowl, but there are times when a cup of simple soup and a big salad hit the spot. On those nights I make a puréed vegetable soup. Even if my pantry and refrigerator are almost empty, I always have the ingredients to make these soups—potatoes or carrots, onions or garlic, chicken broth, milk, and a dried herb or spice. It's about as basic as it gets.

And the technique is as simple as the ingredients are basic. To make puréed vegetable soup, start by bringing 2 cups of chicken broth to a simmer in a large saucepan or Dutch oven. Giving the broth a head start saves cooking time: a vegetable cooks faster when added to simmering broth. While the chicken broth heats, chop an onion or smash a few garlic cloves (or both), adding them as soon as they are prepared.

Vegetables of Choice

With the onion or garlic heating in the broth, turn your attention to the vegetable. The best puréed vegetable soup candidates are root vegetables like potatoes, carrots, turnips, and rutabagas as well as winter squash, broccoli, and cauliflower. Not only are they flavorful, these vegetables are substantial enough once puréed to thicken the soup without any additional starch. On the other hand, soft, moist vegetables like mushrooms, peppers, spinach, zucchini, and onions do not have the necessary body to thicken soup without a starch thickener. So for weeknights, stick to the vegetables that work as a flavor and thickener in one.

For potatoes, carrots, winter squash, turnips, and rutabagas, peel and cut them into a medium dice. Because they will be puréed, size isn't crucial, but the bigger the chunk, the longer the cooking time. Cut broccoli and cauliflower into bite-size florets, and peel and slice broccoli stems. Since broccoli stems are so woody, it is important to peel them well. Otherwise, you'll end up with unpleasant bits of stem. Having prepared the vegetable, add it, along with an herb or dry spice, to the simmering broth, cover the pot, and cook until the vegetables are tender, 10 to 15 minutes.

Once the vegetables are done, put them along with either whole milk or half-and-half in a blender canister. You can also drop in a few sprigs of fresh parsley or other soft fresh herbs at this point, if you like. There's no need to mince them. The blender does it for you. The vegetables can be puréed in a food processor, but they won't have the same smooth silky texture of the blender-puréed ones.

Return the soup to the saucepan, adjust the seasonings with salt and pepper and additional herbs or spices, and reheat it. If the mixture is too thick, add a little extra chicken broth. If using chicken broth means opening a new carton, thin the soup with water. Obviously these soups can be served chilled as well—just cover and refrigerate until ready to serve.

Paired with a hearty salad, puréed soups make a quick weeknight supper. They're also elegant enough to serve as a first course at a nice dinner.

Puréed Vegetable Soup

As is the case with most of this book, the following recipes exemplify the technique, but are by no means exhaustive. I could just as easily team curry with broccoli or carrots with ginger.

2 cups chicken broth

Dried or fresh herb or spice

1 medium onion and/or 3 medium garlic cloves

1 pound potatoes, turnips, rutabagas, carrots, or winter squash, cauliflower, or broccoli

1 cup whole milk or half-and-half

Salt and ground black pepper

1. Bring the broth to a simmer, along with the dried herb or spice, over medium heat. While the broth is heating, cut the onion into medium dice or smash the garlic cloves and remove skin, adding onion and/or garlic to the broth. While broth and onion and/or garlic are heating, prepare the vegetable, adding it to the simmer-ing broth once it is prepared. Cover and simmer until vegetables are tender, about 10 minutes.

2. Transfer the mixture, along with the milk or half-and-half and the fresh herb, to a blender canister or the workbowl of a food processor and purée. (The soup can be cooled to room temperature, refrigerated, and served chilled.) Return the soup to the kettle, seasoning it with salt, if necessary, and ground black pepper, and thinning with additional broth or water if it seems too thick. Heat until soup starts to bubble. Serve.

Broccoli Soup with Red Pepper

VEGETABLE:

1 pound broccoli, cut into bite-size florets, stems peeled well and cut into 1/4-inch rounds

SPICE:

1/2 teaspoon red pepper flakes

Follow the Puréed Vegetable Soup recipe, adding red pepper flakes along with the broth.

Butternut Squash Soup with Ginger

VEGETABLE:

1 pound butternut squash, peeled, seeds removed, and cut into medium dice

SPICE:

½ teaspoon ground ginger

Follow the Puréed Vegetable Soup recipe.

Curried Cauliflower Soup

Garnish this soup, if you like, with a little diced fresh apple.

VEGETABLE:

1 pound cauliflower, trimmed and cut into florets

SPICE:

1 to 1½ teaspoon curry powder

Follow the Puréed Vegetable Soup recipe.

Potato Soup with Parsley and Chives

It is not necessary to mince the parsley. Add the whole sprigs to the blender or food processor.

VEGETABLE:

1 pound potatoes, cut into medium dice

HERBS:

3 or 4 parsley sprigs and 1 tablespoon scallion tops or chives

Follow the Puréed Vegetable Soup recipe, adding parsley and chives to the blender canister when puréeing the soup.

Carrot Soup with Cumin

VEGETABLE:

1 pound carrots, peeled and cut into medium dice

SPICE:

½ teaspoon ground cumin

Follow the Puréed Vegetable Soup recipe (page 50).

Rutabaga Soup with Thyme

VEGETABLE:

1 pound rutabaga, peeled and cut into medium dice

HERB:

½ teaspoon dried thyme

Follow the Puréed Vegetable Soup recipe (page 50).

at-a-glance

PURÉED VEGETABLE SOUP

- Remember the formula—1 onion (or 3 garlic cloves), 1 pound of vegetables, 2 cups of broth, 1 cup of milk or half-and-half, and herbs and/or spices.

- Heat the chicken broth.

- Add the diced onion or smashed garlic to the heating broth.

- Add prepared vegetable (see page 48 for vegetables of choice) to the simmering broth.

- Cover and simmer until vegetables are tender, about 10 minutes.

- Purée the vegetables, along with the cooking liquid and 1 cup of whole milk or half-and-half, in a blender canister (or the workbowl of a food processor).

- Return the soup to the saucepan and bring to a simmer, thinning it with additional broth or water if necessary. Adjust seasonings and serve.

potatoes breakfast all day
fill, fold, cover eggs
cheese fillings whisk

The Big Fat Omelet

Tilt pan and cook till eggs no longer run.

Fill and fold, then cook till barely done.

Until a few years back, I didn't make omelets for family meals. Maybe I'd make one for myself and one other person, but I had trouble making them for four or more.

Unlike those agile omelet cooks seen at breakfast buffets, I proceeded slowly and deliberately. It took me a while to get the feel of it, so my first few omelets always came out of the pan looking like scrambled eggs in semicircular form. Making them one at a time meant we ate in shifts as the omelets came off the stove, or one lucky person got a fresh, hot omelet while the other three got progressively older, oven-warmed versions.

Finally I learned how to serve and make omelets for a crowd the summer we lived in southern France. There were six of us at lunch one day, and our hostess announced she was making omelets. It was hot, we were all tired, and I remember thinking, "What a project!" But about fifteen minutes later, we were all sitting down to a meal of cheeses, cured meats, olives, and a twelve-egg omelet centerpiece. She simply cut the puffed eggs into sixths, giving us each a two-egg wedge. That was it!

Since then, I've never bothered with individual omelets, unless, of course, it's just for me or one other person. To figure out how many eggs go into my omelet, I count the number of eaters, multiply by two, and add an extra egg for the pot.

No matter what I do, sometimes the eggs stick, sometimes they don't, but a thoroughly and evenly heated nonstick skillet is an egg's best friend. Even before you crack the first egg or grate the cheese, turn the heat on low, and let the pan heat slowly while the butter melts. A couple of minutes before you're ready to cook, turn the heat to medium or medium-high depending on the size of the omelet. (The bigger the omelet the lower the heat.) By the time the eggs are beaten and the fillings are ready, the skillet is hot but not scorching, and the butter is nutty brown but not burned.

The temperature of the eggs is almost as important as the temperature of the skillet. Eggs straight from the refrigerator tend to stick, but it isn't necessary to soak them in warm water to get them to room temperature. After setting the skillet over low heat, crack and whisk the eggs, and by the time the skillet's ready, so are the eggs.

Should you add milk to your omelet eggs? Since I don't like puffy omelets, I usually don't. If you do, choose buttermilk over regular milk. Milk dilutes the egg flavor while buttermilk enhances it. When adding buttermilk to omelet eggs (or scrambled eggs for that matter), figure about one tablespoon for every two eggs.

Once you've poured the eggs into the hot skillet, use a plastic or wooden spatula to push back the eggs that have set, tilting the pan so that the uncooked eggs run into the empty areas of the pan. Continue this gentle pushing back and tilting until the omelet top is wet but no longer runny.

To prevent overbrowning, and to avoid working at a frantic pace, turn the burner to low while topping the omelet. Although I've given specific topping amounts in the recipes that follow, there's really no need to measure. Just grab a handful of cheese or a couple of pinchfuls of herbs and sprinkle them on. When making an individual omelet, I fold it into thirds, but when making The Big Fat Omelet, I simply fold it in half once it's topped.

How should this oversized omelet finish cooking? Ideally, it should spend its final minutes in the oven—I like the way the warm enveloping heat finishes cooking the eggs. But unless the oven is on for another purpose, cook it on the stovetop, partially covering the omelet with the lid from another pot and cooking it over low heat.

I've provided recipes, techniques, and cooking times for four- and eight-egg omelets, serving two and four people. Like the eight-egg omelet, a six-egger cooks in a ten-inch skillet. Ten- and twelve-egg omelets can be cooked in a twelve-inch skillet. Just remember to use medium, not medium-high heat.

Since these omelets are done in five to seven minutes, don't put the eggs in the pan until you have prepared all the filling ingredients and set the table.

The Little Big Fat Omelet

Since I often serve French bread with an omelet, the oven is on, heating up the frozen bread. Rather than cover the omelet and finish cooking it stovetop, I prefer to put the omelet in the oven once it has been topped and folded. The slow, even heat of the oven perfectly and gently finishes cooking the eggs.

2 teaspoons butter or other fat

4 to 5 large eggs

Pinch of salt

Ground pepper to taste

Optional Fillings (see pages that follow)

1. Heat the butter over medium-low heat in a 10-inch nonstick skillet (with an oven-proof handle if baking the omelet in the oven) while preparing the eggs and optional fillings. Lightly beat the eggs with salt and pepper; let stand for a few minutes to warm up.

2. Increase the heat to medium high, swirling the butter around to completely coat the pan bottom and up the sides. Once the butter starts to turn golden brown and smells nutty, add the eggs. Using a plastic or wooden spatula to push back the eggs that have set, tilt the pan so that the uncooked eggs run into the empty portion of the pan. Continue pushing back the cooked eggs and tilting the pan until the omelet top is wet but not runny, 1½ to 2 minutes. Reduce the heat to low, and quickly add optional toppings over one half of the omelet. Carefully fold the remaining half over the topped half. Partially cover the pan and cook (or place in a 350 degree oven) until the filling is warm and the eggs are set as desired, 3 to 5 minutes longer. Halve and serve immediately.

The Big Fat Omelet

1 tablespoon butter or other fat

8 or 9 large eggs

¼ teaspoon salt

Ground pepper to taste

Optional fillings (see recipes that follow)

1. Heat the butter over medium-low heat in a 12-inch nonstick skillet while preparing the eggs and optional fillings. Using a fork, lightly beat the eggs with salt and pepper until whites and yolks are blended.

2. Increase the heat to medium high, swirling the butter around to completely coat the pan bottom and sides. Once the butter starts to turn golden brown and smells nutty, add the eggs. Using a plastic or wooden spatula to push back the eggs that have set, tilt the pan so that the uncooked eggs run into the empty portion of the pan. Continue pushing back cooked eggs and tilting the pan until the omelet top is wet but not runny, 1 to 1½ minutes. Reduce the heat to low, and quickly add optional toppings over one half of the omelet. Carefully fold the remaining half over the topped half. Partially cover the pan and cook (or bake in a 350 degree oven) until fillings are warm and eggs are set as desired, 5 to 7 minutes longer. Quarter and serve immediately.

The Big Fat Omelet with Ham and Cheddar

FILLING FOR LITTLE BIG FAT OMELET:

¼ cup diced ham, or 2 thin slices deli-style ham

¼ cup shredded sharp or extra-sharp cheddar cheese

FILLING FOR BIG FAT OMELET:

½ cup diced ham, or 4 thin slices deli-style ham

½ cup shredded sharp or extra-sharp cheddar cheese

Follow either of the Big Fat Omelet recipes (pages 55–56), sprinkling ham and cheese over half the omelet at the appropriate time.

The Big Fat Omelet with Smoked Salmon, Sour Cream, and Chives

FILLING FOR LITTLE BIG FAT OMELET:

2 thin slices smoked salmon (1 to 1½ ounces)

1½ tablespoons sour cream

1 tablespoon snipped chives or minced scallion greens

FILLING FOR BIG FAT OMELET:

4 thin slices smoked salmon (2 to 3 ounces)

3 tablespoons sour cream

2 tablespoons snipped chives or minced scallion greens

Follow either of the Big Fat Omelet recipes (pages 55–56), laying smoked salmon over half the omelet, spreading sour cream over the salmon, and sprinkling chives over the sour cream at the appropriate time.

The Big Fat Omelet with Watercress, Bacon, and Sour Cream

FILLING FOR LITTLE BIG FAT OMELET:

2 bacon slices, cut into ½-inch pieces

⅓ cup stemmed watercress leaves

1½ tablespoons sour cream

FILLING FOR BIG FAT OMELET:

4 bacon slices, cut into ½-inch pieces

⅔ cup stemmed watercress leaves

3 tablespoons sour cream

Fry the bacon in the selected omelet pan over medium heat until crisp and brown, 5 to 7 minutes. Remove bacon with a slotted spoon and pour off all but 2 teaspoons of fat (or 1 tablespoon if making an omelet for 4). Follow either of the Big Fat Omelet recipes (pages 55–56), substituting bacon fat for butter and spreading watercress, bacon, and sour cream over half the omelet at the appropriate time.

The Big Fat Omelet with
Blue Cheese and Bacon

**FILLING FOR
LITTLE BIG FAT OMELET:**

3 bacon slices, cut in ½-inch pieces

1½ tablespoons crumbled blue
cheese

**FILLING FOR
BIG FAT OMELET:**

6 bacon slices, cut in ½-inch pieces

3 tablespoons crumbled blue
cheese

Fry the bacon in the selected omelet pan over medium heat until crisp and brown, 5 to 7 minutes. Remove bacon with a slotted spoon and pour off all but 2 teaspoons of fat (or 1 tablespoon if making an omelet for 4). Follow either of the Big Fat Omelet recipes (pages 55–56), substituting bacon fat for butter and sprinkling bacon and cheese over half the omelet at the appropriate time.

The Big Fat Omelet with
Cream Cheese and Caraway

**FILLING FOR
LITTLE BIG FAT OMELET:**

3 tablespoons cream cheese

Heaping ¼ teaspoon caraway
seeds

**FILLING FOR
BIG FAT OMELET:**

6 tablespoons cream cheese

Heaping ½ teaspoon caraway
seeds

Heat the selected omelet pan over medium heat; add caraway seeds and toast, shaking skillet frequently to ensure even cooking, until fragrant, 2 to 3 minutes; remove seeds and reserve. Follow either of the Big Fat Omelet recipes (pages 55–56), dotting half the omelet with marble-size pieces of cream cheese and sprinkling caraway seeds over cream cheese at the appropriate time.

The Big Fat Omelet with Parmesan and Herbs

**FILLING FOR
LITTLE BIG FAT OMELET:**

2 tablespoons mixed fresh herbs
such as parsley, chives, basil, or
tarragon

3 tablespoons grated Parmesan
cheese

**FILLING FOR
BIG FAT OMELET:**

¼ cup mixed fresh herbs such as
parsley, chives, basil, or tarragon

6 tablespoons grated Parmesan
cheese

Mix herbs and Parmesan. Follow either of the Big Fat Omelet recipes (pages 55–56),
sprinkling herb/cheese over half the omelet at the appropriate time.

The Big Fat Omelet with Onions and Peppers

The sautéed onions and peppers leave natural sugars in the pan, which can
caramelize and cause the omelet to stick. For this reason, sauté the vegetables in a separate skillet or give the pan a quick rinse after cooking the vegetables. Add a cheese of your choice, along with the peppers, if you like.

**FILLING FOR
LITTLE BIG FAT OMELET:**

2 teaspoons butter

½ small onion, sliced thin

½ small red bell pepper, sliced thin

Salt and ground black pepper to taste

**FILLING FOR
BIG FAT OMELET:**

1 tablespoon butter

1 small onion, sliced thin

1 small red bell pepper, sliced thin

Salt and ground black pepper

Heat the butter in the selected omelet pan over medium-high heat until sizzling subsides. Add the onions and peppers; sauté, seasoning with salt and pepper to taste,
until just softened, 4 to 5 minutes. Transfer to a small bowl and set aside. Follow either of the Big Fat Omelet recipes (pages 55–56), sprinkling onions and peppers over
half the omelet at the appropriate time.

The Big Fat Omelet with Mushrooms and Parsley

FILLING FOR LITTLE BIG FAT OMELET:	FILLING FOR BIG FAT OMELET:
2 teaspoons butter	1 tablespoon butter
1/2 cup sliced fresh mushrooms	1 cup sliced fresh mushrooms
Salt to taste	Salt to taste
1 1/2 teaspoons minced fresh parsley	1 tablespoon minced fresh parsley

Heat the butter in the selected omelet pan over medium-high heat until sizzling subsides. Add mushrooms and sauté, seasoning with salt to taste, until lightly browned, 1 to 2 minutes. Transfer to a small bowl; stir in parsley and set aside. Follow either of the Big Fat Omelet recipes (pages 55–56), sprinkling mushrooms over half the omelet at the appropriate time.

The Big Fat Omelet with Spinach and Feta

FILLING FOR LITTLE BIG FAT OMELET:	FILLING FOR BIG FAT OMELET:
2 teaspoons butter	1 tablespoon butter
2 cups washed and stemmed spinach	4 cups washed and stemmed spinach
Salt to taste	Salt to taste
2 tablespoons crumbled feta cheese	1/4 cup crumbled feta cheese

Heat the butter in the selected omelet pan over medium-high heat until sizzling subsides. Add the spinach and sauté, seasoning with salt to taste, until just wilted, about 1 minute. Transfer to a small bowl and set aside. Follow either of the Big Fat Omelet recipes (pages 55–56), sprinkling spinach and feta over half the omelet at the appropriate time.

The Big Fat Omelet with
Asparagus and Parmesan

**FILLING FOR
LITTLE BIG FAT OMELET:**

6 thin asparagus spears, trimmed
to 2 inch tips

Salt to taste

3 tablespoons grated Parmesan
cheese

**FILLING FOR
BIG FAT OMELET:**

12 thin asparagus spears, trimmed
to 2-inch tips

Salt to taste

6 tablespoons grated Parmesan
cheese

In the selected omelet pan bring about ¼ inch of salted water and the asparagus to a boil over medium-high heat; cook asparagus, covered, until just tender, 4 to 5 minutes. Drain and set asparagus aside. Follow either of the Big Fat Omelet recipes (pages 55–56), laying asparagus spears over half the omelet and sprinkling cheese over asparagus at the appropriate time.

The Big Fat Omelet with
Goat Cheese, Tomato, and Basil

**FILLING FOR
LITTLE BIG FAT OMELET:**

3 tablespoons crumbled fresh
goat cheese

1 small plum tomato, cut into small
dice and lightly seasoned with salt

1 tablespoon minced fresh basil
leaves

**FILLING FOR
BIG FAT OMELET:**

6 tablespoons crumbled fresh
goat cheese

2 small plum tomatoes, cut into small
dice and lightly seasoned with salt

2 tablespoons minced fresh basil
leaves

Follow either of the Big Fat Omelet recipes (pages 55–56), sprinkling goat cheese, tomato, and basil over half the omelet at the appropriate time.

The Big Fat Omelet with Salsa, Jack Cheese, and Sour Cream

FILLING FOR LITTLE BIG FAT OMELET:	FILLING FOR BIG FAT OMELET:
3 tablespoons prepared salsa	6 tablespoons prepared salsa
1/4 cup grated Monterey Jack cheese	1/2 cup grated Monterey Jack cheese
1 1/2 tablespoons sour cream	3 tablespoons sour cream

Follow either of the Big Fat Omelet recipes (pages 55–56), spreading salsa, cheese, and sour cream over half the omelet at the appropriate time.

The Big Fat Omelet with Artichokes and Ham

FILLING FOR LITTLE BIG FAT OMELET:	FILLING FOR BIG FAT OMELET:
2 teaspoons butter	1 tablespoon butter
3 small canned artichoke hearts, quartered	6 small canned artichoke hearts, quartered
1/4 cup diced baked ham	1/2 cup diced baked ham
1 tablespoon grated Parmesan cheese (optional)	2 tablespoons grated Parmesan cheese (optional)

Heat the butter in the selected omelet pan over medium-high heat until sizzling subsides. Add the artichokes and ham; sauté until lightly browned, 1 to 2 minutes. Transfer to a small bowl and set aside. Follow either of the Big Fat Omelet recipes (pages 55–56), sprinkling artichoke hearts, ham, and cheese, if desired, over half the omelet at the appropriate time.

The Big Fat Omelet with Crabmeat

FILLING FOR LITTLE BIG FAT OMELET:	**FILLING FOR BIG FAT OMELET:**
2 teaspoons butter	1 tablespoon butter
1 tablespoon diced bell pepper	2 tablespoons diced bell pepper
1 small scallion, sliced thin	2 small scallions, sliced thin
Salt to taste	Salt to taste
$1/3$ cup lump crabmeat, picked over to remove bits of shell	$2/3$ cup lump crabmeat, picked over to remove bits of shell

Heat the butter in the selected omelet pan over medium-high heat until sizzling subsides. Add the peppers and scallions; sauté until just softened, about 1 minute. Add the crabmeat; sauté to warm through. Transfer to a small bowl and set aside. Follow either of the Big Fat Omelet recipes (pages 55–56), sprinkling crab mixture over half the omelet at the appropriate time.

The Big Fat Omelet with Cream Cheese and Chutney

FILLING FOR LITTLE BIG FAT OMELET:	**FILLING FOR BIG FAT OMELET:**
3 tablespoons cream cheese	6 tablespoons cream cheese
2 tablespoons prepared chutney, such as Major Grey's	$1/4$ cup prepared chutney, such as Major Grey's

Follow either of the Big Fat Omelet recipes (pages 55–56), dotting half the omelet with marble-size pieces of cream cheese and spooning chutney over the cream cheese at the appropriate time.

THE BIG FAT OMELET

- Heat butter over low heat in a nonstick skillet.

- Lightly beat eggs with salt and pepper; let stand for a few minutes to warm up.

- Prepare optional fillings.

- Increase the heat to medium until butter starts to turn golden brown and smells nutty. Add the eggs.

- Using a plastic or wooden spatula to push back the eggs that have set, tilt the pan so that the uncooked eggs run into the empty portion of the pan. Continue this process until the omelet top is wet but not runny.

- Reduce the heat to low and quickly add optional toppings over one half of the omelet. Carefully fold the remaining half over the topped half.

- Partially cover the pan and cook (or bake in a 350 degree oven) until the fillings are warm and the eggs are set as desired.

The Big and Bigger Frittata

Cook eggs without stirring till set around the edges.

Bake until puffy, then cut into wedges.

Unless there was a good reason, my mother got up every morning and fixed a bacon-eggs-grits-and-toast breakfast. Like other families of that era, we'd get up and enjoy the meal together before heading off for the day.

Sometimes Mom would fix breakfast again at night. She called it "breakfast for supper," and since I'd already had the same meal once that day, I'd always complain.

Thirty years later, I try to carry on the family breakfast tradition—but barely. I might put on a pot of quick grits, or scramble some eggs, or toast some bagels, but we never sit down to a full breakfast. We're lucky if we have eight minutes together. Which may be why my daughters love eggs for dinner.

I have come to love eggs for dinner too. Supper doesn't get any quicker and simpler. Rather than bacon and eggs, however, I make frittata for four. Dinner is our one shot to get in a vegetable or two for the day, and frittatas pair well with salads and vegetables. And, if there's no time for salad, I can always get a vegetable in the frittata.

Whereas bacon, eggs, toast, and jelly begs for juice and coffee, a frittata meal calls for a glass of wine—another good reason to make the frittata a weeknight regular.

Easier Than an Omelette

Although the ingredients lists may look the same, an omelet and a frittata look different, cook different, and taste different. An omelet's structure is hierarchical, with eggs on top and fillings as hidden support. The frittata structure is a partnership, eggs binding fillings, fillings flavoring eggs.

Omelets may be quick, but frittatas are easy. Unlike omelets, there's no technique to master with frittatas. Once the filling ingredients are cooked, the eggs go into the skillet and the skillet goes into the oven. When the eggs puff, 10 to 12 minutes later, the skillet comes out.

How to Make a Frittata

To make a frittata, start by setting the oven rack in the upper middle position and heating the oven to 400 degrees. Because the frittata will have already gotten enough bottom heat from the burner, bake it mid-oven. Depending on whether you're making a frittata for four or six, pull out a 10- or 12-inch heavy-duty, ovenproof nonstick skillet. To be quick and efficient, cook filling and frittata in the same skillet.

After heating the oven and selecting the skillet, start preparing the filling ingredients, one of which, for me, is always a vegetable. Depending on the vegetable, there are two methods for preparing the filling.

Steam/sauté harder vegetables like potatoes and asparagus. This is done exactly the way it sounds. The vegetable is first steamed or "wet cooked," then sautéed, or "dry cooked" right in the frittata pan. To steam/sauté, place the prepared vegetable and a minced garlic clove in the skillet, along with a few tablespoons of water, some olive oil, and a sprinkling of salt and pepper. Cover the skillet and turn the heat to medium-high. In just a few minutes, the vegetable has steamed and the water in the pan has almost evaporated. At that point remove the lid, and as the last of the water evaporates, the oil will kick in, sautéing the steamed vegetable. (For further information on this technique, see page 202.)

Softer frittata vegetables like peppers, mushrooms, and onions need only a quick sauté. For these, heat the oil while preparing the vegetable. By the time you're done, the oil in the skillet should be shimmering and ready. If vegetable preparation takes longer than the three or four minutes to heat the oil, start the skillet over medium heat, increasing it to medium-high a minute or so before adding the vegetables. When sautéed with the vegetables, the garlic tends to burn by the time the frittata comes out of the oven. For this reason, reduce the heat once the vegetables are cooked, then add the garlic.

While the filling ingredients are cooking, prepare the eggs and grate the cheese. By the time the filling is done, the eggs are ready. And by the time you've added the eggs and they start to set around the edges, the oven is preheated.

I have tried making frittatas stovetop from start to finish with little success. Even with reduced heat and a cover, the frittata bottom overcooks before the eggs cook through. A frittata needs the enveloping oven to cook evenly and to puff.

While the frittata does its oven time, we usually eat a salad or some other simple first course. When we're done, so is the frittata. Even if you don't time it right, frittatas are just as good at room temperature or even chilled.

The Big Frittata

2 tablespoons olive oil

Filling ingredients (see recipes that follow)

Salt and ground black pepper

1 medium garlic clove, minced

8 large eggs

3 tablespoons grated Parmesan cheese

3 ounces additional cheese (optional; see individual recipes)

2 tablespoons minced fresh parsley or basil

1. Adjust the oven rack to the upper-middle position and heat the oven to 400 degrees.

2. **For sautéed filling ingredients,** heat the oil in a 10-inch ovenproof nonstick skillet over medium-high heat until shimmering. Add the prepared ingredients, seasoning them with salt and pepper; sauté until lightly browned, 6 to 8 minutes. Reduce the heat to low, add garlic and cook to blend flavors, about 1 minute longer. **For steam/sautéed filling ingredients,** put oil, 2 to 4 tablespoons water (see recipe for specific amount), filling ingredients, a sprinkling of salt and pepper, and garlic in the 10-inch skillet. Set the skillet over medium-high heat, cover, and steam until the filling ingredients are cooked through (see recipe for specific times). Remove the lid and continue to cook, stirring occasionally, until the liquid evaporates and ingredients start to sauté and lightly brown (see recipe for specific time).

3. Meanwhile, lightly beat the eggs with Parmesan, optional cheese, herb of choice, and salt and pepper to taste.

4. Shake the skillet to evenly distribute the filling ingredients, then add the eggs. Without stirring, cook until they start to set around the edges, about 1 minute. Transfer the pan to the oven and bake until the eggs are puffed and set, 10 to 12 minutes longer. Slide or invert onto a large plate, cut into 4 wedges, and serve.

The Bigger Frittata

Serves 6

3 tablespoons olive oil

Filling ingredients (see recipes below)

Salt and ground black pepper

1 large garlic clove, minced

12 large eggs

¼ cup grated Parmesan cheese

4 ounces additional cheese
(optional; see individual recipes)

3 tablespoons minced fresh parsley
or basil

1. Adjust the oven rack to the upper-middle position and heat the oven to 400 degrees.

2. **For sautéed filling ingredients,** heat the oil in a 12-inch ovenproof nonstick skillet over medium-high heat. Add the prepared ingredients and salt and pepper to taste; sauté until lightly browned, 6 to 8 minutes. Reduce the heat to low, add the garlic, and cook to blend flavors, about 1 minute longer. **For steam/sautéed filling ingredients,** combine the oil with 2 to 4 tablespoons of water (see recipe for specific amount), the filling ingredients, a sprinkling of salt and pepper, and garlic in the 12-inch skillet. Set the skillet over medium-high heat, cover, and steam until the filling ingredients are cooked through (see recipe for specific times). Remove the lid and continue to cook, stirring occasionally, until the liquid evaporates and the ingredients start to sauté and lightly brown (see recipe for specific time).

3. Meanwhile, lightly beat the eggs with the Parmesan, the optional cheese, herb of choice, and salt and pepper to taste.

4. Shake the skillet to evenly distribute the filling ingredients, then add the eggs. Without stirring, cook until the eggs start to set around the edges, about 1 minute. Transfer the pan to the oven and bake until the eggs are puffed and set, 10 to 12 minutes longer. Slide or invert onto a large plate, cut into 6 wedges, and serve.

Frittata with Potatoes and Green Olives

**INGREDIENTS FOR
BIG FRITTATA:**

3 new potatoes, rinsed and cut
into ½ inch-dice

¼ cup pimiento-stuffed olives,
chopped

**INGREDIENTS FOR
BIGGER FRITATTA:**

4 new potatoes, rinsed and sliced
¼-inch thick

6 tablespoons pimiento-stuffed
olives, chopped

Follow the instructions for steam/sautéed filling ingredients (page 68), adding 3 tablespoons of water to the skillet and steaming until the potatoes are just tender, 2 to 3 minutes. Remove the lid and continue to cook until the liquid evaporates and potatoes are lightly browned, 6 to 8 minutes longer.

Frittata with Sausage and Potatoes

**INGREDIENTS FOR
BIG FRITTATA:**

6 ounces mild Italian sausage,
removed from casing

2 new potatoes, sliced thin

**INGREDIENTS FOR
BIGGER FRITATTA:**

8 ounces mild Italian sausage,
removed from casing

3 new potatoes, sliced thin

Follow the instructions for steam/sautéed filling ingredients (page 68), adding ¼ cup of water to the skillet and steaming the ingredients until the sausage loses its raw color and potatoes are just cooked, 4 to 5 minutes. Remove the lid and continue to cook until the liquid evaporates and potatoes and sausage start to brown, 4 to 5 minutes longer.

Frittata with Asparagus and Ham

**INGREDIENTS FOR
BIG FRITTATA:**

8 medium or 12 thin asparagus
spears, trimmed and cut into 1-inch
lengths

4 ounces cooked ham, cut into
¼-inch dice

**INGREDIENTS FOR
BIGGER FRITATTA:**

12 medium or 18 thin asparagus
spears, trimmed and cut into 1-inch
lengths

6 ounces cooked ham, cut into
¼-inch dice

Follow the instructions for steam/sautéed filling ingredients (page 68), adding 2 table-spoons of water to the skillet and steaming until the asparagus is just tender, 2 to 3 minutes. Remove the lid and continue to cook until the liquid evaporates and ham starts to brown, 3 to 5 minutes longer.

Frittata with Spinach and Sausage

**INGREDIENTS FOR
BIG FRITTATA:**

3 cups spinach leaves, chopped
coarse

6 ounces Italian sausage, removed
from casing and crumbled

**INGREDIENTS FOR
BIGGER FRITATTA:**

4 cups spinach leaves, chopped
coarse

8 ounces Italian sausage, removed
from casing and crumbled

Follow the instructions for steam/sautéed filling ingredients (page 68), adding no water to the skillet (since spinach is so moist, it does not need it). Steam until the spinach wilts and sausage loses its raw color, 2 to 3 minutes. Remove the lid and continue to cook until the liquid evaporates, 2 to 3 minutes longer.

Frittata with Tomato and Goat Cheese

INGREDIENTS FOR
BIG FRITTATA:

2 medium plum tomatoes,
sliced ¼-inch thick

3 ounces mild goat cheese,
crumbled

INGREDIENTS FOR
BIGGER FRITATTA:

3 medium plum tomatoes,
sliced ¼-inch thick

4 ounces mild goat cheese,
crumbled

Follow the instructions for sautéed filling ingredients (page 68), making the following changes: Fry the tomato slices in the hot oil in a single layer until lightly browned, 1½ to 2 minutes. Turn the tomatoes, then continue to cook until the other sides are lightly browned, 1½ to 2 minutes longer. Reduce the heat, add garlic, and continue with the recipe, gently stirring the goat cheese, along with Parmesan, into the eggs.

Frittata with Fennel and Fontina

INGREDIENTS FOR
BIG FRITTATA:

1 medium fennel bulb, fronds
removed, halved, cored, and
sliced thin

1 small red onion, halved and
sliced thin

3 ounces shredded fontina or
Swiss (½ cup)

INGREDIENTS FOR
BIGGER FRITATTA:

1 large fennel bulb, fronds
removed, halved, cored, and
sliced thin

1 medium red onion, halved and
sliced thin

4 ounces shredded fontina or
Swiss (¾ cup)

Follow the instructions for sautéed filling ingredients (page 68). Stir the shredded cheese, along with the Parmesan, into the eggs.

Frittata with Zucchini and Mozzarella

**INGREDIENTS FOR
BIG FRITTATA:**

1 medium-large zucchini, sliced
into ¼-inch rounds

½ cup (3 ounces) shredded
mozzarella

**INGREDIENTS FOR
BIGGER FRITATTA:**

2 medium zucchini, sliced
into ¼-inch rounds

¾ cup (4 ounces) shredded
mozzarella

Follow the instructions for sautéed filling ingredients (page 68). Stir the mozzarella,
along with the Parmesan, into the eggs.

Frittata with Chickpeas and Kale

**INGREDIENTS FOR
BIG FRITTATA:**

3 cups coarse-chopped kale

½ cup canned chickpeas, drained
and rinsed

**INGREDIENTS FOR
BIGGER FRITATTA:**

4 cups coarse-chopped kale

¾ cup canned chickpeas, drained
and rinsed

Follow the instructions for steam/sautéed filling ingredients (page 68), adding 3 tablespoons of water to the skillet and steaming until the kale wilts, about 3 minutes.
Remove the lid and cook until the liquid evaporates, 2 to 3 minutes longer.

Frittata with Peppers and Onions

**INGREDIENTS FOR
BIG FRITTATA:**

1 medium bell pepper, cut
into ¼-inch strips

1 medium onion, halved and cut
into ¼-inch wedges

**INGREDIENTS FOR
BIGGER FRITATTA:**

1 large bell pepper, cut
into ¼-inch strips

1 large onion, halved and cut
into ¼-inch wedges

Follow the instructions for sautéed filling ingredients (page 68).

Frittata with Mushrooms, Fontina, and Thyme

**INGREDIENTS FOR
BIG FRITTATA:**

8 ounces mushrooms, sliced

2 teaspoons minced fresh thyme
leaves or ¾ teaspoon dried

½ cup (3 ounces) shredded
fontina cheese

**INGREDIENTS FOR
BIGGER FRITATTA:**

12 ounces mushrooms, sliced

1 tablespoon minced fresh thyme
leaves or 1 teaspoon dried

¾ cup (4 ounces) shredded
fontina cheese

Follow the instructions for sautéed filling ingredients (page 68), adding thyme along with garlic and stirring the fontina, along with Parmesan, into the eggs.

Frittata with Potatoes and Artichoke Hearts

**INGREDIENTS FOR
BIG FRITTATA:**

2 new potatoes, rinsed and cut
into ½-inch dice

4 canned artichoke hearts,
quartered

**INGREDIENTS FOR
BIGGER FRITATTA:**

3 new potatoes, rinsed and cut
into ½-inch dice

6 canned artichoke hearts,
quartered

Follow the instructions for steam/sautéed filling ingredients (page 68), adding 3 tablespoons of water to the skillet and steaming until the potatoes are just tender, 2 to 3 minutes. Remove the lid and continue to cook until the liquid evaporates and potatoes are lightly browned, 6 to 8 minutes longer.

Frittata with Bacon and Onions

Unlike the other frittata recipes, this one uses bacon drippings instead of olive oil. To make this frittata more substantial, feel free to add shredded cheese.

INGREDIENTS FOR BIG FRITTATA:	INGREDIENTS FOR BIGGER FRITTATA:
3 slices bacon, cut into ½-inch pieces	4 slices bacon, cut into ½-inch pieces
1 small onion	1 medium onion

Follow recipe for sautéed filling ingredients (page 68), omitting olive oil and frying bacon until it starts to render its fat. Add onions and continue to cook until bacon is crisp and onion has softened, 6 to 8 minutes.

at-a-glance

FRITTATAS

- Adjust the oven rack to the upper-middle position and heat the oven to 400 degrees.
- Sauté or steam/sauté the filling ingredients in the frittata pan.
- Beat the eggs with Parmesan, herb of choice, and salt and pepper to taste.
- Shake the skillet to evenly distribute filling ingredients; add the eggs and cook until they start to set around the edges.
- Transfer the pan to the oven and bake until the eggs are puffed and set.

Simple Tomato Sauce, Scores of Possibilities

Heat fat and garlic, then cook it for two.

Add canned tomatoes and simmer for a few.

Although my kids will eat most anything once it's on the table, they are prone to complain about it beforehand—unless, of course, it's pasta with tomato sauce. Who could argue? For the cook, the dish is barely a step beyond boiling water. For the diner, this simple entree satisfies the range of tastes, from toddlers and teenagers to vegetarians—even vegans.

When serving pasta with tomato sauce, you may be tempted to use a jarred tomato sauce rather than making one from scratch. Don't do it. The difference in flavor between from-scratch tomato sauce and the jarred variety is significant. Most jarred tomato sauces taste too sweet, too salty, too oily, too chunky, too smooth, too seedy, too cooked, too vegetal, or just too "store-bought."

I might understand jarred-sauce dependency if simple tomato sauce required hours of preparation and cooking, but it doesn't. In its basic form, a quick tomato sauce takes about two minutes to prepare and ten minutes to simmer—less time than it takes to bring a pot of water to boil and cook the pasta. Jarred sauce feeds; homemade sauce nurtures and satisfies.

To make a simple tomato sauce, start by selecting the right pan. A 4-quart saucepan or a 6-quart Dutch oven is perfect for a single recipe of sauce. If making a larger quantity, select a large, deep skillet or soup kettle.

For the simplest tomato sauce, olive oil and butter are the fats of choice. If flavoring the sauce with bacon or sausage, use their drippings instead. To render bacon or sausage fat, fry it first in the pan you've chosen for the sauce. If the sausage or bacon renders more fat than needed, pour some off. If it renders less than 3 or 4 tablespoons, add oil or butter to make up the difference.

Once the fat has been selected, choose an aromatic (onions, garlic, or both). If using garlic only, know that it burns easily in hot oil, which will give the finished sauce a bitter taste. To avoid burning the garlic, heat the minced cloves along *with* the butter or olive oil until it just starts to sizzle and become fragrant. If using drippings or if you have cooked meat or seafood first, cool the pan down a minute or so before adding the garlic. Have the can of tomatoes open and ready to pour in. If pressed for time, you can even get away with crushing the cloves with the broad side of a chef's knife, removing the peel, and tossing the garlic into the heating fat. On the other hand, onions need hot fat to soften them so heat the fat first, then add the onions. Onions are high in moisture, so if using both onions and garlic, it is okay to add the garlic with the onions and sauté them together.

The key to quick tomato sauce is the tomato. Canned crushed tomatoes are ideal when making a simple tomato sauce. The tomatoes are chopped and the juice is thick, eliminating preparation and long simmering, but it's important to buy a quality brand. Some brands contain bitter seeds and bits of peel while others are so smooth-textured they're more like tomato purée.

After tasting dozens of canned tomato products, I recommend three brands of crushed tomatoes. Muir Glen Organic Ground Peeled Tomatoes are the ones I prefer. Located in the organic section of my local grocery store, these canned tomatoes have become so popular I'm never surprised to find the shelf empty. If Muir Glen tomatoes are unavailable, look for Red Pack Crushed or Progresso Crushed. Just open the canned crushed tomatoes and add them to the pot.

If I'm out of crushed tomatoes, whole canned tomatoes packed in purée are my second choice when making a simple tomato sauce. To save time and another dirty bowl, add the tomatoes to the pot and crush them with your fingertips before they've had a chance to heat up. Crush gently, especially at first. If you squeeze too hard before the tomato bursts, you may end up with tomato juice in your eye. If you're not a "hands-on" cook, simply crush the tomatoes in the pot with a potato masher or, if you don't mind having something else to wash, pulse them in a food processor until coarse-chopped.

Different brands of tomatoes contain different amounts of salt, so taste the tomatoes before seasoning the sauce, knowing that the salt flavor will only intensify as the sauce simmers and reduces. Depending on the brand, you may not need to add any salt at all.

Simple tomato sauce may be served as is, but I usually doctor it up by adding a variety of ingredients to the pot, with a few obvious exceptions. Raw seafood such as shrimp and scallops, and uncooked meats such as sausage and boneless chicken thighs, are cooked and removed from the pan before sautéing the onion and/or garlic. How quickly they might overcook determines when they should be returned to the sauce. Since scallops and shrimp easily overcook and toughen, return them to the fully cooked sauce only at the end. Sausage and boneless chicken breasts or thighs should be cooked whole, then returned to the pot cut into bite-size pieces or shredded. Like the other meats, bacon should be cooked before sautéing the aromatics, but it does not need to be removed from the pan.

Since they release so much liquid during cooking and would cause the aromatics to stew rather than sauté, ground meats such as turkey and beef are added after the aromatics have cooked. Raw vegetables such as zucchini, peppers, and mushrooms are best if sautéed along with the garlic and/or onions.

How to Cook and Serve Pasta Fast

Some cooks insist that you need a gallon of water and a tablespoon of salt to boil a pound of pasta. Since it takes nearly 20 minutes to bring this amount of water to a boil, I've found I can get away with less water—much less.

To cook one pound of pasta in less water, bring 2 quarts of water to a full boil over high heat in an 8-quart or larger covered pot. Add 1 tablespoon of salt (1½ times that amount if using kosher salt) and a pound of pasta, stirring it several times at the beginning of cooking to keep it from sticking. (If using spaghetti or other long-strand pasta, press on the strands with a wooden spoon to submerge them.) Boil, partially covered, until just tender. I've actually found that back-of-the-box time suggestions are relatively accurate when pasta is cooked in less water.

For weeknight suppers, I add the pasta to the boiling water once the salad has been dished up. As we eat our salad, I check the pasta once. If it's getting done too quickly, I turn the heat down, and it waits for us. If it's cooking too slowly, I keep the heat cranked up, and we wait for the pasta. Although I know pasta can overcook and become bloated, it is much more resilient than we've been led to believe. From my experience, it's perfectly fine in the pot for a couple minutes—even longer for thick, sturdy pastas. Relax and enjoy your salad.

Some people like to top their pasta with tomato sauce; others prefer to toss the two together before serving. I like my pasta both tossed *and* topped. For tossed and topped pasta, return the drained pasta to the pot. Add about two-thirds of the sauce to the pasta and toss to coat. Transfer a portion of coated pasta to each plate, topping each with portion of the remaining sauce. Grate a generous portion of cheese over each mound of pasta and serve.

To learn how to make tomato sauce without a recipe, always use the same pot. Measure the amount of oil specified, then tilt the pan. Notice what that amount of oil looks like in the pot. Now put away the measuring cups and spoons because the rest is simple—a couple of garlic cloves, a 28-ounce can of crushed tomatoes, and a little chopped parsley if you have it.

Simple Tomato Sauce

Some brands of tomatoes are more acidic than others, so you may want to add a pinch of sugar or even a pinch of baking soda at the end of cooking to neutralize the acidity. If you prefer a lower-fat sauce, use the lesser amount of fat. If you cheat the sauce of too much fat, however, your sauce will lack body and taste like warmed-up tomatoes. Grated Parmesan cheese passed separately goes well with all except for the fresh seafood sauces.

3 to 4 tablespoons fat (extra-virgin olive oil, butter, or rendered meat fat such as sausage or bacon)

AROMATIC:

3 medium garlic cloves, minced, or 1 small onion, halved and sliced thin or chopped fine

1 can (28 ounces) crushed tomatoes or whole tomatoes packed in purée (see page 77)

Ground black pepper and salt

2 tablespoons minced fresh parsley leaves (optional)

In a large saucepan or a Dutch oven, heat garlic and oil together over medium-high heat until garlic starts to sizzle. If using onion, heat oil, add onions, and sauté until soft, 3 to 4 minutes. Stir in tomatoes, bring to a simmer; continue to simmer over medium-low heat until sauce thickens and flavors meld, about 10 to 15 minutes (cooking time varies based on added ingredients). Taste the sauce and season with pepper and salt, if necessary. Stir in optional parsley. Add about ²⁄₃ of the sauce with cooked pasta and toss. Serve, topping each portion with remaining sauce.

Tomato-Basil Cream Sauce

You can substitute 1 teaspoon of dried basil for the fresh, but add it along with the tomatoes. This sauce is best served with fettuccine.

FAT:

3 tablespoons butter

AROMATIC:

1 small onion, halved and sliced thin

EXTRA INGREDIENTS:

½ cup heavy cream

2 tablespoons shredded fresh basil leaves

Follow the Simple Tomato Sauce recipe, adding cream and basil to the fully cooked sauce. Continue to simmer until heated through, 1 to 2 minutes longer.

Tomato Sauce with Wild Mushrooms

Dried mushrooms vary greatly in size. Some look almost like mushroom powder; others are so large they require extra-long soaking times. You can reduce soaking time with the large mushrooms by cutting them into smaller pieces once they are soft enough to cut, then returning them to the soaking liquid.

FAT:

3 to 4 tablespoons extra-virgin olive oil

AROMATIC:

3 garlic cloves, minced

EXTRA INGREDIENTS:

½ ounce (⅓ cup) dried mushrooms

½ teaspoon dried thyme leaves

Add ½ cup of hot tap water to the dried mushrooms. Set a small bowl or some other object over the floating mushrooms so that they are completely submerged in water. Soak until soft, 10–15 minutes. Cut into medium dice.

Meanwhile, follow the Simple Tomato Sauce recipe, adding softened mushrooms, thyme, and the strained mushroom soaking liquid along with the tomatoes.

Tomato Sauce with Fresh Mushrooms and Oregano

FAT:
3 to 4 tablespoons extra-virgin olive oil

AROMATICS:
3 garlic cloves, minced

EXTRA INGREDIENTS:
1/2 pound mushrooms, sliced

1 teaspoon dried oregano

Follow the Simple Tomato Sauce recipe (page 80), adding mushrooms to the garlic; sauté until mushroom liquid evaporates, 3 to 4 minutes. Add oregano with the tomatoes.

Tomato Sauce with Artichokes and Olives

Minced fresh parsley particulary enhances this tomato sauce.

FAT:
3 to 4 tablespoons extra-virgin olive oil

AROMATIC:
3 garlic cloves, minced

EXTRA INGREDIENTS:
1 can (14 ounces) artichoke quarters, drained

16 to 24 piquant black olives, such as Kalamatas, pitted and chopped coarse

Follow the Simple Tomato Sauce recipe (page 80), adding artichokes and olives along with the tomatoes.

Tomato Sauce with Aromatic Vegetables

Give the vegetables a light sprinkling of salt as they sauté.

FAT:
3 to 4 tablespoons butter

AROMATIC:
1 small onion, halved and cut into small dice

EXTRA INGREDIENTS:
1/2 small carrot, cut into small dice

1/2 stalk small celery, cut into small dice

Follow the Simple Tomato Sauce recipe (page 80), sautéing the carrot and celery along with the onion.

Tomato Sauce with Sweet Onions and Thyme

Using a medium-large onion instead of a small one wouldn't hurt this sauce one bit.

FAT:

3 to 4 tablespoons butter

AROMATIC:

1 small onion, halved and sliced thin

EXTRA INGREDIENTS:

Pinch of sugar

1/2 teaspoon dried thyme leaves

Follow the Simple Tomato Sauce recipe (page 80), sprinkling the sautéing onion with a pinch of sugar. Sauté until all moisture evaporates and onion starts to turn golden. Add thyme along with tomatoes.

Tomato Sauce with Zucchini and Basil

So that it doesn't taste bland, salt the zucchini as it sautés. If using fresh basil, add it to the fully cooked sauce.

FAT:

3 to 4 tablespoons extra-virgin olive oil

AROMATIC:

3 garlic cloves, minced, and 1 small onion, halved and sliced

EXTRA INGREDIENTS:

2 medium zucchini, quartered lengthwise and cut into 1/2-inch dice

2 tablespoons minced fresh basil or 2 teaspoons dried

Follow the Simple Tomato Sauce recipe (page 80), adding zucchini to the sautéing garlic and onions; continue to sauté until zucchini are golden, 3 to 4 minutes. Add dried basil along with the tomatoes; add fresh basil to the fully cooked sauce.

Tomato Sauce with Capers and Black Olives

Even if you are not an anchovy fan, you'll never taste them in this sauce. Without making their presence known, they add depth of flavor.

FAT:

3 to 4 tablespoons olive oil

AROMATIC:

3 garlic cloves, minced

EXTRA INGREDIENTS:

4 anchovies, minced (optional)

16 to 24 piquant olives, such as kalamatas, pitted and chopped coarse

2 tablespoons capers, drained

Follow the Simple Tomato Sauce recipe (page 80), stirring anchovies into the sizzling garlic until they soften and adding the olives and capers along with the tomatoes.

Tomato Sauce with Tuna and Olives

When adding the tuna, I prefer to leave it in fairly large chunks rather than break it up as for salad, so stir the sauce lightly. For a heartier sauce, use two cans of tuna. This sauce is also good when made with fresh tuna. Sear the tuna, leaving it medium rare, cut it into chunks, and add it to the fully cooked sauce. Although some purists say Parmesan cheese should never be grated on seafood, I don't think of canned tuna as the same thing, and since it tastes good to me, I shamelessly grate cheese over this dish.

FAT:

3 to 4 tablespoons olive oil

AROMATIC:

3 garlic cloves, minced

EXTRA INGREDIENTS:

1 to 2 (6½-ounce) cans solid white tuna packed in water

16 to 24 piquant black olives, such as kalamata, pitted and chopped coarse, or an equal number of pimiento-stuffed Spanish olives, halved

Follow the Simple Tomato Sauce recipe (page 80), adding tuna and olives with the tomatoes.

Tomato Sauce with Shrimp and Red Pepper Flakes

You can leave the shrimp tails on or take them off, depending on your preference. For a spicier sauce, increase pepper flakes up to $1/2$ teaspoon.

FAT:

4 tablespoons butter or olive oil

AROMATIC:

3 garlic cloves, minced

EXTRA INGREDIENTS:

$2/3$ pound medium shrimp, peeled (and deveined, if desired) and sprinkled with salt and pepper

$1/4$ teaspoon hot red pepper flakes

Follow the Simple Tomato Sauce recipe (page 80), heating oil over medium-high heat. Add the shrimp to the hot oil; sauté until bright pink, 3 to 4 minutes. Remove the pan from the heat; transfer the shrimp to a plate with a slotted spoon. Once the oil has cooled slightly, return the pan to the heat and add red pepper flakes and garlic. Continue with the recipe, adding shrimp to the fully cooked sauce; simmer to blend flavors, 1 to 2 minutes longer.

Tomato Sauce with Mussels and Garlic

Because the mussels are bulky, use a large deep skillet or a soup kettle to make this sauce.

FAT:

3 to 4 tablespoons extra-virgin olive oil

AROMATIC:

3 garlic cloves, minced

EXTRA INGREDIENTS:

$1/2$ cup dry white wine

24 mussels, scrubbed in cold water (and debearded, if necessary)

Follow the Simple Tomato Sauce recipe (page 80), adding wine with the tomatoes and adding mussels after the sauce has simmered for about 10 minutes. Cover and continue to cook over medium heat until the mussels open and the sauce is the desired consistency, about 5 minutes longer.

Tomato Sauce with Clams and Parsley

Since it takes so many fresh clams to make a good sauce, I use half fresh and half canned, cutting down on weeknight preparation and food cost. Since the clam shells are bulky, use a large, deep skillet or soup kettle to make this sauce. For a spicier version, add ½ teaspoon of dried red pepper flakes along with the garlic. Try not to make parsley optional in this sauce.

FAT:

3 to 4 tablespoons extra-virgin olive oil

AROMATIC:

3 garlic cloves, minced

EXTRA INGREDIENTS:

½ cup dry red or white wine

½ teaspoon dried oregano

1 (6.5-ounce) can clams

2 dozen littleneck clams, scrubbed in cold water

Follow the Simple Tomato Sauce recipe (page 80), adding wine, oregano, and canned clam liquid with the tomatoes, and littleneck clams and canned clams after 10 minutes of simmering. Cover and continue to simmer until the clams open, about 5 minutes longer.

Quick Meat Sauce

Give the vegetables a light sprinkling of salt as they sauté.

FAT:

3 to 4 tablespoons butter

AROMATIC:

1 small onion, cut into small dice

EXTRA INGREDIENTS:

½ small carrot, cut into small dice

½ small celery stalk, cut into small dice

½ pound lean ground beef

½ cup dry wine, red or white

Follow the Simple Tomato Sauce recipe (page 80), sautéing the carrot and celery along with the onion and adding the ground beef to the sautéed and softened vegetables. When the beef loses its raw color, add the wine, along with tomatoes.

Tomato Sauce with Sausage and Peppers

Use bulk sausage, if you like. Just remember to cut down on the olive oil and add the meat to the sautéing onions.

FAT:

1 tablespoon extra-virgin olive oil plus drippings from cooked sausages to equal 3 to 4 tablespoons

AROMATIC:

1 small onion, halved and sliced thin

EXTRA INGREDIENTS:

12 ounces Italian sausage in the casing

1 red or yellow bell pepper (or ½ each), halved and cut into thin strips

Bring the sausage, ¼ cup water, and the olive oil to a simmer in a saucepan. Cover and cook over medium heat until the sausage loses its raw color, about 8 minutes. Uncover the pan and cook the sausage until the liquid evaporates, 1 to 2 minutes longer. Fry the sausage, turning it once, until browned on both sides. Remove from the pan; cut into ½-inch slices. (You should have 3 to 4 tablespoons fat in the pan at this point.)

Follow the Simple Tomato Sauce recipe (page 80), sautéing peppers along with the onions, and adding the sausages to the sauce as soon as they are sliced.

Tomato Sauce with Bacon and Olives

FAT:

4 slices thick-cut bacon

AROMATIC:

3 garlic cloves, minced

EXTRA INGREDIENTS:

16 to 24 piquant olives, such as kalamatas, pitted and chopped coarse

In the pan you will use for making the sauce, fry the bacon (cut into ½-inch dice) until crisp, 4 to 5 minutes. Remove the pan from the heat for a minute or so, and add garlic. Follow the Simple Tomato Sauce recipe (page 80), adding olives along with the tomatoes.

Tomato Sauce with Chicken and Red Peppers

In this sauce I prefer the texture of shredded chicken, but if you don't have time or don't want to wait until it is cool enough to handle, simply cut it into bite-size pieces.

FAT:

3 to 4 tablespoons extra-virgin olive oil

AROMATICS:

3 garlic cloves and 1 small onion, halved and sliced thin

EXTRA INGREDIENTS:

4 boneless, skinless chicken thighs, sprinkled with salt and pepper

1 medium red or green bell pepper (or 1/2 red and 1/2 green), cut into thin strips

Heat the oil over medium-high heat in the pan you will use to cook the sauce. Add the thighs; cook, turning once, until lightly browned, 4 to 5 minutes. Remove from the skillet; cut into bite-size pieces or shred when cool enough to handle. Follow the Simple Tomato Sauce recipe (page 80), sautéing the pepper strips along with the onions and garlic and adding chicken to the sauce as soon as it is cut or shredded.

Tomato Sauce with Ground Turkey and Oregano

Ground turkey is a wonderful stand-in for ground beef.

FAT:

3 tablespoons extra-virgin olive oil

AROMATIC:

1 small onion, halved and sliced thin

EXTRA INGREDIENTS:

1/2 pound 93% lean ground turkey

1 teaspoon dried oregano or 2 tablespoons fresh

Follow the Simple Tomato Sauce recipe (page 80), adding ground meat to the sautéed onions. Continue to cook until the meat has lost its raw color, 4 to 5 minutes. If using dried oregano, add with the tomatoes. If using fresh, add it to the fully cooked sauce.

Tomato Sauce with Bacon, Bay Scallops, and Basil

I am not a bay scallop fan, except in tomato sauce. If you don't want to use bacon, butter can be substituted.

FAT:

3 to 4 tablespoons rendered fat from 4 slices thick-cut bacon, cut into ½ inch pieces

AROMATIC:

3 minced garlic cloves

EXTRA INGREDIENTS:

¾ pound bay scallops, sprinkled with salt

2 tablespoons minced fresh basil leaves

In the pan used to make the sauce, fry bacon over medium-high heat until most of its fat has rendered and it is almost crisp, 4 to 5 minutes. Add scallops; sauté until just opaque, 2 to 3 minutes. Remove pan from heat; transfer scallops to a plate with a slotted spoon. Once oil has cooled slightly, return pan to heat and add garlic. Follow recipe for Simple Tomato Sauce (page 80), adding scallops and fresh basil to cooked sauce; simmer to blend flavors, 1 to 2 minutes longer.

at-a-glance

SIMPLE TOMATO SAUCE

- Select a large (4-quart) saucepan or a 6-quart Dutch oven to make the sauce.
- Figure on 3 to 4 tablespoons of fat—butter, olive oil, or bacon or sausage drippings.
- Heat garlic and fat together. When the garlic starts to sizzle, add the canned crushed tomatoes.
- If using onions (or a combination of onions and garlic), add them to the hot oil and sauté until softened.
- Add extra ingredients—vegetables, meats, seafood, pantry ingredients, and diced and fresh herbs—at the appropriate time.

Pasta with Vegetables

Simmer firm vegetables in salted pasta water,

Sauté garlic in oil, then toss them all together.

This basic technique goes for leafy greens, too.

Just boil them with the pasta 'til they're limp and cooked through.

Cook tender vegetables with garlic and oil,

Then toss in some pasta that's fresh from the boil.

Although our family gets its share of fruit at breakfast and lunch, dinner is when we usually get our daily dose of vegetables. For this reason, pasta tossed with vegetables shows up regularly on our supper menu. Zucchini goes down a whole lot easier with my kids when it's tossed with ziti.

Although there's no one way to make pasta with vegetables, I've developed my own formula over the years. The technique starts with a pot of pasta boiling in salted water and a skillet with minced garlic or sliced onion sautéing in olive oil or sometimes butter. Many pasta-with-vegetable recipes require yet another pot to cook the vegetable, but for weeknight meals, I will not dirty three pots for one dish. Either the vegetable boils with the pasta or it sautés with the garlic. But how do you know which vegetables should cook with the pasta and which ones should sauté with the garlic and oil?

There are three kinds of vegetables—firm, tender, and leafy. Taking pasta out of the equation, I realized that each category of vegetable demands a particular cooking method. When I asked myself if I would ever sauté raw broccoli, cauliflower, asparagus, or kale, the answer was "Not likely." Would I ever boil bell peppers, onions, mushrooms, or zucchini? The answer was "Probably not." After that, the decision about which pot or pan the vegetables should cook in was obvious.

Firm vegetables like broccoli, cauliflower, asparagus, cabbage, snow peas, sugar snaps, carrots, and potatoes need moist heat to soften them up, so they boil with the pasta. Not only does this technique save an extra pot, but the vegetables flavor the pasta water as it cooks, resulting in a light broth that is used to moisten the finished pasta dish.

Bitter leafy greens—turnip, mustard, collard, kale, and broccoli rabe—like firm vegetables, cook with the pasta. The boiling water tames the bitter greens' assertive flavor and tenderizes their tough texture.

On the other hand, tender, high-moisture vegetables, like bell peppers, onions, mushrooms, leeks, eggplant, zucchini, yellow squash, and fennel need the high, dry heat of the sauté pan to evaporate juices and intensify flavor.

Since I usually sauté tender greens—spinach, Swiss chard, and beet greens—they are the only types of vegetables that don't follow the pattern. While they're great sautéed as a side dish, these greens tend to clump up and are difficult to distribute evenly throughout the pasta. For this reason, boil them with the pasta.

Because the pasta water, in combination with the fat, makes a "sauce," it must be as flavorful as it can be. Boil the pasta (along with firm and leafy vegetables) in a small quantity of water. Obviously, the shallower the cooking liquid, the more intensely flavored it will be. As the pasta cooks, it releases starch (pasta is, after all, just flour and water) into the water. This starch lightly thickens the water, giving it a pleasant body. When pasta is cooked in larger quantities of water, the diluted thickener is barely noticeable.

As when boiling a pound of pasta for tomato sauce (see page 78), bring a mere two quarts of water to boil and season it with a full tablespoon of salt. So that the pasta cooks more evenly in this smaller quantity of water, partially cover the pot. To keep the pasta and vegetable water from boiling over, however, it is important to cook them in a large (at least 8-quart) soup kettle.

Although this chapter is organized by the type of vegetable—firm vegetables, leafy greens, and tender vegetables—once you've mastered the technique, you can mix vegetables from the different categories. Make pasta with bell peppers (from the tender vegetable category) and spinach (from the greens category). Try a mix of half each leeks and asparagus, or mushrooms and greens.

FIRM VEGETABLES

Many vegetables fall into the firm category. Although this list is not comprehensive (salsify, for example is a firm vegetable, but not one that would likely be featured in a pasta dish), the obvious candidates for pasta dishes made with firm vegetables are included.

- **Asparagus.** Pencil-thin to medium asparagus usually come bound with one or two rubber bands. Leaving the asparagus bundled, whack off the tough bottom $1\frac{1}{2}$ or 2 inches. Still leaving the asparagus bundled, slice the bunch into 1-inch pieces, removing the rubber band only when necessary. Thicker asparagus spears are woodier and should be snapped off individually. Holding the tip end of the asparagus in one hand, snap the spear. It will break naturally at the tender part. Cut trimmed asparagus into 1-inch lengths.

- **Broccoli.** Cut florets from the thick stalk, cutting florets into bite-size pieces; set aside. Starting at one end of the stalk, grasp the tough outer peel with a paring knife and pull to remove. Repeat pulling peel from the stalk to remove completely. Cut florets into large bite-size pieces and stems into $\frac{1}{4}$-inch-thick coins.

- **Butternut squash.** Peel and halve the squash; scoop out seeds. Cut each half into approximate 1-inch chunks.

- **Cabbage.** Quarter the cabbage; cut out core from each quarter. Separate the leaves into manageable piles, press to flatten, and shred with a chef's knife. Although I don't think it's worth dirtying a food processor for a half cabbage or less, you can also machine-shred it.

- **Carrots.** Peel and cut (on the diagonal, if you like) into $\frac{1}{4}$-inch-thick coins.

- **Cauliflower.** Remove green leaves from cauliflower; cut out core. Snap florets from the head, cutting florets into bite-size pieces.

- **New or red potatoes.** Quarter if small, or cut into 1-inch chunks if large.

- **Snow peas.** Stem and remove strings if necessary.

- **Sugar snap peas.** Stem and remove strings if necessary.

Pasta with Firm Vegetables

I find the back-of-the-box times are usually quite accurate when cooking pasta in a smaller quantity of water, as I do here. Using those cooking times as a guide, drop the vegetables into the boiling pasta about 5 minutes before they should be done. Angel hair pasta is not the ideal pasta for this dish. It cooks more quickly than the vegetables and its fine texture requires a moister sauce. Short stubby pastas, such as penne, fusilli, and bowties, are ideal.

1 pound firm vegetables, such as broccoli, cauliflower, asparagus, potatoes, cabbage, winter squash, snow peas, sugar snap peas, carrots

Salt

1 package (1 pound) pasta

4 tablespoons fat (olive oil, butter, or bacon fat)

AROMATIC:

3 garlic cloves and/or 1 medium onion

Optional flavorings and/or dried/fresh herbs (see recipes that follow)

Parmesan cheese to taste

Ground black pepper

1. Prepare selected vegetable.

2. Meanwhile, bring 2 quarts of water to a boil over medium-high heat in an 8-quart soup kettle; add 1 tablespoon of salt and the pasta to the boiling water. Using back-of-the-box cooking times as a guide, cook the pasta, partially covered and stirring frequently, until about 5 minutes from doneness. Add the selected vegetable to the pot of partially cooked pasta; cook, partially covered, until pasta is al dente and vegetables are just cooked, about 5 minutes longer.

3. Meanwhile, in a medium skillet, heat fat and garlic together over medium-high heat until garlic starts to sizzle. If using onion, heat fat, add onions, and sauté until soft, 3 to 4 minutes. Stir in optional flavorings and dried herbs; sauté to blend flavors, about 1 minute, and set aside.

4. Drain the pasta and vegetables, reserving ½ cup pasta cooking liquid. Return pasta to pot, add contents of skillet, pasta cooking liquid, optional fresh herbs, and a generous sprinkling of Parmesan cheese; toss to coat. Taste, adjusting seasonings, including pepper to taste. Serve, with additional cheese passed separately.

Pasta with Broccoli, Garlic, and Red Pepper Flakes

VEGETABLE:

1 bunch broccoli (1–1½ pounds),
cut into bite-size florets; stems peeled
and cut into ½-inch coins

FAT:

4 tablespoons olive oil

AROMATIC:

3 medium garlic cloves

FLAVORINGS:

½ teaspoon hot red pepper flakes

1 medium tomato, cut into small dice

Follow the Pasta with Firm Vegetables recipe, heating red pepper flakes along with the garlic and adding tomato once it starts to sizzle.

Pasta with Cabbage, Potatoes, Bacon, and Thyme

You can substitute ½ teaspoon dried caraway seeds for the thyme, if you like.

VEGETABLE:

¼ small cabbage (about 8 ounces),
chopped coarse

2 medium red potatoes,
cut into medium dice

FAT:

4 tablespoons rendered bacon fat
from 4 slices thick-cut bacon, cut
into ½-inch pieces

AROMATIC:

3 medium garlic cloves

HERB:

½ teaspoon dried thyme leaves

In the skillet used for sautéing the garlic, fry the bacon over medium heat until crisp, about 5 minutes. Remove bacon with a slotted spoon; set aside. Using bacon renderings as the fat, follow the Pasta with Firm Vegetables recipe, adding thyme to the sautéing garlic. Add bacon with Parmesan cheese; toss to coat.

Pasta with Cauliflower, Tomato, and Olives

VEGETABLE:

1 small head cauliflower (1–1½ pounds), trimmed and cut into bite-size florets, or 1 pound florets

FAT:

4 tablespoons olive oil

AROMATIC:

3 medium garlic cloves

FLAVORINGS AND HERB:

1 large plum tomato, cut into small dice

16 piquant olives, such as kalamata, pitted

¼ cup minced fresh parsley leaves

Follow the Pasta with Firm Vegetables recipe (page 94), adding tomato and olives to sizzling garlic and parsley when tossing pasta.

Pasta with Butternut Squash, Bacon, and Thyme

Use short stubby pasta, like rotelle (wagon wheels) or orecchiette, to complement the small chunks of squash.

VEGETABLE:

½ medium butternut squash, peeled and cut into medium dice

FAT:

4 tablespoons rendered bacon fat from 4 slices thick-cut bacon, cut into ½-inch pieces

AROMATIC:

3 medium garlic cloves

HERB:

½ teaspoon dried thyme leaves

In the skillet used for sautéing the garlic, fry the bacon over medium heat until crisp, about 5 minutes. Remove bacon with a slotted spoon; set aside. Using bacon renderings for fat, follow the Pasta with Firm Vegetables recipe (page 94), adding thyme to the sautéing garlic. Add bacon with Parmesan cheese; toss to coat.

Pasta with Asparagus, Lemon, and Parsley

If you like, you can add ½ cup of frozen green peas to the boiled pasta and asparagus right before draining it.

VEGETABLE:

1 bunch thin or medium asparagus spears (about 1¼ pounds), tough ends cut off, spears cut into 1-inch lengths

FAT:

4 tablespoons butter

AROMATIC:

1 medium onion

FLAVORING AND HERB:

1 teaspoon fine-grated zest from 1 lemon

2 tablespoons snipped chives or ¼ cup chopped fresh parsley leaves

Follow the Pasta with Firm Vegetables recipe (page 94), adding lemon zest to the sautéing garlic and chives (or parsley) when tossing pasta.

Quick Pasta Primavera

VEGETABLE:

5 to 6 ounces each: asparagus, carrots, sugar snap peas

FAT:

4 tablespoons butter

AROMATIC:

1 medium onion, halved and sliced thin

FLAVORING AND HERBS:

1 medium tomato, cut into medium dice

¼ cup minced fresh parsley leaves

2 tablespoons snipped fresh chives

Follow the Pasta with Firm Vegetables recipe (page 94), adding tomato to sautéing onion. Add the parsley and chives when tossing the pasta.

LEAFY GREENS

When I serve greens as a side dish, I figure about half a pound per person, so cleaning and preparing two or three pounds of greens is not a weeknight project. Teaming pasta with greens, however, means I don't have to clean quite so many.

Because many varieties of greens are gritty, they must be thoroughly washed. To accomplish this quickly, fill the sink with cold water. As the water fills the sink, start cleaning the greens. Stem them over the sink, allowing the stemmed leaves to drop into the water.

The technique for greens is the same as that for firm vegetables—boil them in the same pot with the pasta. The following greens are all perfect pasta partners:

- **Beet greens.** Hold each leaf between thumb and index finger of one hand while pulling back the stem with the other, then coarse-chop washed leaves.

- **Bok choy.** Cut crisp edible stem crosswise into thin slices. Coarse-chop leaves.

- **Broccoli rabe.** Peel stems. Coarse-chop washed leaves.

- **Collard greens.** Slash down both sides of each leaf with a sharp knife, then coarse-chop washed leaves.

- **Curly endive.** Trim root ends; coarse-chop greens.

- **Escarole.** Trim root ends; coarse-chop greens.

- **Kale.** Slash down both sides of each leaf with a sharp knife, then coarse-chop washed leaves.

- **Mustard greens.** Slash down both sides of each leaf with a sharp knife, then coarse-chop washed leaves.

- **Spinach.** For large mature spinach with tough stems, hold each leaf between thumb and index finger of one hand while pulling back the stem with the other. For young spinach, hold the bunch by the root, leaf end down, and pinch the leaves from the stems.

- **Swiss chard.** Slash down both sides of each leaf with a sharp knife, then coarse-chop washed leaves.

- **Turnip greens.** Hold each leaf between thumb and index finger of one hand while pulling back the stem with the other, then coarse-chop large leaves.

Pasta with Leafy Greens

Greens and garlic are a natural pairing, but feel free to add or substitute an onion.

1½ pounds greens, such as beet greens, bok choy, broccoli rabe, collard greens, curly endive, escarole, kale, mustard greens, spinach, Swiss chard, turnip greens

Salt

1 package (1 pound) pasta

4 tablespoons fat (olive oil, butter, or bacon fat)

3 garlic cloves

Optional flavorings and/or dried/fresh herbs (see recipes below)

Parmesan cheese to taste

Ground black pepper

1. Prepare selected greens.

2. Bring 2 quarts of water to a boil over medium-high heat in a large kettle; add 1 tablespoon of salt and the pasta to the boiling water. Using back-of-the-box cooking times as a guide, cook the pasta, partially covered and stirring frequently, until about 5 minutes away from being done. Add the prepared greens to the pot of the partially cooked pasta; cook, stirring to wilt greens, until pasta is al dente and greens are just tender, about 5 to 7 minutes longer.

3. Meanwhile, in a medium skillet, heat the fat and garlic together over medium-high heat until the garlic starts to sizzle. Stir in optional flavorings and/or dried herbs; sauté to blend flavors, about 1 minute, and set aside.

4. Drain the pasta, reserving ½ cup of the pasta cooking liquid. Return pasta to the pot, add contents of the skillet, reserved cooking liquid, optional fresh herbs, and a generous sprinkling of Parmesan cheese; toss to coat. Taste, adjusting seasonings, including pepper to taste. Serve, with additional cheese passed separately.

Pasta with Leafy Greens, Bacon, and Red Pepper Flakes

VEGETABLE:

Any leafy green, washed, trimmed or stemmed, and chopped coarse

FAT:

4 tablespoons rendered bacon fat from 4 slices thick-cut bacon, cut into 1/2-inch pieces

FLAVORINGS:

1/2 teaspoon hot red pepper flakes

In the skillet used for sautéing the garlic, fry the bacon over medium heat until crisp, about 5 minutes, then follow the recipe for Pasta with Leafy Greens.

Pasta with Leafy Greens, Lemon, and Red Pepper Flakes

VEGETABLE:

Any leafy green, washed, trimmed or stemmed, and chopped coarse

FAT:

4 tablespoons olive oil

FLAVORINGS:

1/2 teaspoon hot red pepper flakes

1 teaspoon lemon zest

Follow the recipe for Pasta with Leafy Greens.

Pasta with Leafy Greens, Tomatoes, and Olives

VEGETABLE:

Any leafy green, washed, trimmed or stemmed, and chopped coarse

FAT:

4 tablespoons olive oil

FLAVORINGS:

1 large plum tomato, cut into small dice

16 piquant black olives, such as kalamata, pitted

Follow the recipe for Pasta with Leafy Greens (page 98).

at-a-glance

PASTA WITH FIRM AND LEAFY VEGETABLES

- Bring 2 quarts of water seasoned with 1 tablespoon of salt to a boil in a large soup kettle. Cook pasta until about 5 minutes away from being done.
- Add desired firm or leafy vegetable and cook until pasta is al dente and vegetables are just tender. Drain, reserving 1/2 cup of pasta water. Return pasta and vegetables to the pot.
- Heat 4 tablespoons of fat in a large skillet.
- If using garlic, heat along with the fat until the garlic just starts to sizzle. If using onions or a combination of onions and garlic, add them to the hot fat and sauté them until softened.
- Stir optional flavorings into the softened garlic and/or onions; cook to blend flavors.
- Toss together the drained pasta and vegetables, pasta cooking liquid, contents of the skillet, and Parmesan cheese in the pot.

TENDER VEGETABLES

Although this list of high-moisture vegetables is not comprehensive (celery, for example, is a tender vegetable, but not one that would likely be featured in a pasta dish), it includes the obvious candidates for vegetable pasta dishes made with tender vegetables.

- **Bell peppers.** Cut about $\frac{1}{2}$ inch off the base and stem end, removing the stem from the top slice. After removing the core, make a slit down one side of the pepper and open it up so that the pepper lies flat. Cut into $\frac{1}{4}$-inch strips. Thin-slice the base and stem as well.

- **Eggplant.** Trim off ends. Cut eggplant into $\frac{1}{2}$-inch-thick rounds. In stacks of 3 or 4, cut rounds into $\frac{1}{2}$-inch cubes.

- **Fennel.** Trim the fennel bulb of fronds and stalks; reserve fronds. Halve, core, and cut each fennel half crosswise into thin slices.

- **Leeks.** Trim off the tough dark green tops and discard. Quarter lengthwise, then cut crosswise into $\frac{1}{2}$-inch-thick slices. Wash in a sink of cold water, letting any grit sink to the bottom.

- **Mushrooms.** Domestic white and porcini: Trim stem ends, rinse, and slice $\frac{1}{4}$ inch thick. Portobellos: remove and trim stems, rinse stems and caps, and slice both thin.

- **Onions.** Peel, halve from root to stem end, and slice thin crosswise.

- **Yellow squash.** Trim ends, quarter lengthwise, and cut into medium dice.

- **Zucchini.** Trim ends, quarter lengthwise, and cut into medium dice.

Pasta with Tender Vegetables

1 to 1¼ pounds selected tender vegetables (such as bell peppers, zucchini, yellow squash, mushrooms, eggplant, onions, leeks, or fennel)

1 tablespoon salt

1 package (1 pound) pasta

4 tablespoons fat (olive oil, butter, or bacon fat)

AROMATIC:

3 garlic cloves and/or an onion

Ground black pepper

Optional flavorings and/or dried/fresh herbs (see recipes below)

Parmesan cheese to taste

1. Prepare selected vegetable.

2. Bring 2 quarts of water to a boil in a large kettle. Add salt and pasta to the boiling water. Using package cooking times as a guide, cook the pasta, partially covered and stirring frequently, until al dente.

3. Meanwhile, in a large skillet, heat fat and garlic over medium-high heat until the garlic just starts to sizzle. If using onion, heat the fat, add the onion, and sauté until soft, 3 to 4 minutes. Add the prepared vegetable to the pan, sprinkling generously with salt and pepper; sauté until tender, 5 to 7 minutes longer. Stir in optional flavorings and dried herbs; cook to blend flavors, about 1 minute longer. Remove from heat and set aside, uncovered, until the pasta is done.

4. Drain the pasta, reserving ½ cup of the cooking liquid. Return pasta to the pot; add the contents of the skillet, pasta cooking liquid, optional fresh herbs, and a generous sprinkling of Parmesan cheese; toss to coat. Taste, adjust seasonings, including pepper to taste. Serve, with additional cheese passed separately.

Pasta with Zucchini, Tomato, and Oregano

VEGETABLE:

2 medium zucchini, trimmed, quartered lengthwise, and cut into medium dice

FAT:

4 tablespoons olive oil

AROMATIC:

1 medium onion

FLAVORINGS AND HERB:

1 plum tomato, cut into small dice

½ teaspoon dried oregano

Follow the Pasta with Tender Vegetables recipe, adding tomato and oregano to sautéed zucchini.

Pasta with Fennel, Red Onion, and Parsley

VEGETABLE:

2 small fennel bulbs (1¼ pounds)

FAT:

4 tablespoons olive oil

AROMATIC:

1 medium red onion

HERB:

¼ cup minced fresh parsley leaves

Follow the Pasta with Tender Vegetables recipe, adding parsley when tossing pasta.

Pasta with Mushrooms, Rosemary, and Garlic

VEGETABLE:

1 pound mushrooms, trimmed and sliced thin

FAT:

4 tablespoons olive oil

AROMATIC:

3 medium garlic cloves

HERBS:

1½ tablespoons minced fresh rosemary* or 1½ teaspoons dried

2 tablespoons minced fresh parsley leaves

Follow the Pasta with Tender Vegetables recipe, adding rosemary to the sautéed mushrooms and parsley when tossing the pasta.

*NOTE: Fresh rosemary is the exception to the dried herb/fresh herb rule. To tame its pungent flavor, I add it to the sautéing mushrooms rather than adding it at the end.

Pasta with Bell Peppers, Capers, and Basil

VEGETABLE:

3 medium red and/or yellow bell
peppers (about 1 pound)

FAT:

4 tablespoons olive oil

AROMATIC:

3 medium garlic cloves

FLAVORINGS AND HERB:

1 Italian plum tomato, cut into
small dice

2 tablespoons drained capers

1/4 cup chopped fresh basil leaves

Follow the Pasta with Tender Vegetables recipe (page 102), adding tomato and capers
to the sautéed peppers and basil when tossing the pasta.

Pasta with Eggplant, Tomato, and Rosemary

VEGETABLE:

1 medium eggplant

FAT:

4 tablespoons olive oil

AROMATIC:

3 medium garlic cloves

FLAVORINGS AND HERB:

1 large plum tomato, cut into
small dice

1 1/2 teaspoons minced fresh rosemary
leaves (see note page 103)

1/4 cup minced fresh parsley leaves

Follow the Pasta with Tender Vegetables recipe (page 102), adding tomato and rosemary to the sautéed eggplant and parsley when tossing the pasta.

PASTA WITH TENDER VEGETABLES

- Bring 2 quarts of water seasoned with 1 tablespoon of salt to a boil in a large soup kettle. Cook pasta until al dente. Drain, reserving ½ cup of pasta water. Return pasta to pot.

- Heat 4 tablespoons of fat in a large skillet.

- If using garlic, heat along with fat until the garlic just starts to sizzle. If using onions or a combination of onions and garlic, add them to the hot fat and sauté them until softened.

- Add desired tender vegetable and sauté until just tender.

- Stir optional flavorings into the softened vegetables; cook to blend flavors.

- Toss together the drained pasta, pasta cooking liquid, contents of the skillet, and Parmesan cheese in the pot.

quick ricotta filling
wonton/egg roll sauce
wrappers herbs

Weeknight Ravioli and Lasagna

For ravioli and lasagna, homemade in a pinch,

Use wonton, egg roll wrappers, and the process is a cinch.

I own a manual pasta machine. I have an electric one, too. I've also got all the other little gadgets for making stuffed pasta—crimpers, cutters, rollers, and wheels. But all that paraphernalia is down in the basement now, and I may even sell it at a yard sale someday. From-scratch stuffed pasta is just too time-consuming and difficult for me to make on a regular basis.

A couple of years ago, my husband and I went to our friends' house for dinner. There were eight of us that night, and the first course was mushroom ravioli. As our hosts brought them to the table, I was impressed that they had attempted such a temperamental dish for so many guests. As I looked more closely, I noticed that these ravioli had not only made it to the table, they were beautiful. The pasta was sturdy yet sheer, revealing the filling within. One bite and I knew I had never before eaten or made ravioli this good. They tasted earthy yet ethereal, substantial yet tender. I immediately asked how she managed to serve such perfect ravioli. Her secret, she said, was wonton wrappers.

Since that dinner, I have never made from-scratch stuffed pasta again. When I get a taste for ravioli, I simply buy wonton wrappers, which are in fact egg pasta that has been perfectly mixed, rolled, and cut, ready for me to stuff, seal, and simmer.

QUICK RAVIOLI

Wonton ravioli make an elegant first course, and if you choose a filling that's as simple as the herbed ricotta one, they're easy enough to put together for weeknight dinner. To make them, start by bringing a generous two quarts of water to a simmer over medium-high heat in a large deep sauté pan (11 to 12 inches in diameter and about 3 to 4 inches high). If you don't have a large sauté pan, you can use a soup kettle, but it's easier to fish ravioli out of a shallow rather than a deep pan. Since you may be using the ravioli cooking liquid as a sauce, season it generously with 1 tablespoon of table salt (or 1 1/2 tablespoons kosher), and drizzle a teaspoon or so of oil into the simmering water to keep the ravioli from sticking.

Unlike long sheets of cut pasta that dry out quickly and become difficult to work with, wonton wrappers stay moist in their packaging. Pull out about a dozen wrappers at a time, laying six on a dry countertop. After dropping a tablespoon of filling in the center of each wonton square, dip your index finger in a bowl of water, and quickly run it around the perimeter of each wrapper. Pastry brushes and egg washes are unnecessary, awkward, and messy.

Working with one wonton at a time, lay another wrapper over the topped one, sealing it on all four sides and pressing as much air out as possible. As you transfer the finished ravioli to a large wire rack, give them one last quick pinch around the perimeter.

Because the dough is perfectly textured and machine cut, wonton ravioli can be made quickly. In fact, I can stuff and seal two dozen in about twelve minutes. If you are making ravioli ahead for a dinner party, leave them at room temperature on a wire rack loosely covered with plastic wrap. If dinner is more than an hour away, refrigerate them. The combination of loose plastic and the wire rack creates an environment that is neither too dry, causing the ravioli to turn brittle, nor too moist, making them sticky.

Since fresh pasta cooks quickly, simmer the ravioli in batches. (If you want them done more quickly, use two skillets.) When making them for four or less, drop eight ravioli into the simmering water, stirring lightly at first to keep them from sticking. Set the timer for three minutes and go about your business. They're done when the pasta over the filling starts to wrinkle and the ravioli turn from opaque to translucent.

Like pancakes, ravioli are best eaten right away. If not, they start to dry out and get cold. To avoid this, transfer two hot ravioli to each pasta plate with a large solid—not slotted—spoon. The attendant cooking liquid keeps the ravioli warm and separate while the remaining ones cook. Don't pick up too much water, however, or you'll end up with soup.

Transferring ravioli to individual plates rather than a large bowl also means they're moved only once—less hassle and less chance for breakage. Repeat the cooking process, and just three minutes later the remaining hot ravioli warm up the ones on the plate. Drizzle them with a little melted butter which, when combined with the cooking liquid already on the plate, becomes an instant sauce. A little grated cheese, a grinding of fresh pepper, and you're ready to eat.

Before sitting down, drop the final eight ravioli into the water, but don't wait for them. Eat while they cook. Those who want another one or two get them hot a few minutes later.

When serving ravioli as a first course, cook them in two skillets, not just the one, and heat the pasta plates in a warm oven. The shorter cooking time and the hot plates ensure perfect ravioli every time.

Quick Ravioli

To avoid cooking them in three batches, simmer the ravioli in two pans. Because of its simplicity (and because it tastes so good), I like drizzling the cooked ravioli with a little melted butter. Simple Tomato Sauce (see page 80) also makes an excellent topping.

1 recipe ravioli filling (see recipes that follow)

1 tablespoon table salt (or 1½ tablespoons kosher salt)

1 teaspoon vegetable oil

1 (12-ounce) package wonton wrappers

2 tablespoons melted butter or warmed extra-virgin olive oil or flavored butter (see below)

Grated Parmesan cheese and ground black pepper for topping

1. Make the filling. Bring a generous 2 quarts of water to simmer in a large, deep sauté pan if cooking the ravioli immediately after filling. When water starts to simmer, add the salt and oil. Heat oven to 200 degrees and warm 4 pasta plates.

2. With a large wire rack and a small bowl of water close by, lay 6 wonton wrappers on a clean, dry countertop. Drop 1 tablespoon of filling onto each wrapper. Moisten the perimeter of each wrapper by dipping an index finger in the water bowl. Working with one at a time, top each wrapper with another wrapper, pressing as much air out as possible to seal completely. Transfer to a wire rack, wipe work surface dry, and repeat the filling and sealing process with the remaining wonton wrappers and filling. (The ravioli can be covered loosely with plastic wrap and left at room temperature up to 1 hour or refrigerated up to 4 hours.)

3. Drop 8 ravioli into the simmering water. Cook until the pasta over the filling starts to wrinkle and the ravioli turn from opaque to translucent, 3 to 4 minutes. With a large solid (not slotted) spoon, transfer a portion of cooked ravioli, along with a little of the cooking liquid, to the warmed plate. Repeat with the remaining ravioli. Drizzle with a portion of butter or oil, sprinkle with Parmesan cheese and pepper, and serve immediately.

Herbed Ricotta Filling

Makes about 1 1/2 cups, or enough to fill 24 wonton wrappers

The ricotta filling can be made very quickly and is perfect for weeknight ravioli. Substitute fresh goat cheese for the ricotta if you like.

1¼ cups ricotta cheese

¼ cup grated Parmesan cheese

2 garlic cloves, minced

2 tablespoons minced fresh parsley leaves

1 teaspoon dried basil leaves (or 1 tablespoon chopped fresh)

½ teaspoon dried oregano

1 large egg

Salt and ground black pepper

Mix all ingredients, including salt and pepper to taste, in a medium bowl. Proceed with the Quick Ravioli recipe (page 109).

Watercress Filling with Beans and Bacon

Makes about 1 1/2 cups, or enough to fill 24 wonton wrappers

4 ounces (5 to 6 slices) bacon, cut into 1-inch pieces

2 packed cups tender bitter greens, such as watercress or arugula, rinsed and chopped coarse

3 garlic cloves, minced

½ teaspoon minced fresh rosemary

1 (16-ounce) can white beans, such as cannellini, drained and rinsed

Fry the bacon in a medium skillet over medium-high heat until crisp, 4 to 5 minutes. Add the greens, garlic, and rosemary; cook until the greens wilt and flavors blend, 1 to 2 minutes longer. Put the greens mixture, along with the beans, in a food processor fitted with the steel blade; pulse until the mixture is chopped coarse. Transfer to a small bowl and proceed with the Quick Ravioli recipe (page 109).

Wild Mushroom Filling

*Makes about 1 1/2 cups, or enough
to fill 24 wonton wrappers*

To soak dried mushrooms, microwave 1 cup of water in a 2-cup Pyrex measuring cup to boiling. Drop in the dried mushrooms and set a custard cup or similar small dish over them to weight them down.

1 ounce dried porcini (or other dried mushrooms), soaked in boiling water until soft, about 10 minutes, then squeezed dry (see above)

2 garlic cloves, peeled

1 (8-ounce) package sliced white mushrooms

2 tablespoons olive oil

1/2 teaspoon dried thyme leaves

Salt and ground black pepper

3/4 cup ricotta cheese or fresh goat cheese

1 large egg

1. Mince the dried mushrooms and garlic in a food processor fitted with the steel blade. Add the sliced mushrooms; pulse until chopped fine.

2. Heat the oil in a medium skillet over medium-high heat. When the oil starts to shimmer, add the mushrooms and sauté, seasoning with thyme and salt and pepper to taste, until the liquid completely evaporates, about 5 minutes. Transfer the mixture to a medium bowl and stir in the ricotta; adjust seasoning. Stir the egg into the warm filling. Proceed with the Quick Ravioli recipe (page 109).

Spinach Ricotta Filling

Makes about 1 ¹/₂ cups, or enough to fill 24 wonton wrappers

2 garlic cloves

1 (10-ounce) package frozen whole-leaf spinach, thawed and squeezed dry

2 tablespoons olive oil

¹/₂ teaspoon grated nutmeg

Salt and ground black pepper

¹/₂ cup ricotta cheese

2 tablespoons grated Parmesan cheese

1 large egg

1. Mince the garlic cloves in a food processor fitted with the steel blade. Add the spinach; pulse until chopped fine.

2. Heat the oil in a medium skillet over medium-high heat until shimmering. Add the spinach mixture and sauté, seasoning with nutmeg and salt and pepper to taste, until the liquid evaporates, 1 to 2 minutes. Transfer the mixture to a medium bowl, stir in the ricotta and Parmesan cheeses, and adjust seasoning. Stir the egg into the warm filling. Proceed with the Quick Ravioli recipe (page 109).

at-a-glance

QUICK RAVIOLI

- Choose a ravioli filling and make it.
- Bring a generous 2 quarts of water to a simmer in a large, deep sauté pan. When water starts to simmer, add 1 tablespoon of salt and 1 teaspoon of oil.
- Fill and seal wonton wrappers, transferring them to a wire rack.
- Cooking in batches, simmer ravioli until they turn from opaque to translucent, 3 to 4 minutes. Transfer a portion, along with a little of the cooking liquid, to each warm soup plate. Repeat cooking process.
- Drizzle with butter or oil (or Simple Tomato Sauce, page 80), and sprinkle with Parmesan cheese and pepper.

QUICK LASAGNA

With quick ravioli under my belt, it wasn't long before I realized that the larger egg roll wrappers could be used to make quick individual lasagnas. What was once a weekend-only dish immediately became a weeknight favorite.

Like traditional lasagna, this quicker version sandwiches a filling between sheets of pasta. Unlike more traditional lasagnas, these quick lasagnas are composed of just three layers—a filling in between two cooked egg roll wrappers—and they are not baked. The lasagna starts with a cooked egg roll wrapper, followed by a flavorful filling like herbed ricotta simmered in tomato sauce, eggplant slices sprinkled with Parmesan-flavored breadcrumbs, a portobello mushroom stuffed with cheese, or a tomato sauce enriched with Italian sausage. Draped over this generous, highly seasoned filling is another egg roll wrapper.

Quick Lasagna is simple enough to make for supper, yet elegant enough for a dinner party, but with two caveats. Cooking and assembly is last minute and, unlike traditional lasagna, these pastas must be eaten right away. Because of the last-minute preparation, this dish is difficult to make for more than four people, unless you have a second skillet and an extra pair of hands.

The cooking setup for Quick Lasagna is the same as for ravioli (see How to Turn Egg Roll Wrappers into Lasagna Noodles, page 114). Since each batch of pasta cooks in about 45 seconds, do not start cooking them until the fillings and sauces are almost done. If the first course is a salad, the lasagnas can be kept warm in a 200 degree oven up to five minutes.

How to Turn Egg Roll Wrappers into Lasagna Noodles

I like the way the egg roll wrapper naturally creases and pleats as I lay it on the plate, but occasionally the wrapper slides off the spoon too quickly and lands in a heap. To more easily spread the wrapper, I've found that a very light coating of vegetable oil cooking spray on the plate makes the difference between a noodle that sticks and one that glides.

1. Bring 2 quarts of water to a simmer over high heat in a large, deep sauté pan (11 to 12 inches by 3 to 4 inches). When the water starts to simmer, add 1 tablespoon of salt and 1 teaspoon of oil. Set 4 pasta or dinner plates, lightly coated with vegetable oil cooking spray if desired (see note above), next to the pan of simmering water.

2. Once the fillings and/or sauces are a couple of minutes away from being done, drop 4 egg roll wrappers into simmering water, moving them around with a large slotted spoon to keep them from sticking together. Simmer until tender, about 45 seconds. One at a time, transfer wrappers and attendant cooking liquid to plates, spreading the wrappers out as much as possible. Drop remaining 4 wrappers into the simmering water. While the final 4 are cooking, spoon or arrange a portion of filling and/or sauce over the wrappers on the plate, then drape the remaining 4 cooked wrappers over each portion of filling, spreading them out as much as possible. Sauce or garnish and serve.

Quick Lasagna with Herbed Ricotta and Parmesan

Along with the Sausage Ragu (see page 117), this one is the simplest to make and appeals to the widest range of tastes.

8 egg roll wrappers

HERBED RICOTTA FILLING

1¼ cups ricotta cheese

¼ cup grated Parmesan cheese

2 garlic cloves, minced

2 tablespoons minced fresh parsley leaves

1 teaspoon dried basil leaves (or 1 tablespoon chopped fresh)

½ teaspoon dried oregano

1 large egg

Salt and ground black pepper

QUICK TOMATO SAUCE

3 tablespoons olive oil

2 medium garlic cloves

1 (28-ounce) can crushed tomatoes (preferably Red Pack or Progresso)

Grated Parmesan cheese for topping

1. Prepare the egg roll wrappers for simmering (see box opposite).

2. *For the filling,* mix all ingredients, including salt and pepper to taste, in a small bowl; set aside.

3. *For the sauce,* heat oil and garlic in a Dutch oven. When the garlic starts to sizzle, add the tomatoes and bring to a simmer. Drop the herbed ricotta filling in approximate ⅓-cup portions into the tomato sauce. Cover, reduce the heat to low, and cook until each portion of ricotta has set and the tomatoes have thickened to sauce consistency, about 10 minutes.

4. A few minutes before serving, cook the egg roll wrappers. Top each cooked wrapper with a portion of ricotta and a little sauce. Drape each remaining cooked wrapper over each plate of filling. Spoon some tomato sauce over each, sprinkle with Parmesan, and serve immediately.

Quick Eggplant Lasagna with Toasted Breadcrumbs

Serves 4

Since tomato sauce is not the main feature in this dish, top it with the jarred variety if you like. Remember, however, that Quick Tomato Sauce takes only 2 minutes to prepare and cooks in 10 minutes.

8 egg roll wrappers

EGGPLANT FILLING

1 medium-large eggplant (about 1 pound), cut into twelve ½-inch-thick rounds

¼ cup extra-virgin olive oil

Salt and ground black pepper

¼ cup grated Parmesan cheese

¼ cup dry breadcrumbs

1 garlic clove, minced

2 tablespoons minced fresh parsley leaves

1 cup Quick Tomato Sauce (see page 115) or 1 cup jarred spaghetti sauce, heated

1. Adjust the oven rack to the upper middle position and heat the oven to 425 degrees. Prepare the egg roll wrappers for simmering (see box on page 114).

2. *For the filling,* brush the eggplant rounds with 3 tablespoons of oil and sprinkle generously with salt and pepper. Arrange in a single layer on a large shallow baking sheet; roast until the eggplant is soft and the bottom has browned, 10 to 15 minutes.

3. Mix the Parmesan, breadcrumbs, garlic, and parsley with the remaining tablespoon of oil in a small bowl. Remove the eggplant from the oven, turn the slices over, and top with half the crumb mixture. Scatter the remaining crumb mixture on the baking sheet in a thin even layer off to the side. Return the pan to the oven and continue to bake until the crumbs on both eggplant and pan are a rich golden brown, 2 to 3 minutes.

4. During the eggplant's final minutes in the oven, cook the egg roll wrappers (see page 114). Place 3 eggplant rounds on each of four cooked wrappers. Drape each remaining cooked wrapper over the eggplant. Spoon a little tomato sauce over each portion of lasagna, sprinkle with the remaining breadcrumbs, and serve immediately.

Quick Lasagna with Sausage Ragu

Serves 4

Although I prefer this sauce with pork sausage, it can be made with Italian-style turkey sausage as well.

8 egg roll wrappers

SAUSAGE RAGU

12 ounces Italian sausage, in the casing

3 tablespoons olive oil

3 garlic cloves, minced

1 (28-ounce) can crushed tomatoes

Parmesan cheese for topping

Minced fresh parsley (optional)

1. Prepare the egg roll wrappers for simmering (see box on page 114).

2. *For the ragu,* bring the sausage, 1/2 cup of water, and 1 tablespoon of the olive oil to a simmer in a Dutch oven. Cover and cook over medium heat until the sausage loses its raw color, 5 to 6 minutes. Remove the cover, increase the heat to medium-high, and cook until all the liquid evaporates and the sausage starts to sizzle and brown. Continue to cook, turning once or twice during the process, until the sausages are brown on both sides. Remove the sausage and set aside.

3. Put the remaining 2 tablespoons of oil and the garlic in the Dutch oven. To the sizzling garlic, add the tomatoes and bring to a simmer. Cover, reduce the heat to low, and cook until the tomatoes have thickened to sauce consistency, about 10 minutes. Cut the sausage into 1/2-inch-thick slices and add them to the simmering sauce.

4. A few minutes before serving, cook the egg roll wrappers. Top the first 4 cooked wrappers with a portion of Sausage Ragu, leaving a little plain tomato sauce for topping. Drape each remaining cooked wrapper over the ragu. Top with a little of the remaining sauce, sprinkle with Parmesan and optional parsley, and serve immediately.

Lasagna with Portobellos, Mozzarella, and Parmesan

Serves 4

Don't let the wrong size portobellos keep you from making this dish. Use two or three small ones for every medium-large portobello (decreasing the cooking time). If you can only find extra-large ones, roast them whole (increasing the cooking time) and cut them into reasonably sized portions. Then sandwich them between the two pasta wrappers.

8 egg roll wrappers

PORTOBELLO FILLING

4 medium-large portobello mushrooms
(10 to 12 ounces total)

3 tablespoons olive oil

Salt and ground black pepper

4 ounces shredded mozzarella cheese
(about 1$\frac{1}{3}$ cups)

$\frac{1}{4}$ cup grated Parmesan cheese, plus
extra for sprinkling

BALSAMIC BUTTER

2 tablespoons butter, heated

1 tablespoon balsamic vinegar

1. Adjust the oven rack to the upper-middle position and heat the oven to 425 degrees. Prepare the egg roll wrappers for simmering (see box on page 114).

2. *For the filling,* brush the mushrooms with the oil and sprinkle generously with salt and pepper. Place the mushrooms, gill side up, on a shallow baking pan (lined with foil if you don't want a dirty pan) and roast until soft, but not shriveled, 8 to 12 minutes, depending on mushroom size. Sprinkle a portion of mozzarella, then of Parmesan in each cap. Return to the oven and continue to roast until the mozzarella melts and Parmesan turns nutty brown, about 2 minutes longer.

3. During the mushrooms' final minutes in the oven, cook the egg roll wrappers. Place a mushroom cap on each of the first 4 cooked wrappers. Drape each remaining cooked wrapper over a mushroom. Whisk the balsamic into the butter and drizzle a little over each plate. Sprinkle with a little extra Parmesan, if you like. Serve immediately.

Quick Lasagna with Asparagus, Crabmeat, and Lemon Sauce

Serves 4

Thick asparagus makes this lasagna too lumpy. If that's all you can find, halve the spears lengthwise before cooking them.

8 egg roll wrappers

LEMON SAUCE

3/4 cup low-sodium chicken broth

1/4 cup lemon juice

2 tablespoons butter

1 bunch thin asparagus (about 1 pound), bottom 2 inches cut off

8 ounces lump or backfin crabmeat, picked over to remove bits of shell

4 scallions, trimmed and sliced thin cross-wise

1. Prepare the egg roll wrappers for simmering (see box on page 114).

2. Meanwhile, bring the broth and lemon juice to a boil in a small saucepan over medium-high heat. Continue to simmer until the broth has reduced by half, about 5 minutes. Whisk in the butter. Cover and keep warm.

3. While the sauce is cooking, put the asparagus in the water that will be used to simmer the egg roll wrappers; simmer until just tender, 3 to 4 minutes. Transfer to a plate with a slotted spoon; set aside. Heat the crabmeat in the microwave until just warm.

4. Cook the egg roll wrappers. Top each of the first 4 cooked wrappers with a portion of warm asparagus, crabmeat, scallions (reserving a little for garnish), and a tablespoon of the lemon sauce. Drape each remaining cooked wrapper over each portion of asparagus and crab, drizzle with remaining lemon sauce, garnish with remaining scallions, and serve immediately.

at-a-glance

QUICK LASAGNA

- Choose a filling and sauce and make them both.

- Meanwhile, bring 2 quarts of water to a simmer over high heat in a large, deep sauté pan. When the water starts to simmer, add 1 tablespoon of salt and 1 teaspoon of oil.

- Lightly coat 4 dinner plates with vegetable oil cooking spray and place next to the pan of simmering water.

- When the fillings and/or sauces are a couple of minutes away from being done, cook 4 egg roll wrappers until tender, about 45 seconds. Transfer wrappers to plates, spreading them out as much as possible. Drop the remaining 4 wrappers into the simmering water.

- Spoon or arrange a portion of the filling and/or sauce over the plated wrappers.

- Drape the remaining cooked wrappers over each portion of filling, spreading them out as much as possible. Sauce or garnish and serve.

quick soy sauce
bean sprouts crunch
scallions snow peas

Weeknight Stir-Fries

With onion, garlic, and ginger, stir-fry a pound each of vegetables and meat,

Then stir in a flavoring sauce for a meal satisfying and complete.

Long ingredients lists, lengthy preparation, and a foreign cooking process often make stir-fries seem impossible for weeknight cooking. For that very reason, I set out a few years back to demystify stir-fry. At the time, my goal was to make myself as comfortable stir-frying as I was with searing or sautéing.

Working with that formula over the years, I've modified the recipe to make it even more supper-friendly. My stir-fry consists of 1 pound of flavored meat (or poultry, seafood, or tofu), 1 pound of vegetables, 1 onion, 1 tablespoon each of garlic and ginger, 1 recipe of flavoring sauce, a little cornstarch for thickener, and oil for stir-frying.

To make a simple stir-fry, set a large (12-inch) heavy-bottomed nonstick or cast-iron skillet over low heat, then prepare the meat, chicken, fish, or tofu you've selected. I find the following require minimal preparation and cook quickly:

- **Medium shrimp.** Shelled and deveined, tails removed or left on as desired. Rock shrimp, which are often sold peeled and ready to use, are perfect.
- **Sea scallops.** Make sure to purchase dry scallops (see page 188 for further explanation). Halve these large scallops horizontally.

121

- **Boneless, skinless chicken breasts or thighs.** Cut them into bite-size chunks or strips.

- **Pork tenderloin.** Slice thin crosswise. Although other tender cuts of pork will work, I find thin slices of tenderloin ideal for stir-frying. Usually packaged in twos, they weigh 12 to 16 ounces each. Use one for stir-fry and freeze the other one for later.

- **Beef.** Almost any steak (sirloin, New York strip, rib-eye, tenderloin) sliced thin across the grain. Flank and skirt steak are also good candidates and must be also sliced across the grain, and on a slight angle.

- **Tofu.** Select the firm style and cut it into ¾-inch chunks.

After preparing one of the above, mix it with a tablespoon each of soy sauce and sherry. This quick dunk may seem like a frivolous step, but it isn't. The flavor difference between meat that has been marinated and meat that has not is dramatic. Surrounded by highly seasoned sauce and vegetables, nonmarinated meat tastes bland, throwing off the balance of flavors. The meat doesn't need to marinate long—just make it the first thing you do after setting the skillet over low heat.

Since most domestic stoves just don't have the BTUs to stir-fry a large quantity of meat and vegetables at the same time, you must cook the meat in batches. If you don't, the meat will not sear properly and the skillet will cool down significantly, causing problems for the vegetables in the next step.

Regardless of the stir-fry I'm making, I always start with a medium-large (8-ounce) onion, which can be peeled and cut into wedges very quickly. When choosing the remaining vegetables, avoid hard thick ones like broccoli or cauliflower florets, thick asparagus, and carrot rounds that must be parboiled. Instead, stick to high-moisture or already-cooked vegetables that stir-fry quickly and require little or no preparation.

Canned sliced water chestnuts and baby corn require nothing more than opening a can, draining the liquid, and rinsing them. Fresh bean sprouts and prepared fresh vegetables like sliced mushrooms and shredded cabbage and carrots are merely "snip and dump."

Bell peppers can be quickly cut into large dice or strips. Snow peas that have had their strings removed require nothing more than a quick rinse. Scallions and pencil-thin asparagus just need to be trimmed and cut into 1-inch lengths. Zucchini, yellow squash, and eggplant can be sliced or diced in seconds.

The following vegetables cook quickly and are good candidates for a quick stir-fry:

- **Pencil-thin asparagus.** Trimmed and cut into 1-inch lengths.

- **Fresh bean sprouts.** Simply open the plastic bag and dump. Fresh bean sprouts are crisp compared to canned ones and should be used when possible.

- **Green cabbage.** Quartered, cored, and coarsely shredded. Packaged shredded cabbage, though a little fine, works well. Napa cabbage, with its more tender leaves, waters down a stir-fry.

- **Carrots.** Packaged shredded carrots are perfect—simply snip and dump.

- **Celery.** Cut crosswise into $1/2$-inch chunks.

- **Eggplant.** Trim ends and cut crosswise into $3/4$-inch-thick slices, then into $3/4$-inch-thick chunks.

- **Green beans.** The thinner, the better. Pinch off stem ends.

- **Sliced white mushrooms.** Packaged presliced white mushrooms are perfect for weeknight stir-fries. Presliced portobello mushrooms, however, are too thick to fully cook in this particular cooking method.

- **Onions.** Peeled, halved pole to pole, each half cut into 8 wedges.

- **Yellow, red, and green bell peppers.** Stemmed, seeded, and cut into 1-inch squares or $1/2$-inch strips.

- **Pineapple.** Peeled, quartered, cored, and cut into bite-size chunks. Though not a vegetable, pineapple is a must in a sweet-and-sour stir-fry. Canned pineapple chunks packed in their own juice are not bad in stir-fries and, unlike fresh pineapple, the quality is at least consistent.

- **Scallions.** Trimmed and cut into 1-inch lengths.

- **Snow peas.** Strings removed. (Many stores sell snow peas with strings removed. If you can find them, buy them. They save precious preparation time.)

- **Canned water chestnuts and baby corn.** Open the can, drain, and rinse. When calculating the $1 1/2$ pounds of vegetables you need for a stir-fry, remember to count the drained weight only. Avoid canned bamboo shoots and bean sprouts, which are watery and limp.

- **Zucchini or yellow squash.** Trim each end and cut into $1/2$-inch-thick rounds or into julienne strips 2 inches long and $1/4$ inch thick.

For the same reason that the meat must be cooked in batches, the vegetables must be added to the skillet incrementally. Always start with the onion. If the skillet is good and hot, the onion wedges will turn brown in less than a minute.

It's usually pretty simple to figure out which of the two remaining vegetables should be added to the skillet first. There's usually one vegetable that naturally takes a little longer to cook through. Water chestnuts, baby corn, bean sprouts, and scallions need very little cooking time and should always be added last. Thin asparagus, for example, needs longer stir-frying time than mushrooms; peppers need longer than pineapple; snow peas need longer than shredded carrots. If it's not obvious, just pick a vegetable and start. You're not going to ruin the stir-fry. Staggering vegetables is more about keeping the skillet hot. If one vegetable ends up slightly over- or undercooked—no big deal. Just keep it in mind next time you stir-fry.

Mincing garlic and ginger for stir-fry can be the most tedious of the preparation steps. In an attempt to save time, I've tried using bottled minced garlic and sliced ginger. As much as I want to like these convenience products, I can't. Each tastes strong and distinct, and muddies the stir-fry's otherwise fresh, clear flavors. There is, however, a quick way to mince them both. Slice peeled garlic cloves and gingerroot crosswise about 1/4 inch thick. Line up the garlic and ginger slices on a countertop or other hard surface. Place the flat side of a chef's knife over the slice and hit the side of the knife with your fist. The smashing action causes the ginger and garlic instantly to mince. If you haven't hit it hard enough, re-position the knife over the slice and smash it again.

Add the garlic and ginger to the stir-fry after the onion has stir-fried but before adding the next vegetable. You want to add them as soon as possible so they flavor the entire dish. If you add them too soon, however, they burn and make the stir-fry taste bitter.

For weeknight stir-fries, I keep the flavoring sauces simple. With the exception of the Basil Stir-Fry Sauce, which requires a fresh herb, I've limited the flavoring sauce ingredients to pantry items. Use common sense when pairing sauces with meats. The Soy-Sesame Stir-Fry Sauce and the Basil Stir-Fry Sauce are compatible with just about any meat and vegetable—beef, pork, poultry, fish, or tofu. Limit the Lemon Stir-Fry Sauce to poultry and seafood and the Sweet and Sour Stir-Fry Sauce to poultry, pork, and seafood.

Thickening the stir-fry with a little cornstarch is an extra step I'm willing to take. I like the body and sheen it provides, but don't add it until after you've added the flavoring sauce. Otherwise the sauce will not absorb into the vegetables and meat.

Weeknight Stir-Fry

Once you've cooked through this master recipe a couple of times, you'll memorize the formula. After that, you'll only need to refer to the flavoring sauces that follow. Serve with Steamed Rice (page 235).

1 pound beef, pork, poultry, seafood, or tofu, cut into bite-size pieces (see pages 121–122)

1 tablespoon each: soy sauce and dry sherry

1 medium-large onion (about 8 ounces), halved from pole to pole, each half cut into 8 wedges

1 pound vegetables (see page 123), cut in approximate size of the selected meat or seafood

1 tablespoon each: minced garlic and ginger

1 recipe flavoring sauce

2 teaspoons cornstarch mixed with 2 tablespoons canned chicken broth, plus extra broth if necessary

3 tablespoons peanut or vegetable oil

1. While preparing ingredients in steps 2–6, set an 11- to 12-inch heavy-bottomed skillet over low heat. Three to four minutes before stir-frying, turn on the exhaust fan and increase the heat to high.

2. Toss the protein of choice with soy sauce and sherry in a medium bowl; set aside.

3. Prepare the onion and vegetables and transfer to a medium large bowl, keeping them separate.

4. Mince the garlic and ginger and place in a small bowl; set aside.

5. Mix flavoring sauce in a small bowl; set aside.

6. Mix the cornstarch with chicken broth in a small bowl; set aside.

7. When ready to stir-fry, drizzle 1 tablespoon of the oil to coat the pan completely. Add half the protein of choice; stir-fry until seared and just cooked through, 2 to 3 minutes. Transfer to a clean bowl; stir-fry the remaining protein, adding it to the bowl when cooked.

(continued)

8. Drizzle the remaining oil (1½ to 2 tablespoons) into the hot skillet. Add the onion; stir-fry until browned but still crisp, about 1 minute. Add the garlic and ginger, then the second vegetable; continue to stir-fry until softened but still crisp, 1 to 2 minutes longer. Add the final vegetable; sauté until all vegetables are tender-crisp, 1 to 2 minutes longer. Return the protein to the pan.

9. Stir in the flavoring sauce; stir-fry to coat all ingredients. Stir the cornstarch mixture and add to the skillet; stir until the juices become saucy and glossy. If the pan juices look too thick, add a couple more tablespoons of chicken broth. Serve immediately.

Stir-Fried Chicken with Baby Corn and Zucchini

PROTEIN:

1 pound boneless, skinless chicken breasts, cut crosswise and into bite-size pieces

VEGETABLES:

8 ounces zucchini, cut into ½-inch-thick rounds or into julienne strips 2 inches long and ¼ inch thick

1 (14-ounce) can baby corn (drained weight 8 ounces)

FLAVORING SAUCE:

Basil (or Cilantro) Flavoring Sauce (page 132)

Follow the Weeknight Stir-Fry recipe (page 125), adding zucchini to the skillet before the corn.

Stir-Fried Chicken with Asparagus and Mushrooms

PROTEIN:

1 pound boneless, skinless chicken breasts, cut crosswise and into bite-size pieces

VEGETABLES:

8 ounces pencil-thin asparagus, trimmed and cut into 1-inch pieces

1 (8-ounce) package sliced mushrooms

FLAVORING SAUCE:

Lemon Flavoring Sauce (page 132)

Follow the Weeknight Stir-Fry recipe (page 125), adding asparagus to the skillet before the mushrooms.

Stir-Fried Chicken, Snow Peas, and Water Chestnuts

PROTEIN:

3/4 to 1 pound boneless, skinless chicken breasts, cut crosswise and into bite-size pieces

VEGETABLES:

12 ounces snow peas, strings removed

1 (8-ounce) can sliced water chestnuts (drained weight 5 ounces)

FLAVORING SAUCE:

Lemon Flavoring Sauce (page 132)

Follow the Weeknight Stir-Fry recipe (page 125), adding snow peas to the skillet before the water chestnuts.

Stir-Fried Scallops with Cabbage and Scallions

To save shredding time, use packaged shredded cabbage.

PROTEIN:

1 pound dry sea scallops, halved
horizontally

VEGETABLES:

12 ounces shredded green cabbage,
trimmed and cut into 1-inch pieces

1 bunch (4 ounces) scallions, ends
trimmed and cut into 1-inch lengths

FLAVORING SAUCE:

Soy-Sesame Flavoring Sauce
(page 131)

Follow the Weeknight Stir-Fry recipe (page 125), adding cabbage to the skillet before the scallions.

Stir-Fried Shrimp with Peppers and Scallions

PROTEIN:

3/4 to 1 pound medium shrimp, shelled
and deveined if necessary

VEGETABLES:

2 medium red or yellow bell peppers
(12 ounces), cut into 1-inch squares
or 1/2-inch-thick strips

1 bunch (4 ounces) scallions, ends
trimmed and cut into 1-inch lengths

FLAVORING SAUCE:

Basil (or Cilantro) Flavoring Sauce
(page 132)

Follow the Weeknight Stir-Fry recipe (page 125), adding bell peppers to the skillet before the scallions.

Stir-Fried Tofu with Haricots Verts and Eggplant

Since whole green beans take too long to cook through, haricots verts or very thin green beans are used here. If halved lengthwise, however, whole green beans cook faster and will work. Zucchini can be substituted for the haricots verts as well.

PROTEIN:

3/4 to 1 pound firm tofu, cut into 3/4-inch cubes

VEGETABLES:

8 ounces eggplant, ends trimmed, cut into 3/4-inch-thick chunks

8 ounces haricots verts, ends trimmed (see note above)

FLAVORING SAUCE:

Basil (or Cilantro) Flavoring Sauce (page 132)

Follow the Weeknight Stir-Fry recipe (page 125), adding eggplant to the skillet before the beans.

Stir-Fried Beef with Cabbage and Mushrooms

PROTEIN:

3/4 to 1 pound flank steak, sliced thin on a slight angle, or other steak (see page 122 for options), sliced thin

VEGETABLES:

8 ounces shredded cabbage

8 ounces sliced mushrooms

FLAVORING SAUCE:

Soy-Sesame Flavoring Sauce (page 131)

Follow the Weeknight Stir-Fry recipe (page 125), adding cabbage to the skillet before the mushrooms.

Stir-Fried Beef with Celery and Water Chestnuts

Sprinkle this stir-fry with roasted cashews if you like.

PROTEIN:

¾ to 1 pound flank steak, sliced thin on a slight angle, or other steak, sliced thin

VEGETABLES:

10 to 12 ounces celery, trimmed and sliced crosswise ¼ inch thick

1 (8-ounce) can sliced water chestnuts (drained weight 5 ounces), rinsed

FLAVORING SAUCE:

Soy-Sesame Flavoring Sauce (page 131)

Follow the Weeknight Stir-Fry recipe (page 125), adding celery to the skillet before the water chestnuts.

Stir-Fried Pork with Snow Peas and Shredded Carrots

PROTEIN:

1 pork tenderloin (¾ to 1 pound), sliced thin crosswise

VEGETABLES:

12 ounces snow peas, strings removed

2 medium carrots, shredded coarse, or 4 ounces packaged shredded carrots

FLAVORING SAUCE:

Basil (or Cilantro) Flavoring Sauce (page 132)

Follow the Weeknight Stir-Fry recipe (page 125), adding snow peas to the skillet before the carrots.

Sweet-and-Sour Pork with Peppers and Pineapple

PROTEIN:

1 pork tenderloin (³/₄ to 1 pound),
sliced thin crosswise

VEGETABLE/FRUIT:

1¹/₂ medium yellow or red bell
peppers, cut into 1-inch chunks
or ¹/₂-inch strips

¹/₂ already peeled and cored fresh
pineapple (8 ounces), cut into 1-inch
chunks, or 1¹/₄ cups drained canned
pineapple packed in juice

FLAVORING SAUCE:

Sweet-and-Sour Flavoring Sauce
(page 132)

Follow the Weeknight Stir-Fry recipe (page 125), adding peppers to the skillet before
the pineapple.

Soy-Sesame Flavoring Sauce

Enough to flavor one recipe Weeknight Stir-Fry

¹/₄ cup canned low-sodium
chicken broth

¹/₄ cup soy sauce

2 teaspoons rice wine vinegar

2 teaspoons toasted sesame oil

1 teaspoon hot red pepper flakes

1 teaspoon sugar

Mix all ingredients in a small bowl and set aside.

Sweet-and-Sour Flavoring Sauce

Enough to flavor one recipe Weeknight Stir-Fry

For a spicier sauce, substitute 1 jalapeño, halved, stemmed, seeded, and minced, for the hot red pepper flakes. If using canned pineapple, 1/4 cup of the pineapple juice can be substituted for the chicken broth.

1/4 cup canned chicken broth

2 tablespoons soy sauce

2 tablespoons cider, balsamic, or rice wine vinegar

1 tablespoon brown sugar

1/2 teaspoon hot red pepper flakes

Mix all ingredients in a small bowl and set aside.

Basil (or Cilantro) Flavoring Sauce

Enough to flavor one recipe Weeknight Stir-Fry

1/4 cup canned chicken broth

1/4 cup soy sauce

2 teaspoons rice wine vinegar

1/2 teaspoon sugar

1/4 cup shredded fresh basil leaves *or* 1/4 cup chopped fresh cilantro

Mix all ingredients in a small bowl and set aside.

Lemon Flavoring Sauce

Enough to flavor one recipe Weeknight Stir-Fry

1/4 cup lemon juice plus 1 teaspoon lemon zest

1/4 cup canned chicken broth

1 tablespoon soy sauce

2 tablespoons sugar

Mix all ingredients in a small bowl and set aside.

WEEKNIGHT STIR-FRY

- Set an 11- to 12-inch heavy-bottomed skillet over low heat.
- Toss selected meat with soy sauce and sherry.
- Prepare onion and other stir-fry vegetables.
- Mince garlic and ginger.
- Mix flavoring sauce.
- Mix cornstarch with chicken stock.
- Increase heat to high and turn on exhaust fan 3 to 4 minutes before start of cooking.
- Stir-fry selected protein in two batches; set aside.
- Starting with the onion, stir-fry vegetables, staggering additions to avoid cooling off the skillet.
- Return cooked protein to skillet.
- Stir in flavoring sauce, then cornstarch mixture, adding a couple more tablespoons of chicken stock if necessary.

ginger scallion
sesame oil soy sauce
stir-fry shrimp
rice

More Asian Fast Food Lo Mein,
Fried Rice, and Pad Thai

Lo mein ratios are different—1/2 pound of vegetables and 1/4 of meat.

Add 1/2 pound of cooked spaghetti and don't forget the heat.

With fried rice there's no sauce to make, no thickener to mix,

one egg and some cooked rice make it the simplest to fix.

Pad Thai takes eggs like Fried Rice and noodles like Lo Mein,

Though flavorings change—fish sauce and lime—the method is the same.

E ven more than stir-fry, my daughters love to eat fried rice and lo mein. With cooked rice or pasta on hand, I can have either of these dishes on the table in less than twenty minutes.

Although the flavorings and ingredients differ slightly, the method for making lo mein and fried rice is almost identical. As with stir-fry, the skillet must be searing hot and the meat and vegetable additions are staggered so that the ingredients fry instead of stew.

Except for pineapple, which is good only in sweet-and-sour stir-fries, most of the suggested stir-fry meats or vegetables (see pages 121–123) work equally well in lo mein or fried rice. Since the meat and vegetables are supporting rather than featured ingredients in these dishes, cut them slightly smaller than you would for a meat-and-vegetable-only stir-fry.

I often use leftover meat, poultry, and shrimp in fried rice and lo mein. If using leftover meat, you'll only need about 4 ounces. If using fresh meat, poultry, or seafood, figure about 6 ounces.

If making lo mein or fried rice with cooked meat and a raw vegetable, give the vegetable a head start, stir-frying it first. If using a cooked vegetable (e.g. water chestnuts or baby corn) and raw meat, start with the meat. If both meat and vegetable are either raw or cooked, stir-fry the meat first, giving it a little head start.

Although pad thai doesn't quite offer the flexibility of ingredients that fried rice and lo mein do, the dish is definitely a close cousin. The technique is identical—keep the skillet hot, stagger the meat and vegetable additions, and add a cooked starch. Like fried rice, pad thai contains eggs. Like lo mein, noodles are the starch of choice. Only the flavorings change: fish sauce takes soy's place and lime juice stands in for vinegar.

Simple Lo Mein

1 medium-large onion, halved from pole to pole, each half cut into eight wedges

4 to 6 ounces beef, pork, poultry, seafood, or tofu, cooked or raw, cut into bite-size pieces

8 ounces vegetables, cut into bite-size pieces

1½ teaspoons minced garlic

1½ teaspoons minced fresh ginger

1 recipe Lo Mein Flavoring Sauce (page 138)

1 tablespoon soy sauce

2 tablespoons vegetable oil

4 heaping cups of leftover cooked spaghetti (about 8 ounces uncooked)

1. Heat a large (12-inch) heavy-bottomed skillet over low heat while preparing onion, meat, vegetables, garlic, and ginger, and the flavoring sauce. Marinate the meat in 1 tablespoon of soy sauce. Three to four minutes before stir-frying, turn on the exhaust fan and increase the heat to high.

2. Put 1 tablespoon of oil and the onion in the skillet; stir-fry until the onion is still crisp but starts to turn brown, about 1 minute. Add the raw meat; stir-fry until lightly browned, about 1 minute. Add the first vegetable; stir-fry until tender-crisp, about 1 minute. Add the second vegetable; stir-fry about 1 minute longer. Stir in garlic and ginger. Transfer to a plate and set aside. (If using a cooked meat, add it between the two vegetables.)

3. Put the remaining 1 tablespoon of oil in the skillet; heat until shimmering. Add the spaghetti; stir-fry until heated through, about 2 minutes. Return the meat/vegetable mixture to the pan, along with Lo Mein Flavoring Sauce (page 138); stir-fry to combine and heat through. Serve immediately.

Pork Lo Mein with Mushrooms and Cabbage

MEAT:

4 ounces roast pork, cut into bite-size pieces, or 6 ounces pork tenderloin, sliced thin

VEGETABLE:

½ package sliced mushrooms (4 ounces)

4 ounces shredded cabbage

Follow the Simple Lo Mein recipe, adding roast pork between the mushrooms and the cabbage. (If using fresh pork tenderloin, stir-fry it before adding the cabbage and mushrooms.)

Chicken Lo Mein with Celery and Water Chestnuts

MEAT:

1 boneless, skinless chicken breast half (about 6 ounces), cut crosswise into ½-inch slices

VEGETABLE:

2 large celery stalks, sliced thin (about 4 ounces)

1 (8-ounce) can water chestnuts, drained (5 ounces drained weight)

Follow the Simple Lo Mein recipe, adding chicken to the skillet, followed by the celery, then the water chestnuts.

Shrimp Lo Mein with Snow Peas and Scallions

MEAT:

6 ounces medium shrimp, shelled and cut into ½-inch pieces

VEGETABLE:

4 ounces snow peas, strings removed

1 large bunch (4 ounces) scallions, trimmed and cut into 1-inch lengths

Follow the Simple Lo Mein recipe, adding shrimp to the skillet, followed by the snow peas, then the scallions.

Lo Mein Flavoring Sauce

Enough to flavor one recipe Lo Mein

¼ cup low-sodium chicken broth	2 teaspoons toasted sesame oil
¼ cup soy sauce	1 teaspoon hot red pepper flakes
2 teaspoons rice wine vinegar	1 teaspoon sugar

Mix in a small bowl; set aside.

at-a-glance

SIMPLE LO MEIN

- Make sure to have 4 cups (8 ounces) of cooked spaghetti on hand.
- Heat a large (12-inch) skillet over low heat while preparing meat, vegetables, and sauce.
- Increase the heat to high and turn on the exhaust fan 3 to 4 minutes before start of cooking.
- Starting with the onion, stir-fry meat and vegetables, staggering additions to avoid cooling off the skillet. Transfer meat/vegetable mixture to a plate.
- Stir-fry spaghetti until heated through. Return the meat/vegetable mixture to the skillet, along with Lo Mein Sauce; stir-fry until heated through.

Simple Fried Rice

The rice needs to stir-fry in a generous amount of oil. (It's fried rice, after all.) If you don't use enough oil, the dish starts to taste more like a rice casserole. Note that except for the 2 eggs, 1 onion, and 1 garlic clove, all the other ingredients begin with 4.

1 medium onion, halved from pole to pole; each half cut into 6 wedges

4 to 6 ounces meat of choice, cooked or raw, cut into bite-size pieces

4 to 6 ounces vegetable of choice, cooked or raw, cut into bite-size pieces

1 large garlic clove, minced

2 large eggs, beaten

4 tablespoons soy sauce

4 tablespoons vegetable oil

4 cups cooked rice

4 scallions, white and green parts, minced

1. Set a heavy-bottomed 12-inch nonstick or cast iron skillet over low heat while preparing meat, vegetable, garlic, and eggs. Marinate the meat in 1 tablespoon of soy sauce. Three to four minutes from making the fried rice, increase the heat to high and turn on the exhaust fan.

2. Put 1 tablespoon of oil and the onion in the skillet; stir-fry until the onion is still crisp but starts to turn brown, about 1 minute. Add the raw meat or vegetable; stir-fry until crisp-tender for vegetables or lightly browned for meat, about 1 minute. Add the cooked meat or vegetable; stir-fry until lightly browned, about 1 minute longer. (If both meat and vegetables are raw or cooked, stir-fry the meat first, giving it a little head start.) Stir in the garlic, then transfer the mixture to a plate; set aside.

3. Put the remaining 3 tablespoons oil in the skillet; heat until shimmering. Add the rice; stir-fry, breaking up clumps, until heated through, about 2 minutes. Add the egg; stir until scrambled, about 1 minute. Return the meat/vegetable mixture, along with the remaining 3 tablespoons of soy sauce and the scallions, to the pan and stir to combine. Serve immediately.

Fried Rice with Pork and Mushrooms

MEAT:

4 ounces roast pork, sliced ¼ inch
thick, then into ¼-inch matchsticks

VEGETABLE:

½ package sliced mushrooms
(4 ounces)

Follow the Simple Fried Rice recipe (page 139), adding mushrooms first to the onions; stir-fry until lightly browned, 1 to 2 minutes. Add pork and continue with the recipe.

Fried Rice with Shrimp and Water Chestnuts

MEAT:

6 ounces medium shrimp, shelled and
cut into ½-inch pieces

VEGETABLE:

1 (8-ounce) can water chestnuts,
drained and rinsed (5 ounces
drained weight)

Follow the Simple Fried Rice recipe (page 139), adding shrimp first to the onions; stir-fry until lightly browned, 1 to 2 minutes. Add the water chestnuts and continue.

Fried Rice with Celery, Peppers, and Mushrooms

MEAT:

None (doubled vegetable quantity)

VEGETABLE:

1 celery stalk, cut into small dice

½ package sliced mushrooms
(4 ounces)

½ medium red bell pepper, cut into
medium dice

Follow the Simple Fried Rice recipe (page 139), adding celery first to the onions; stir-fry until lightly browned, about 1 minute. Add the mushrooms, then the peppers, allowing mushrooms to stir-fry about 30 seconds before adding peppers.

Fried Rice with Chicken and Celery

MEAT:

1 boneless, skinless chicken breast
half (4 to 6 ounces), cut into
1/2-inch pieces

VEGETABLE:

2 celery stalks, cut into small dice

Follow the Simple Fried Rice recipe (page 139), adding chicken first to the onions; stir-fry until lightly browned, 1 to 2 minutes. Add the celery and continue with the recipe.

at-a-glance

FRIED RICE

- Make sure to have 4 cups of cooked rice on hand.
- Heat a large (12-inch) skillet over low heat while preparing fried rice ingredients.
- Increase the heat to high and turn on the exhaust fan 3 to 4 minutes before start of cooking.
- Starting with the onion, stir-fry the meat and vegetables, staggering additions to avoid cooling off the skillet. Transfer to a plate.
- Stir-fry the rice to heat through; add the egg; stir until scrambled.
- Return the meat/vegetable mixture to the skillet, along with soy sauce and scallions; stir-fry until heated through.

Weeknight Pad Thai

Since rice noodles, the traditional pad thai filler, are not always easy to find, I've found that spaghetti, more readily available and always in the pantry, works just as well.

1 recipe Pad Thai Sauce (see opposite)

1 medium onion, halved from pole to pole, each half cut into 8 wedges

6 ounces shrimp, chicken, or tofu, cut into bite-size pieces

1 large garlic clove, minced

6 scallions, white and green part, cut into 1-inch lengths

6 ounces (2 cups) bean sprouts, rinsed

2 large eggs, lightly beaten

1/4 cup roasted peanuts, coarsely chopped

1 lime, cut into 6 wedges

2 tablespoons vegetable oil

4 cups cooked spaghetti (8 ounces), patted dry

Cilantro leaves for garnish (optional)

1. Set a heavy-bottomed 12-inch nonstick or cast-iron skillet or wok over low heat while preparing Pad Thai Sauce, onion, shrimp, garlic, scallions, bean sprouts, eggs, peanuts, and lime. Three to four minutes before starting to cook, increase the heat to high and turn on the exhaust fan.

2. Put 1 tablespoon of oil and the onion in the skillet; stir-fry until the onion is still crisp but starts to turn brown, 30 to 45 seconds. Add the shrimp; stir-fry until lightly browned, about 1 minute. Stir in the garlic, then scallions and bean sprouts; stir-fry until the vegetables wilt slightly, about 1 minute. Make a well in the center of the pan; pour in the eggs. Cook until partially set, then scramble into the vegetable mixture. Transfer to a plate, pour half the pad thai sauce over the vegetable mixture, toss to coat, and set aside.

3. Heat the remaining tablespoon of oil in the hot skillet until shimmering. Toss the spaghetti with the remaining Pad Thai Sauce; put in the skillet and stir-fry until heated through, about 2 minutes. Return the vegetable mixture to the skillet; stir-fry until heated through. Transfer to a serving platter. Squeeze 2 of the lime wedges over the noodles, sprinkle with peanuts, and garnish with cilantro and remaining lime wedges. Serve immediately.

Pad Thai Sauce

Enough to flavor 1 recipe Weeknight Pad Thai

Thai or Vietnamese fish sauce, also known as nam pla or nuoc nam, is available at Asian specialty markets or in the Asian section of many grocery stores across the country.

6 tablespoons Thai or Vietnamese
fish sauce

2 tablespoons sugar

1 teaspoon red pepper flakes

Mix all ingredients; stir until sugar is dissolved.

at-a-glance

WEEKNIGHT PAD THAI

- Be sure to have 4 cups (8 ounces) cooked spaghetti on hand.
- Heat a large (12-inch) skillet over low heat while preparing meat, vegetables, and sauce.
- Increase the heat to high and turn on the exhaust fan 3 to 4 minutes before start of cooking.
- Starting with the onion, stir-fry meat and vegetables, staggering additions to avoid cooling off the skillet.
- Scramble the eggs into the meat/vegetable mixture, transfer to a plate, pour on half the pad thai sauce, and toss to coat.
- Toss the spaghetti with the remaining Pad Thai Sauce; stir-fry until heated through.
- Return the vegetable mixture to the skillet; stir-fry until heated through.
- Transfer to a serving platter; squeeze on lime juice, sprinkle with peanuts, and garnish with cilantro.

If You've Made One Sauté, You've Made Them All Sautéed Chicken and Turkey Cutlets, Boneless Pork Chops, Fish Fillets, and Duck Breasts, with Pan Sauces and Relishes

Heat butter and oil, swirling them around.

Add meat, seasoned and coated, and cook until beautifully browned.

As a child, I ate chicken, fish, and pork chops pan-fried and on the bone. I didn't cook my first boneless, skinless chicken breast until the late 70s. The recipe was Suprêmes de Volaille à Blanc from *Mastering the Art of French Cooking*. You couldn't buy boneless, skinless chicken breasts back then, so I selected whole ones and carefully halved, boned, skinned, and trimmed them myself. With all the special preparation and the fancy French title, those precious morsels were definitely dinner party fare. Now, just a generation later, boneless, skinless chicken breasts are a once-a-week entree at our house.

I still like to crunch on fried fish tails, gnaw pork chop bones, and suck on chicken drumsticks, but I prefer sautéed boneless cuts—chicken, turkey, pork, duck breasts, fish fillets—for weeknight cooking. With a steam-sautéed vegetable or a quick salad, I can pull off a dinner in fifteen minutes. Sautéing is a simple technique, and once you learn it, you can cook a variety of boneless meats and fish.

CHICKEN CUTLETS

To sauté chicken breasts properly, you must start by heating the pan before you ever touch the chicken. Since neither oil nor butter is ideal, use a combination of the two—butter for flavor, oil to increase the smoking point. As soon as you turn on the burner, put the butter and oil in the pan. The slow, steady heat keeps the fat from wild sizzling, spitting, smoking, and burning.

Just as important as heating the oil to the right temperature is choosing the right size skillet. The chicken breasts should fit in the pan comfortably with only a little space in between. For four chicken breasts, you'll need a skillet measuring 12 inches across the top; for three, choose a 10-inch skillet and for two breasts select an 8-inch skillet.

While the fat slowly comes up to the right temperature, prepare the meat. Depending on the style of chicken breast, trimming can be minimal or extensive. Some processing plants remove the whole breast from the bone, leaving the two half breasts attached. Held together by cartilage, the breasts need to be separated. To split and trim them in one step, cut down each side of the cartilage. If there's excess fat around the edges, trim that off too. Since the tenderloin thickens up the breast and keeps the center from getting done quickly, simply pull it out and cook it separately. Removing the tenderloin makes the breast an almost even thickness, guaranteeing fast, even cooking.

If available, trim-free chicken breasts are perfect for weeknight cooking. Split, trimmed, and tenderloins removed, these chicken breasts are practically skillet-ready right out of the package.

Should chicken breasts be dredged in flour before sautéing? I think so. Compared with a floured version, the unprotected surface of an uncoated chicken breast tends to turn leathery from the high heat. I also like the almost fried look and flavor of coated chicken breasts.

Once you're a couple of minutes away from sautéing, increase the heat to medium-high until the oil is hot but not smoking and the flecks of milk solids in the butter turn golden brown and smell nutty. Just to be sure, flick a pinch of the dredging flour into the pan. If the flour sizzles for a split second and immediately turns golden, the pan is ready. Add the chicken breasts and sauté until golden brown, about three minutes. At that point, turn them and sauté for another three minutes. That's it. There's no need to pinch, prod, poke, and push around the chicken. If the oil temperature and the pan size are right, the chicken breasts should be done with one turn in about six minutes.

I'll occasionally serve sautéed chicken breasts with a wedge of lemon, a salsa, or an uncooked relish. But more often, I make a quick pan sauce once I remove the chicken breasts from the skillet. I hate washing all the pan drippings down the drain. And besides, this initial "wash" loosens up the brown bits, making cleanup no more than a sponge wipe and quick rinse. For more information on making pan sauces, see page 158.

Since chicken breasts are sautéed most frequently, I have chosen them as my sauté model, but other boneless cuts such as turkey cutlets, boneless pork chops, and fish fillets are sautéed in exactly the same way (see recipes that follow). Regardless of what you sauté, the method is the same.

TURKEY CUTLETS

Since we eat a lot of white meat at our house (neither of my daughters eat pork, beef, or lamb), turkey cutlets often stand in for chicken. Like many meat cuts, packaged turkey cutlets tend to be sliced a little thin for my tastes. For this reason—and because it's usually cheaper, I often buy a boneless, skinless turkey breast (sometimes called turkey London broil) and make my own turkey cutlets.

Since there are no bones, skin, or fat to remove, this butchering exercise is simple. To turn a boneless, skinless turkey breast into cutlets, remove the very large tenderloin from its cut (as opposed to its skinned) side, then cut the turkey breast, crosswise, into $^{1}/_{2}$-inch thick slices. Depending on the turkey breast size, there may be enough for two meals. If so, refrigerate or freeze the remaining cutlets.

Sautéed Boneless, Skinless Chicken Cutlets

2 tablespoons butter

1 tablespoon oil

4 boneless chicken breast halves, trimmed of fat and tenderloin removed, and pounded with the dull side of a chef's knife until more or less even textured

Salt and ground black pepper

$1/4$ cup flour measured into a pie plate or other shallow pan

Lemon wedges, or a pan sauce or uncooked relish

1. Heat the butter and oil in an 11- to 12-inch skillet over low heat. While the pan is heating, sprinkle chicken breasts and tenderloins on both sides with salt and pepper, then dredge in flour.

2. A couple of minutes before sautéing, increase the heat to medium-high. When the butter stops foaming and starts to smell nutty, arrange the chicken breasts, skinned side up, and tenderloins in the skillet. Cook, turning only once, until chicken breasts are rich golden brown, about 3 minutes per side (tenderloins will be done a little sooner). Remove chicken from skillet.

3. Serve immediately with lemon wedges or an uncooked relish. Or make a pan sauce by adding $1/2$ cup liquid to the skillet; boil until the liquid is reduced to about $1/4$ cup. Tilting the skillet so that the reduced liquid is at one side of the pan, whisk in butter or other enrichments until the sauce is smooth and glossy. Spoon a portion of sauce over each sautéed chicken breast and serve immediately.

Uncooked Relish Possibilities (pages 171–173): All-Purpose Salsa; Parsley Relish with Capers and Cornichons; Tomato Relish with Pine Nuts, Green Olives, and Lemon Zest; Roasted Pepper Relish with Olives, Capers, and Rosemary.

Pan Sauce Possibilities (pages 159–170): Red Wine–Dijon Pan Sauce; Marsala Wine Pan Sauce; Sauterne Pan Sauce with Figs and Pistachios; Sweet Vermouth Pan Sauce with Prunes; Port Wine Pan Sauce with Dried Cranberries; Tomato-Tarragon Pan Sauce; Tomato-Rosemary Pan Sauce; Tomato-Anchovy Pan Sauce; Tomato Sauce with Black Olives and Provençal Herbs; Cooked Tomato Relish with Onion and Mint; White Wine Vinegar Pan Sauce; Balsamic Vinegar Pan Sauce; Apple Cider Pan Sauce; Orange-Dijon Pan Sauce with Rosemary; Orange Pan Sauce with Pernod; Lemon-Caper Pan Sauce; Quick Velouté; Mustard Cream Sauce; Mushroom–Goat Cheese Pan Sauce; Green Grape–Rosemary Pan Sauce; Curried Chutney Pan Sauce; Asian-style Sweet-and-Sour Sauce.

Sautéed Turkey Cutlets

Serves 4 to 6

Sautéed chicken breasts and turkey cutlets are similar in flavor, so all of the pan sauces, the salsa, and the uncooked relishes can be used for either cut.

2 tablespoons butter	Salt and ground black pepper
1 tablespoon oil	¼ cup flour measured into a pie plate or other shallow pan
1 boneless, skinless turkey breast half (about 1½ pounds), cut into six 1-inch-thick cutlets, or 6 precut turkey cutlets	Lemon wedges, or a pan sauce or uncooked relish

1. Heat the butter and oil in an 11- to 12-inch skillet over low heat. While the pan is heating, sprinkle turkey cutlets on both sides with salt and pepper, then dredge in flour.

2. A couple of minutes before sautéing, increase the heat to medium-high. When the butter stops foaming and starts to smell nutty brown, arrange the cutlets in the skillet. Cook, turning only once, until they are a rich golden brown, 3 to 4 minutes per side. Remove cutlets from skillet.

3. Serve immediately with lemon wedges or an uncooked relish. Or make a pan sauce by adding ½ cup liquid to the skillet; boil until the liquid is reduced to about ¼ cup. Tilting the skillet so that the reduced liquid is at one side of the pan, whisk in butter or other enrichments until the sauce is smooth and glossy. Spoon a portion of sauce over each portion of cutlets and serve immediately.

Uncooked Relish Possibilities (pages 171–173): All-Purpose Salsa; Parsley Relish with Capers and Cornichons; Tomato Relish with Pine Nuts, Green Olives, and Lemon Zest; Roasted Pepper Relish with Olives, Capers, and Rosemary.

Pan Sauce Possibilities (pages 159–170): Red Wine–Dijon Pan Sauce; Marsala Wine Pan Sauce; Sauterne Pan Sauce with Figs and Pistachios; Sweet Vermouth Pan Sauce with Prunes; Port Wine Pan Sauce with Dried Cranberries; Tomato-Tarragon Pan Sauce; Tomato-Rosemary Pan Sauce; Tomato-Anchovy Pan Sauce; Tomato Sauce with Black Olives and Provençal Herbs; Cooked Tomato Relish with Onion and Mint; White Wine Vinegar Pan Sauce; Balsamic Vinegar Pan Sauce; Apple Cider Pan Sauce; Orange-Dijon Pan Sauce with Rosemary; Orange Pan Sauce with Pernod; Lemon-Caper Pan Sauce; Quick Velouté; Mustard Cream Sauce; Mushroom–Goat Cheese Pan Sauce; Green Grape–Rosemary Pan Sauce; Curried Chutney Pan Sauce; Asian-style Sweet-and-Sour Sauce.

BONELESS PORK CHOPS

As a Southerner, I grew up eating pork once or twice a day. If it wasn't bacon for breakfast, it was ham for lunch, or pork chops for supper. Back then, pork chops were meaty and flavorful, framed by a generous border of fat. Mom never thought to trim off the fat before cooking a pork chop, and I certainly never thought to trim it off before eating. I can still remember the burst of flavorful juice and fat as I bit into one.

But the pig was a different animal back then. In recent decades the lack of demand for lard, coupled with a trend toward healthier diets, has caused the industry to dramatically lean up pork. Industry's success at eliminating the pig's surface fat has resulted in the loss of its intramuscular fat as well. Known as marbling, this fat traps and retains juices during cooking and gives pork its flavor and body.

Without marbling, bone-in pork chops are practically impossible to cook well, and until they figure out how to put the marbling back in, I won't buy them. For starters, they don't brown evenly. The bone sits on the pan surface while the lean meaty part of the chop draws up and pulls away from the pan. Short of pan frying—cooking the chop in a larger amount of fat—there's no way for a bone-in chop to brown evenly in a film of fat.

With any roast, chop, or steak, the meat nearest the bone is the last to get done. With beef or lamb, most people don't mind that the meat next to the bone is a little more rare. Pork is different, and most cooks end up overcooking the chop to get the bone meat done. If the meat is marbled, a little overcooking isn't a problem. But with today's lean pork, a big portion of the chop overcooks, losing juice and drying out, waiting for the meat nearer the bone to get done.

So why not just buy packaged boneless pork chops? I generally find that most boneless pork chops—even the thick-cut style—are too thin. In an attempt to create 4- or 5-ounce portions for today's health-conscious eaters, butchers cut the chops so thin there's no way for them to brown on the outside before they've cooked through and dried out. If you can find 1 to 1¼-inch-thick boneless pork chops, buy them.

Since I usually can't, I buy a small boneless loin roast from the rib end nearest the shoulder (the more flavorful section of the pork loin) and cut it into 1-inch-thick boneless chops. This technique doesn't require special butchering skills. With a moderately sharp knife, these five or six cuts should take less than a minute and are no more difficult than slicing meat from a boneless deli ham. Better to cook one thick chop and split it between two people than to cook two thin ones.

Sautéed Boneless Pork Chops

Serves 4 to 6

If using store-cut thinner chops, reduce the cooking time by a minute or so.

2 tablespoons butter

1 tablespoon oil

1 boneless rib end pork loin roast (about 1½ pounds), cut into 6 generous 1-inch-thick chops, each chop pressed lightly with fingertips to flatten, or 6 thick-cut boneless pork chops

Salt and ground black pepper

¼ cup flour measured into a pie plate or other shallow pan

A pan sauce or uncooked relish

1. Heat the butter and oil in an 11- to 12-inch skillet over low heat. While the pan is heating, sprinkle the chops on both sides with salt and pepper, then dredge them in flour.

2. A couple of minutes before sautéing, increase the heat to medium-high. When the butter stops foaming and starts to smell nutty brown, arrange the chops in the skillet. Cook, turning only once, until they are a rich golden brown, about 3 minutes per side. Remove from skillet.

3. Serve with an uncooked relish. Or make a pan sauce by adding ½ cup of liquid the skillet; boil until the liquid is reduced to about ¼ cup. Tilting the skillet so that the reduced liquid is at one side of the pan, whisk in butter or other enrichments until the sauce is smooth and glossy. Spoon a portion of sauce over each chop and serve immediately.

Uncooked Relish Possibilities (pages 171–173): All-Purpose Salsa; Parsley Relish with Capers and Cornichons; Tomato Relish with Pine Nuts, Green Olives, and Lemon Zest; Roasted Pepper Relish with Olives, Capers, and Rosemary.

Pan Sauce Possibilities (pages 159–170): Red Wine–Dijon Pan Sauce; Marsala Wine Pan Sauce; Sauterne Pan Sauce with Figs and Pistachios; Sweet Vermouth Pan Sauce with Prunes; Port Wine Pan Sauce with Dried Cranberries; Tomato-Tarragon Pan Sauce; Tomato-Rosemary Pan Sauce; Tomato-Anchovy Pan Sauce; Tomato Sauce with Black Olives and Provençal Herbs; Cooked Tomato Relish with Onion and Mint; Balsamic Vinegar Pan Sauce; Balsamic Pan Sauce with Pine Nuts and Raisins; Apple Cider Pan Sauce; Orange-Dijon Pan Sauce with Rosemary; Orange Pan Sauce with Pernod; Lemon-Caper Pan Sauce; Mustard Cream Sauce; Mushroom–Goat Cheese Pan Sauce; Green Grape–Rosemary Pan Sauce; Black Pepper Molasses Pan Sauce; Curried Chutney Pan Sauce; Asian-style Sweet-and-Sour Sauce.

FISH FILLETS

Buying meat is wonderfully predictable. Most grocery stores display cases full of segregated meats, neatly packaged on Styrofoam trays, all looking and weighing about the same. A meat purchase requires very little thought—simply drop a package in the grocery cart and keep moving.

Buying fish is a little more of an adventure. Other than a few farm-raised varieties, fish are wild and are affected by season, weather, and overfishing. Halibut may be cheap and plentiful one week, scarce and pricey the next. Last week's grouper may be available in 8-ounce fillets; this week's grouper fillets may weigh 12 pounds.

And with a global market, there's so much choice—perch from Uganda, sea bass from Chile, salmon from Norway. In fact, buying fish these days is a little like buying wine. It helps to be informed. Do you want steaks or fillets, farm-raised or wild, oily or lean, thick or thin, light or dark, imported or domestic, mild or assertively flavored? Do you want to spend $3.99 or $16.99 a pound. Do you want catfish, grouper, snapper, or sole? Is the orange roughy fresh, or would perch or tilapia be better? No wonder chicken breasts are so popular.

So how do you decide what to buy? Besides making friends with the fishmonger, I start with an open mind. I don't usually decide what I'm going to buy until I get to the counter. After eyeing the case, I buy what looks good. How do you know? While there are many perfectly fine fish-buying tips, I think most of us can tell instinctively whether fish is fresh or not. Selecting pristine fish over those that have crossed the line is as simple as picking fresh flowers over ones that are starting to fade.

Unlike old fish that look hangdog dull and limp, and are often sitting in a puddle of their own juice, fresh fish are perky, bright, glistening, and moist. If in doubt after inspection, ask. If still in doubt, smell. Although I am not bold enough to ask at the counter, I smell packages of questionable fish before I leave the store. Looks may deceive, but odor never will.

When buying fish for sautéing, avoid fillets that are less than ½ inch thick. Super-thin fillets like gray sole may be great for rolling, stuffing, and baking, but when sautéed, they overcook before they start to brown and they easily fall apart. Look for fillets from ½ inch up to 1¼ inches thick. Fillets in this range are thin enough to cook quickly, yet thick enough to hold together in the pan. Potential candidates for such fillets include tilapia, catfish, perch, orange roughy, black sea bass, and the thicker flounder/sole varieties like lemon sole, dabs, and fluke. Striped bass, grouper, and snapper are equally good, but these fish range dramatically in size. Small ones are perfect for sautéing, but if these fillets are much over 1¼ inches thick, I usually ask the fishmonger to cut them crosswise into 1-inch-thick medallions.

Despite the variety in size, shape, thickness, and color, a fish fillet is prepared and sautéed just as you would a chicken breast, turkey cutlet, or boneless pork chop—plus or minus a minute's sauté time. A ½-inch-thick fillet usually cooks in about 4 minutes (2 minutes per side), while a 1-inch-thick fillet usually takes about 6 minutes.

When sautéing fish, there are two potential problems. If cooking more than two or three fillets, they rarely fit in one pan, even a large skillet. To solve the problem, I've tried folding under the tail end of the fillet to decrease surface area. I've even tried sautéing them in two different skillets at the same time. Since thin fish fillets cook so quickly, however, I prefer to cook the fish in two batches in the same skillet. Less fat, less mess.

The larger the fish, the more likely it is to fall apart during cooking. For this reason, cut large whole fish fillets (anything much over 8 ounces) into manageable pieces, making them much easier to turn. Most fish come skinned these days. If they aren't, score the skin to keep the fillet from curling during the cooking process.

Unlike other meats, fish fillets vary wildly in size. Buy what you want and vary portion sizes. If you can get only 10-ounce fillets, serve 5-ounce portions and a few extra potatoes. If the fillets weigh in at 8 ounces, buy one for each person and skip the starch. With fish, you have to be flexible.

For cooking instructions on steaklike fish, such as tuna, swordfish, halibut, shark, Chilean sea bass, and salmon, see If You Can Sauté, You Can Sear (page 174).

Sautéed Fish Fillets
(Flounder, Catfish, Snapper, Tilapia, Grouper, and Other Thin, White-Fleshed Fish)

2 tablespoons butter

1 tablespoon oil

4 small fish fillets or 1½ pounds fish fillets cut into 4 pieces

Salt and ground black pepper

¼ cup flour measured into a pie plate or other shallow pan

Lemon wedges, or a pan sauce or uncooked relish

1. Heat the butter and oil in an 11- or 12-inch skillet over low heat. While the pan is heating, sprinkle the fish on both sides with salt and pepper, then dredge in flour.

2. A couple of minutes before sautéing, increase the heat to medium-high. When the butter stops foaming and starts to smell nutty brown, arrange 2 fillets in the skillet. Cook until light golden brown and a crust forms, 2 to 3 minutes. Turn with a thin metal spatula and continue to cook until light golden brown on the other side, about 1 to 3 minutes longer, depending on the thickness of the fish. Transfer the fish to a plate; keep warm on the warm stovetop or set the plate in a warm oven while the remaining fish cooks. Put the two remaining pieces of fish in the skillet; repeat sautéing process.

3. Serve immediately with lemon wedges, salsa, or an uncooked relish. Or make a pan sauce by adding ½ cup liquid to the skillet; boil until the liquid is reduced to about ¼ cup. Tilting the skillet so that the reduced liquid is at one side of the pan, whisk in butter or other enrichments (see suggestions below) until the sauce is smooth and glossy. Spoon a portion of sauce over each fillet and serve immediately.

Uncooked Relish Possibilities (pages 171–173): All-Purpose Salsa; Parsley Relish with Capers and Cornichons; Tomato Relish with Pine Nuts, Green Olives, and Lemon Zest; Pickled Pink Onions; Roasted Pepper Relish with Olives, Capers, and Rosemary.

Pan Sauce Possibilities (pages 159–170): Tomato-Tarragon Pan Sauce; Tomato-Anchovy Pan Sauce; Cooked Tomato Relish with Onion and Mint; White Wine Vinegar Pan Sauce; Orange Pan Sauce with Pernod; Lemon-Caper Pan Sauce; Quick Velouté; Mustard Cream Sauce; Green Grape–Rosemary Pan Sauce; Horseradish Pan Sauce.

HOW TO SAUTÉ

- Choose the right size skillet so that the pieces of meat have neither too much nor too little space between them.

- Before preparing the meat, set the skillet over medium-low heat, immediately adding a mix of oil and butter, so that they heat up with the skillet.

- While the skillet is heating, prepare the meat, sprinkling both sides of each piece with salt and pepper, then dredging each side in flour.

- A couple of minutes before sautéing, increase the heat to medium-high. When the oil is hot but not smoking and the flecks of milk solids in the butter turn golden brown and smell nutty, add the meat.

- Cook the meat, turning only once, until golden brown on each side.

- Make a pan sauce or serve with an uncooked sauce or relish.

DUCK BREASTS

There are few worse dishes than poorly sautéed duck breast at a mediocre continental restaurant. More than likely, the cook has sautéed the duck at medium-high heat, causing the skin to turn a rich dark brown very quickly. Mistakenly thinking the duck breast is done, he removes it from the skillet, slicing it and fanning it on the plate. The skin, not having had a chance to render its fat, is nearly as thick as the breast itself and is greasy, unappetizing, and inedible. It's unfortunate, because when cooked right, crisp duck skin is better than the meat itself. So even though the sauté method in this chapter doesn't work for duck breasts, the technique is simple. Besides, many of the pan sauces for chicken breasts and pork chops partner well with sautéed duck breasts.

There are four varieties of duck in this country—Mallard, Moulard, Muscovy, and Pekin. Mallards are generally sold whole and only in the fall. Only the Moulard, Muscovy, and Pekin duck breasts are packaged and sold separately.

Raised primarily for foie gras, the Moulard duck breast is large (each half weighing 12 to 14 ounces) with dark, rich, and beefy meat and an especially thick skin. The Muscovy drake (or male) breast is also large, about the same size as a Moulard, but with a lighter flavor and significantly less fat. The Muscovy hen breast is much smaller, the whole breast weighing 14 to 16 ounces. Like its male counterpart, it is less fatty and its meat is sweet and tender. The Pekin, or Long Island, duck breast is also small, the whole breast weighing 9 to 10 ounces, but like the Moulard, it has a thick covering of fat.

Since duck breasts are not widely available, you may not have a choice. But regardless of what you get, the cooking principles are the same. You don't need lots of cooking experience to sauté a duck breast—just a little patience.

Sautéed Duck Breasts

Serves 4

From my experience, the Moulard breasts need the full 30 minutes to be rendered of their fat. Half a Moulard or Muscovy duck breast serves two people. You need half a Pekin or Muscovy hen duck breast for each person.

2 to 4 duck breast halves, skin (but not breast) scored crosswise, about every inch (see above)

Salt and ground black pepper

A pan sauce or uncooked relish

1. Heat a 10- or 12-inch skillet (depending on size and number of breasts, do not overcrowd or leave too much vacant space in the pan) over medium-low heat. Arrange the duck breasts, skin side down, in the hot pan and cook slowly, pouring accumulated drippings from the pan occasionally, until the fat has almost competely rendered and the skin is crisp and mahogany brown, 15 to 30 minutes (see note above). Pour off all but 1 tablespoon of fat, increase the heat to medium, and turn the duck breasts skin side up. Continue to cook until the breasts are medium rare to medium (135–140 degrees), 5 to 10 minutes longer. Let the breasts sit for 5 minutes while making the sauce.

2. Pour the fat from the skillet but do not wipe it clean. Make one of the uncooked relishes. Or make a pan sauce by putting 1/2 cup of liquid in the skillet and boiling until it is reduced to about 1/4 cup. Tilting the skillet so that the reduced liquid is at one side of the pan, whisk in butter or other enrichments. Thin-slice each duck breast half, transferring a portion to each dinner plate. Spoon a tablespoon of relish or sauce over each portion and serve immediately.

Uncooked Relish Possibilities (pages 171–173): All-Purpose Salsa; Parsley Relish with Capers and Cornichons; Tomato Relish with Pine Nuts, Green Olives, and Lemon Zest; Roasted Pepper Relish with Olives, Capers, and Rosemary.

Pan Sauce Possibilities (pages 159–170): Red Wine–Dijon Pan Sauce; Marsala Wine Pan Sauce; Sauterne Pan Sauce with Figs and Pistachios; Sweet Vermouth Pan Sauce with Prunes; Port Wine Pan Sauce with Dried Cranberries; Balsamic Vinegar Pan Sauce; Balsamic Pan Sauce with Pine Nuts and Raisins; Apple Cider Pan Sauce; Orange-Dijon Pan Sauce with Rosemary; Black Pepper Molasses Pan Sauce; Curried Chutney Pan Sauce.

HOW TO SAUTÉ DUCK BREASTS

- Score the fat, but not the meat, of each breast every inch or so.

- Heat a medium or large skillet, depending on the size and quantity of duck breasts, over medium-low heat.

- Place the duck breasts in the hot pan, skin side down, and cook very slowly until nearly every ounce of fat is rendered and the skin is crisp. Throughout the cooking process, pour the fat from the pan.

- Turn the duck breasts over and continue to cook over medium heat until the breast is medium rare to medium (135 to 140 degrees), 5 to 10 minutes longer.

- Cut the duck breast into thin slices on the diagonal.

PAN SAUCES

Pan sauces are the simplest and most natural way to flavor a chicken cutlet, fish fillet, pork chop, or steak. Many classic pan sauce recipes, however, require the reduction of fairly large quantities of wine, stock, juice, or cream, tacking on ten minutes or more to an otherwise quick dish. Unless the sautéed meat, fish, or poultry is held in a warm oven, it oftens become soggy and cold by the time the sauce is done. In addition, many pan sauces are enriched and thickened with large quantities of butter or heavy cream. I don't mind the extra time or calories for a special meal, but for weeknights, I want a sauce that is flavorful, quick, and light.

A classic pan sauce often starts with sautéing garlic or shallots in the empty skillet. To speed up the process, I eliminate that step. While there's hardly a pan sauce that wouldn't benefit from a little shallot or garlic, for time's sake I usually leave them out. In the few sauces where garlic is crucial, I simply add it along with the liquid and let it soften while the liquid is reducing.

To transform chicken stock, juice, or wine from a thin liquid to a thicker sauce, it must be reduced by at least half. Reducing 1½ or 2 cups of liquid—the quantity called for in many recipes—takes more time and effort than I usually have on a Tuesday night. Plus, we just don't need a quarter cup of rich sauce per person for a family meal. I've found that ½ cup of liquid reduces to the proper consistency in just a couple of minutes. With flavorful additions like capers or dried fruit and a modest amount of butter for enrichment, there is an overflowing tablespoon of flavorful sauce for each person— more than enough for a weeknight dinner.

Liquids such as low-sodium chicken broth and orange juice and sweet fortified wines such as marsala, madeira, sweet vermouth, and port make fine sauces on their own. Reduce ½ cup of any of these liquids in a pan of chicken drippings and you'll get a good sauce. Acidic liquids, however, need taming. A sauce made from straight lemon juice or vinegar, for example, is too harsh. For these, use six tablespoons of chicken broth, sweet fortified wine, or fruit juice for every two tablespoons of lemon juice or vinegar (for a total of ½ cup of liquid).

Though not harsh, pan sauces made with straight red or white wine taste weak, sour, and off kilter. Cutting the wine with an equal amount of low-sodium chicken broth balances the sauce. For wine sauces use ¼ cup each chicken broth and wine (for a total of ½ cup liquid). And if making a red wine pan sauce, it benefits from other flavorings as well.

There are, of course, exceptions to the rule. Asian-style Sweet-and-Sour Sauce (see page 170) calls for $1/4$ cup chicken broth, 2 tablespoons soy sauce, and 2 tablespoons rice wine vinegar rather than 6 tablespoons chicken broth and 2 tablespoons vinegar (but still a total of $1/2$ cup liquid).

When using two different liquids in a pan sauce, some recipes call for reducing one liquid before adding the other. Not these. While the chicken sautés, measure all the pan sauce ingredients into a measuring cup and pour them into the skillet where they simmer together.

How quickly the sauce reduces depends on the heat and heaviness of the pan. If the skillet is hot and heavy-duty, the liquid reduces almost as soon as it hits the pan. In a cooler skillet the reduction may take a couple of minutes. Once the sauce reduces to $1/4$ cup—don't measure, just eyeball it—it's time to add a little butter or cream.

While I want my pan sauce to be light, I find that a pan sauce without a little fat is brash and intense. Not only does butter, heavy cream, or olive oil enrich and soften flavors, it also thickens the sauce and gives it much-needed body. A small amount of sauce, however, requires only a small amount of butter. Just one miraculous tablespoon of butter or olive oil (or two tablespoons of heavy cream) takes a sauce from puckery to pleasant.

at-a-glance

HOW TO MAKE A PAN SAUCE

- Measure pan sauce ingredients in a measuring cup (liquid always totals $1/2$ cup).

- Pour liquid into hot skillet once meat, poultry, or fish has been removed.

- Reduce liquid to $1/4$ cup.

- Tilt the skillet and whisk in butter or cream, and spoon over each portion and serve.

Red Wine–Dijon Pan Sauce

For chicken and turkey cutlets, boneless pork chops and tenderloin, duck breasts, steaks and burgers.

LIQUID:

¼ **cup canned low-sodium chicken broth**

¼ **cup full-bodied red wine**

FLAVORING:

1 **teaspoon Dijon mustard**

FAT:

1 **tablespoon butter**

Measure broth, wine, and mustard in a measuring cup. Follow instructions for making a pan sauce in individual sauté or sear recipe, or see page 159.

Marsala Wine Pan Sauce

For chicken and turkey cutlets, boneless pork chops and tenderloin, and duck breasts.

LIQUID:

½ **cup marsala wine**

FAT:

1 **tablespoon butter**

Follow the instructions for making a pan sauce in individual sauté or sear recipe, or see page 159.

Sauterne Pan Sauce with Figs and Pistachios

For chicken and turkey cutlets, boneless pork chops and tenderloin, and duck breasts. Gewürztraminer or riesling can also be used.

LIQUID:

½ **cup sauterne or other sweet dessert wine**

FLAVORINGS:

8 **dried figs, quartered**

2 **tablespoons coarse-chopped pistachios**

FAT:

1 **tablespoon butter**

Combine the sauterne and figs in a measuring cup. Follow instructions for making a pan sauce in individual sauté or sear recipe, or see page 159. Sprinkle pistachios.

Sweet Vermouth Pan Sauce with Prunes

For chicken and turkey cutlets, boneless pork chops and tenderloin, and duck breasts. If you think of it, soak the dried fruit in the port while the chicken breasts are sautéing.

LIQUID:

6 tablespoons sweet vermouth or cream sherry

2 tablespoons cider vinegar

FLAVORING:

¼ cup chopped prunes

FAT:

1 tablespoon butter

Combine the sherry, vinegar, and prunes in a 1-cup Pyrex measuring cup. Follow instructions for making a pan sauce in individual sauté or sear recipe, or see page 159.

Port Wine Pan Sauce with Dried Cranberries

For chicken and turkey cutlets, boneless pork chops and tenderloin, and duck breasts. Dried cherries can be substituted for the cranberries, if you like. If you think of it, soak the dried fruit in the port while the chicken breasts are sautéing.

LIQUID:

½ cup port wine

FLAVORING:

2 tablespoons dried cranberries

2 teaspoons seedless raspberry jam *or* red currant jelly

FAT:

1 tablespoon butter

Combine the port, cranberries, and jam in a measuring cup. Follow instructions for making a pan sauce in individual sauté or sear recipe, or see page 158.

Tomato-Tarragon Pan Sauce

For chicken and turkey cutlets, boneless pork chops and tenderloin, fish steaks, and scallops.

LIQUID:

¼ cup canned low-sodium chicken broth

¼ cup dry vermouth or white wine

FLAVORINGS:

4 canned tomatoes, chopped coarse, about ¾ cup

1 teaspoon minced fresh tarragon or scant ½ teaspoon dried

FAT:

1 tablespoon butter

Combine the broth and vermouth with the tomatoes and tarragon. Follow instructions for making a pan sauce in individual sauté or sear recipe, or see page 159.

Tomato-Rosemary Pan Sauce

For chicken and turkey cutlets, boneless pork chops and tenderloin, steaks, filet mignon, and burgers.

LIQUID:

¼ cup canned low-sodium chicken broth

¼ cup dry vermouth or white wine

FLAVORINGS:

4 canned tomatoes, chopped coarse

½ teaspoon minced fresh rosemary

FAT:

1 tablespoon butter

Measure broth, vermouth, tomatoes, and rosemary in a small bowl. Follow instructions for making a pan sauce in individual sauté or sear recipe, or see page 159.

Tomato-Anchovy Pan Sauce

For chicken and turkey cutlets, boneless pork chops and tenderloin, and fish fillets and steaks.

LIQUID:

½ cup canned low-sodium chicken broth

FLAVORING:

1 tablespoon tomato paste

1 teaspoon minced anchovies or anchovy paste

FAT:

1 tablespoon butter

Combine the broth with the tomato paste and anchovy. Follow instructions for making a pan sauce in individual sauté or sear recipe, or see page 159.

Tomato Sauce with Black Olives and Provençal Herbs

For chicken and turkey cutlets, steaks, burgers, boneless pork chops and tenderloin, and fish steaks. In this sauce, olive oil, not butter, is drizzled in off the heat.

LIQUID:

¼ cup canned low-sodium chicken broth

¼ cup dry white wine

FLAVORING:

4 canned tomatoes, chopped coarse

2 garlic cloves, minced

½ teaspoon herbes de Provence or dried thyme

2 tablespoons coarse-chopped piquant black olives

FAT:

1 tablespoon extra-virgin olive oil

Combine the broth and wine with the tomatoes, garlic, herb, and olives. Follow instructions for making a pan sauce in individual sauté or sear recipe, or see page 159. Off the heat, drizzle in 1 tablespoon extra-virgin olive oil.

Cooked Tomato Relish with Onion and Mint

For chicken and turkey cutlets, boneless pork chops and tenderloin, fish steaks, and burgers.

LIQUID:

¼ cup canned low-sodium chicken broth

¼ cup canned crushed tomatoes, undrained

FLAVORINGS:

1 small onion, halved and sliced thin

2 tablespoons minced fresh mint, basil, or parsley leaves

FAT:

1 tablespoon butter

Combine the broth and tomatoes in a measuring cup. Sauté onion in the empty skillet until translucent but still crisp, 2 to 3 minutes. Follow instructions for making a pan sauce in individual sauté or sear recipe, or see page 159. Whisk mint, then butter into the reduced liquid.

White Wine Vinegar Pan Sauce

For chicken and turkey cutlets, fish fillets and steaks, and scallops.

LIQUID:

6 tablespoons canned low-sodium chicken broth

2 tablespoons white wine vinegar

FLAVORING:

2 tablespoons Dijon mustard

FAT:

1 tablespoon butter

Combine the broth, vinegar, and mustard in a measuring cup. Follow instructions for making a pan sauce in individual sauté or sear recipe, or see page 159.

Balsamic Vinegar Pan Sauce

For chicken and turkey cutlets, boneless pork chops and tenderloin, duck breasts, steaks, and burgers.

LIQUID:	FLAVORING:
¼ cup balsamic vinegar	None
¼ cup canned low-sodium chicken broth	FAT:
	1 tablespoon butter

Combine vinegar and broth with a measuring cup. Follow instructions for making a pan sauce in individual sauté or sear recipe, or see page 159.

Balsamic Pan Sauce with Pine Nuts and Raisins

For boneless pork chops and tenderloin, and duck breasts.

LIQUID:	FLAVORING:
¼ cup balsamic vinegar	2 tablespoons raisins
¼ cup canned low-sodium chicken broth	2 tablespoons toasted pine nuts
	FAT:
	1 tablespoon butter

Combine the vinegar and broth with the raisins and pine nuts. Follow instructions for making a pan sauce in individual sauté or sear recipe, or see page 159.

Apple Cider Pan Sauce

For chicken and turkey cutlets, boneless pork chops and tenderloin, and duck breasts.

LIQUID:	FLAVORING:
6 tablespoons apple cider	None
2 tablespoons balsamic vinegar	FAT:
	1 tablespoon butter

Follow instructions for making a pan sauce in individual sauté or sear recipe, or see page 159.

Orange-Dijon Pan Sauce with Rosemary

For chicken and turkey cutlets, boneless pork chops and tenderloin, and duck breasts. When making this pan sauce for pork or duck, add 1 tablespoon brown sugar along with the mustard.

LIQUID:

½ cup orange juice

FLAVORING:

1 teaspoon Dijon mustard

½ teaspoon minced fresh rosemary leaves

FAT:

1 tablespoon butter

Combine the juice with the mustard and rosemary. Follow instructions for making a pan sauce in individual sauté or sear recipe, or see page 159.

Orange Pan Sauce with Pernod

For chicken and turkey cutlets, boneless pork chops and tenderloin, and fish fillets, steaks, and scallops.

LIQUID:

¼ cup canned low-sodium chicken broth

¼ cup orange juice

FLAVORINGS:

1 teaspoon finely grated orange zest

1 tablespoon Pernod

FAT:

1 tablespoon butter

Combine the broth, juice, zest, and Pernod. Follow instructions for making a pan sauce in individual sauté or sear recipe, or see page 159.

Lemon-Caper Pan Sauce

For chicken and turkey cutlets, boneless pork chops and tenderloin, fish fillets, steaks, and scallops. If you don't like capers, simply leave them out.

LIQUID:

6 tablespoons low-sodium chicken broth

2 tablespoons lemon juice

FLAVORING:

2 teaspoons drained capers

FAT:

1 tablespoon butter

Combine the broth, lemon juice, and capers in a measuring cup. Follow instructions for making a pan sauce in individual sauté or sear recipe, or see page 159.

Quick Velouté

For chicken and turkey cutlets, fish steaks, and scallops.

LIQUID:

¼ cup canned low-sodium chicken broth

¼ cup dry vermouth

FAT:

2 tablespoons heavy cream

Measure the broth and vermouth in a 1-cup glass measuring cup. Follow instructions for making a pan sauce in individual sauté or sear recipe, or see page 159.

Mustard Cream Sauce

For chicken and turkey cutlets, steaks, burgers, boneless pork chops and tenderloin, and fish steaks and fillets.

LIQUID:

½ cup canned low-sodium chicken broth

FLAVORING:

2 tablespoons coarse-grained mustard

FAT:

2 tablespoons heavy cream

Combine the broth and mustard. Follow instructions for making a pan sauce in individual sauté or sear recipe, or see page 159.

Mushroom–Goat Cheese Pan Sauce

For chicken and turkey cutlets, boneless pork chops and tenderloin, steaks, and burgers. You can't offer a series of pan sauces without a mushroom one. I have chosen shiitakes, since they sauté more quickly than other mushrooms. Rather than using cream or butter, enrich this sauce with fresh goat cheese.

Liquid:

¼ cup canned low-sodium chicken broth

¼ cup full-bodied red wine

FLAVORINGS:

½ pound shiitake mushrooms, stems removed and discarded, caps sliced thin

2 tablespoons minced fresh parsely leaves

FAT:

2 tablespoons fresh goat cheese

Measure the broth and wine in a measuring cup. Put the mushrooms in the empty skillet; sauté until wilted, 2 to 3 minutes. Follow instructions for making a pan sauce in individual sauté or sear recipe, or see page 159. Stir parsley and then goat cheese into the reduced liquid.

Green Grape–Rosemary Pan Sauce

For chicken and turkey cutlets, boneless pork chops and tenderloin, and fish fillets.

LIQUID:

½ cup canned low-sodium chicken broth

FLAVORINGS:

1 cup green grapes, halved

½ teaspoon minced fresh rosemary

FAT:

2 tablespoons heavy cream

Combine the broth with the grapes and rosemary. Follow instructions for making a pan sauce in individual sauté or sear recipe, or see page 159.

Horseradish Pan Sauce

For fish fillets and steaks, steaks, and burgers.

LIQUID:

¼ cup canned low-sodium
chicken broth

¼ cup dry vermouth or white wine

FLAVORING:

2 tablespoons prepared horseradish

FAT:

1 tablespoon butter

Combine broth, vermouth, and horseradish in a measuring cup. Follow instructions for making a pan sauce in individual sauté or sear recipe, or see page 159.

Black Pepper Molasses Pan Sauce

For boneless pork chops and tenderloin, duck breasts, seared steaks, and burgers. To boost the pork flavor in this dish, use bacon drippings rather than butter to brown the meat. Fry 3 strips of thick-cut bacon, cut into small pieces, in the skillet until crisp. Remove bacon bits and add enough vegetable oil to equal about 3 tablespoons. Sauté the meat and make the sauce, adding the bacon bits back into the finished sauce.

LIQUID:

¼ cup canned low-sodium chicken
broth

¼ cup full-bodied red wine

FLAVORING:

2 tablespoons molasses
Several grinds fresh ground
black pepper

FAT:

1 tablespoon butter

Combine the broth, wine, molasses, and pepper in a measuring cup. Follow instructions for making a pan sauce in individual sauté or sear recipe, or see page 159.

Curried Chutney Pan Sauce

For chicken and turkey cutlets, pork tenderloin and boneless chops, and duck breasts.

LIQUID:

6 tablespoons canned low-sodium chicken broth

2 tablespoons rice wine vinegar

FLAVORING:

2 tablespoons prepared chutney, such as Major Grey's

1/4 teaspoon curry powder

FAT:

1 tablespoon butter

Combine the broth and vinegar with the chutney and curry powder. Follow instructions for making a pan sauce in individual sauté or sear recipe, or see page 159.

Asian-style Sweet-and-Sour Pan Sauce

For chicken and turkey cutlets, pork tenderloin, and boneless chops. Unlike the other sauces, this one doesn't have an enrichment. Sprinkle the sauced chicken breasts with sliced scallions, if you like. For a Thai-flavored sauce, use the fish sauce in place of the soy.

LIQUID:

1/4 cup canned low-sodium chicken broth

2 tablespoons distilled white vinegar

2 tablespoons soy sauce *or* Vietnamese fish sauce

FLAVORING:

2 tablespoons brown sugar

2 garlic cloves, minced

FAT:

None

Combine the broth and vinegar with the soy sauce, brown sugar, and garlic. Follow instructions for making a pan sauce in individual sauté or sear recipe, or see page 159— but omit butter.

RELISHES

I've organized a wardrobe that works almost year round. Most of my clothes work whether it's fall, winter, or spring. Only during the summer do I switch to shorts, sleeveless shirts, and sandals. It's the same with my pan sauces. They offer enough variety to take me through fall, winter, and spring. But come summer, I need a change. It's time to switch to uncooked relishes.

Except for the pickled onions, the relishes that follow work with almost any sautéed or seared meat, poultry, or seafood. I particularly like the All-Purpose Salsa because the formula works regardless of the fruit I have on hand. The other relishes are made mostly with pantry ingredients, so if you're well-stocked, you should be able to make them without a trip to the store. And actually, they can be made year round as well.

All-Purpose Salsa

Makes 2 cups

Depending on the ingredients, this salsa can be served with chicken and turkey cutlets, pork tenderloin and chops, duck breasts, fish fillets and steaks, and steaks and burgers. This salsa works with any of the following: tomatoes, avocado, peaches, nectarines, grapes, oranges, grapefruits, apricots, plums, pineapple. The formula works when making a corn salsa as well. For a black bean and corn salsa, use equal parts of corn and black beans.

1½ cups fine-diced tomato, avocado, or other fruit (see note above), or 8 ounces frozen corn, thawed (about 1½ cups)

¼ medium red onion, cut into small dice, or 2 scallions, sliced thin

¼ yellow or red bell pepper, cut into small dice

1 jalapeño pepper, seeded and minced

1 tablespoon minced fresh cilantro *or* parsley leaves

2 tablespoons juice from a lime *or* 2 tablespoons rice wine vinegar

½ teaspoon cumin or chili powder (optional)

Salt and ground black pepper to taste

Mix all ingredients in a medium bowl; let stand, if possible, for juices to release and flavors to blend, 5 to 10 minutes.

Parsley Relish with Capers and Cornichons

Serves 4

For chicken and turkey cutlets, pork tenderloin and chops, duck breasts, fish fillets and steaks, and steaks and burgers. Cornichons are available at specialty food stores and in the gourmet section of many grocery stores. Although the taste will be slightly different, 2 tablespoons sliced baby dill pickle can be substituted for the cornichons.

½ cup parsley leaves, chopped coarse

3 cornichons, sliced thin, plus 1 teaspoon cornichon juice

2 tablespoons capers

½ medium shallot or 1 scallion, sliced thin

¼ cup olive oil

Salt and ground black pepper to taste

Mix all ingredients in a small bowl.

Tomato Relish with Pine Nuts, Green Olives, and Lemon Zest

Serves 4

For chicken and turkey cutlets, pork tenderloin and chops, duck breasts, fish fillets and steaks, and steaks and burgers.

4 canned tomatoes, chopped coarse

2 garlic cloves, lightly smashed and slivered

2 tablespoons olive oil

¼ cup loosely packed parsley leaves

1 tablespoon toasted pine nuts

4 green olives, pitted and chopped coarse

2 (1-inch) strips lemon zest, sliced as thin as possible

Salt and ground black pepper

Mix all ingredients in a medium bowl.

Pickled Pink Onions

Serves 4

For fish fillets and steaks and burgers.

> ½ **medium-large red onion, sliced thin**
>
> 3 **tablespoons red wine vinegar**
>
> **Salt and ground black pepper**

Mix in a medium bowl; let sit until ready to serve.

Roasted Pepper Relish with Olives, Capers, and Rosemary

Makes about a scant cup or enough for 4 servings

For chicken and turkey cutlets, pork tenderloin and chops, duck breasts, fish fillets and steaks, and steaks and burgers. This recipe can be easily doubled or even more, and it holds well in the refrigerator for at least a week.

> 4 **medium garlic cloves, peeled**
>
> 2 **tablespoons extra-virgin olive oil**
>
> 3 **jarred roasted red peppers, cut into medium dice (½ cup total)**
>
> 3 **piquant black olives, such as kalamatas, pitted and quartered**
>
> 1 **teaspoon drained capers**
>
> 2 **teaspoons fresh rosemary leaves**
>
> **Ground black pepper to taste**

1. Heat the garlic and olive oil in a small saucepan over low heat. When the garlic starts to sizzle and turn golden, remove from the heat. Remove the garlic from the oil, and when cool enough to handle, quarter each clove lengthwise.

2. Meanwhile, mix the remaining ingredients in a small bowl. Add olive oil and garlic. Toss to coat and serve.

If You Can Sauté, You Can Sear
Seared Steaks, Filet Mignon, Burgers, Pork Tenderloin, Salmon Fillets, Fish Steaks, and Scallops, with Flavored Butters

The only trick to searing is a pan that's good and hot
The only other thing you need is a fan that vents a lot.

If you can sauté, you can sear or pan-broil. The big difference between the two is the turn of a knob—from medium-high to high. As with sautéing, start by choosing the right size pan for the job. Most cooks know not to overcrowd a pan, but few think about the consequences of searing in a pan that is too large. Choose a 12-inch skillet to sear one steak and the unused surface will smoke excessively. Try cramming four New York strips in the same skillet, and you'll kill the heat and steam the meat. If in doubt about size, lay the meat in the cold pan before you start to cook to see if it fits. The pieces of meat should never touch, nor should there be more than an inch or so between them.

For searing, the weight of the pan is almost more important than the size. In order to build up and maintain high heat but keep the meat from burning, a heavy-bottomed skillet is crucial. Cast-iron skillets work well, but avoid them when making pan sauces.

Iron can react with highly acidic ingredients such as wine, citrus juices, and vinegar, resulting in an off-flavored, metallic sauce. When making a pan sauce, use a heavy-duty nonstick skillet.

Start by heating the pan over low heat for 5 to 10 minutes. If heated quickly at a high temperature, the pan doesn't have a chance to build up heat and will cool as soon as the meat hits the surface. If heated gradually and slowly, the pan builds up a reserve that maintains the heat level even after the meat has been added.

While the pan is slowly heating, prepare the vegetable or salad, set the table, measure the ingredients for a sauce, or make a flavored butter, knowing that you'll be ready to eat soon after you drop the meat into the pan. If you've got help with these predinner tasks, and there's less time to preheat, start the pan on medium for a few minutes rather than on low.

Three or four minutes before searing, turn the heat from low to high and turn on the exhaust fan. As it starts to get hot, the residual oils in the pan will send up little wisps of smoke. To avoid excessive pan smoke but still get the fat needed for cooking, rub the meat with oil first rather than adding the oil directly to the pan.

To neatly and efficiently oil and season the meat or fish, set the pieces on a plate, drizzle them with oil, and turn them to coat. Once oiled, the surface easily attracts salt and pepper. After seasoning one side, turn the pieces over and season the other side as well.

When the skillet is hot, drop in the seasoned meat or fish and cook until it forms a rich brown crust on one side, 2 to 4 minutes, depending on thickness and type of cut. Turn it, and continue to cook it to the same state on the other side. If the skillet is hot and not overcrowded, the meat or fish should be done 2 to 4 minutes later. (See specific recipes for exact times.)

Where there's searing, there's smoke, but even a mediocre exhaust fan should suck it out of the kitchen. Only when I forget to turn on the fan does my smoke alarm go off.

Since I could very easily be talking on the phone, washing a few dishes, listening to a kid's problem, chatting with my husband, or serving the salad while the meat is searing, it's easy to lose track of time. For this reason, I usually set my timer to remind myself when to turn the pieces.

So how do you know what to sear? Sear any meat or fish you want heavily crusted and medium-rare to medium. Obvious candidates are steaks—boneless strip steaks (also known as New York strips, Kansas City steaks, or club sirloins), boneless beef rib steaks (also known as rib-eye steaks or Delmonicos), and filet mignons. Meaty steaklike fish—tuna, swordfish, salmon, shark—sear well, as do sturdy white-fleshed fish—Chilean sea bass and halibut, as well as monkfish, trimmed and cut into medallions. Jumbo sea scallops are also among my favorite seared dishes.

Pork can be either seared or sautéed. Because I like boneless pork chops breaded and sautéed, I've included them in the sautéing chapter, but I prefer to sear pork tenderloin that I have cut into medallions.

If the cuts of meat or fish are 1 to 1 1/4 inches thick, they should be medium rare to medium by the time they've seared on both sides. If you prefer your meat or fish cooked medium well, reduce the heat once both sides are crusted, and let them continue to cook without further browning.

Whether searing or sautéing, the method for making a pan sauce is the same. Remove the meat or fish from the pan and pour 1/2 cup of liquid into the empty pan. The liquid will reduce to 1/4 cup within a minute or so. Stir in just 1 tablespoon of butter (or 2 of cream) to the reduced liquid. To further understand how to make a pan sauce, see pages 158–159.

Searing can be messy. Cooked over high heat, meat and fish naturally sputter and spit, and the stovetop does get greasy. A splatter screen, designed to keep the fat in the pan while allowing the moisture to escape, helps only a little. In the end, there's still a film of fat on the stove. Whether I use a screen or not, there's still a mess to clean up, so why bother?

On sear nights, I hose down the stove with glass cleaner or degreaser and wipe it clean with a wad of paper towels. That's it. A small price to pay for wonderfully crusted meat and fish.

Although cooking times may vary by a minute or two and pan size may change, searing is searing. Whether you're cooking sea scallops or hamburgers, the technique is exactly the same.

STEAK

I'll order a prime T-bone or porterhouse at a great steak house, but when I'm cooking, I generally stick to boneless steaks. Just like pork, today's beef is so lean it's difficult to cook a bone-in steak well. When seared, the steak bone sits on the pan surface while the lean meat draws up and pulls away from the pan, resulting in only a spotty brown surface.

When selecting a steak for searing, choose one of three boneless cuts—the boneless strip steak (also known as a New York strip, Kansas City steak, or club sirloin), the boneless beef rib steak (also known as a rib-eye or Delmonico), or the filet mignon.

In addition to looking for boneless cuts, choose thick-cut steaks, 1 to 1¼ inches thick. A steak less than 1 inch thick will likely overcook by the time it's had a chance to sear on both sides, even over high heat. Since a 1-inch-thick strip or rib steak generally weighs about 12 ounces, buy one steak for two people. It's better to buy one thick steak and split it than to buy two thin steaks and be disappointed.

Since filet mignons are cut from the long, tapered beef tenderloin, sizes can vary depending from which section they are cut. Look for filets in the 6-ounce range.

Seared Rib-Eye or Strip Steak

2 steaks, rib-eye or New York strips, each about 1 inch thick and weighing 12 ounces

2 tablespoons olive or vegetable oil

Salt and ground black pepper

A pan sauce, uncooked relish, or flavored butter

1. Set a heavy-bottomed 12-inch skillet over low heat for 5 to 10 minutes, or medium heat for 3 to 4 minutes, while preparing the meal and seasoning the steaks. Three to four minutes before searing the steaks, turn on the exhaust fan and increase the heat to high.

2. Set the steaks on a plate and drizzle with oil; turn to coat. Sprinkle with salt and pepper.

3. A minute or so after the residual oils in the skillet send up wisps of smoke, put the steaks in the pan. Cook over high heat until the meat develops an even, rich brown crust, about 3 minutes. Turn steaks and continue to cook over high heat until the remaining sides develop an even, rich brown crust and the meat is medium rare to medium, 3 to 3½ minutes longer. (For more well-done meat, turn the heat to low and cook, turning once, for a minute or two longer.) Remove to a serving dish and let stand 5 minutes.

4. Serve with an uncooked relish or flavored butter. Or make a pan sauce by adding ½ cup liquid to the skillet; boil until the liquid is reduced to about ¼ cup. Tilting the skillet so that the reduced liquid is at one side of the pan, whisk in butter or other enrichments until the sauce is smooth and glossy.

Uncooked Relish Possibilities (pages 171–173): All-Purpose Salsa; Parsley Relish with Capers and Cornichons; Tomato Relish with Pine Nuts, Green Olives, and Lemon Zest; Pickled Pink Onions; Roasted Pepper Relish with Olives, Capers, and Rosemary.

Flavored Butter Possibilities (pages 191–192): Parsley-Shallot-Garlic Butter; Horseradish Butter; Blue Cheese Butter.

Pan Sauce Possibilities (pages 159–170): Red Wine–Dijon Pan Sauce; Tomato-Rosemary Pan Sauce; Tomato Sauce with Black Olives and Provençal Herbs; Balsamic Vinegar Pan Sauce; Mustard Cream Sauce; Mushroom–Goat Cheese Pan Sauce; Horseradish Pan Sauce; Black Pepper Molasses Pan Sauce.

Seared Filet Mignon

Serves 4

Because these steaks are smaller than rib and strip steaks, they tend to fit into a 10-inch skillet, and because they are slightly thicker, they cook a minute or two longer.

4 filet mignon steaks, each about 6 ounces and 1¼ inches thick

2 tablespoons olive or vegetable oil

Salt and ground black pepper

A pan sauce, uncooked relish, or flavored butter

1. Set a heavy-bottomed 10-inch skillet over low heat for 5 to 10 minutes, or medium heat for 3 to 4 minutes, while preparing the meal and seasoning the steaks. Three to four minutes before searing the steaks, turn on the exhaust fan and increase heat to high.

2. Set the steaks on a plate and drizzle with oil; turn steaks to coat. Sprinkle with salt and pepper.

3. A minute or so after the residual oils in the skillet send up wisps of smoke, put the steaks in the pan. Cook over high heat until the meat develops an even, rich brown crust, 3½ to 4 minutes. Turn the steaks and continue to cook over high heat until the sides develop a rich brown crust and the meat is medium rare, 3½ to 4 minutes. (For medium filets, turn the heat to low and cook, turning once, for a minute or two longer.) Remove to a plate and let stand 5 minutes.

4. Serve with an uncooked relish or flavored butter. Or make a pan sauce by adding ½ cup liquid to the skillet; boil until the liquid is reduced to about ¼ cup. Tilting the skillet so that the reduced liquid is at one side of the pan, whisk in butter or other enrichments until the sauce is smooth and glossy.

Uncooked Relish Possibilities (pages 171–173): All-Purpose Salsa; Parsley Relish with Capers and Cornichons; Tomato Relish with Pine Nuts, Green Olives, and Lemon Zest; Pickled Pink Onions; Roasted Pepper Relish with Olives, Capers, and Rosemary.

Flavored Butter Possibilities (pages 191–192): Parsley-Shallot-Garlic Butter; Horseradish Butter; Blue Cheese Butter.

Pan Sauce Possibilities (pages 159–170): Red Wine–Dijon Pan Sauce; Tomato-Rosemary Pan Sauce; Tomato Sauce with Black Olives and Provençal Herbs; Balsamic Vinegar Pan Sauce; Mustard Cream Sauce; Mushroom–Goat Cheese Pan Sauce; Horseradish Pan Sauce; Black Pepper Molasses Pan Sauce.

HAMBURGER

Most of us think of a hamburger first as a sandwich, but when prepared with the right grind of meat, formed with a light hand, and seared properly, a well-made burger rivals a great steak.

Buying the right cut of beef is key. Ground chuck, one of the most flavorful cuts of beef, makes the best burger. But just because the package says it's ground chuck doesn't necessarily mean that it is. Most stores do not segregate beef scraps by cut. Instead, they are tossed into one big bin. The scraps are then ground with varying amounts of fat and labeled ground sirloin, ground round, ground chuck, and ground beef.

To ensure that I'm getting the real thing, I usually select a chuck roast from the meat case and ask the butcher to grind it for me while I continue to shop. Before checking out, I pick up my freshly ground 100 percent ground chuck. This effortless step at the store guarantees I get what I want. And since mass-ground beef can be risky these days, it reduces the chances of getting tainted beef.

In addition to buying the right ground beef, it is also important to season and form the burgers properly. To do this, break up the ground beef and sprinkle it with salt and pepper, tossing the meat lightly before forming the patties. Overworking the meat can result in tough, tight-grained, rubbery burgers. To prevent this, divide the ground chuck into 5-ounce portions. Working with one at a time, toss the meat lightly from hand to hand to form a rough ball. With fingertips, lightly press the ball into a 1-inch-thick patty.

Although there's nothing like the flavor of a charcoal-grilled burger, there's nothing like the crust of a pan-seared burger. If you buy real ground chuck, fully season it, lightly form it, and give it a thick crust, you'll leave the buns in the basket and the trimmings on the plate, because all this burger needs is a pan sauce and a glass of red wine.

Pan-Seared Burgers

Because of their high fat content, burgers don't need an oil coating. Ground chuck is the most flavorful meat for burgers.

1¼ pounds 100 percent ground chuck

¾ teaspoon salt

¼ teaspoon ground black pepper

A pan sauce, uncooked relish, or flavored butter

1. Place the ground chuck in a large bowl and break it up with your fingers. Sprinkle with salt and pepper; toss lightly to distribute seasonings. Divide the meat into four equal portions. With cupped hands, toss one portion of meat back and forth to form a loose ball. Pat lightly with fingertips to form a 1-inch-thick burger. Repeat with remaining portions of meat.

2. Set a heavy-bottomed 12-inch skillet over low heat for 5 to 10 minutes, or medium heat for 3 to 4 minutes, while preparing the meal and seasoning and forming the burgers. Three to four minutes before searing the burgers, turn on the exhaust fan and increase the heat to high.

3. A minute or so after the residual oils in the skillet send up wisps of smoke, put the burgers in the pan. Cook over high heat until the meat develops a thick, rich brown crust, about 4 minutes for medium rare and 5 minutes for medium. Turn the burgers and continue to cook over high heat until the remaining sides develop a thick, rich brown crust, and burgers are cooked to desired doneness, about 4 minutes longer. Remove to a plate and let stand 5 minutes.

4. Serve with an uncooked relish or flavored butter. Or make a pan sauce by adding ½ cup liquid to the skillet; boil until the liquid is reduced to about ¼ cup. Tilting the skillet so that the reduced liquid is at one side of the pan, whisk in butter or other enrichments until the sauce is smooth and glossy.

Uncooked Relish Possibilities (pages 171–173): All-Purpose Salsa; Parsley Relish with Capers and Cornichons; Tomato Relish with Pine Nuts, Green Olives, and Lemon Zest; Pickled Pink Onions; Roasted Pepper Relish with Olives, Capers, and Rosemary.

Flavored Butter Possibilities (pages 191–192): Parsley-Shallot-Garlic Butter; Horseradish Butter; Blue Cheese Butter.

Pan Sauce Possibilities (pages 159–170): Red Wine–Dijon Pan Sauce; Tomato-Rosemary Pan Sauce; Tomato Sauce with Black Olives and Provençal Herbs; Balsamic Vinegar Pan Sauce; Mustard Cream Sauce; Mushroom–Goat Cheese Pan Sauce; Horseradish Pan Sauce; Black Pepper Molasses Pan Sauce.

PORK TENDERLOIN

Back in the late 1980s, when the pork tenderloin was first introduced to the market, I wasn't exactly sure how to cook it. When I treated it like a roast and baked it, the tenderloin never browned. When I treated it like a steak and cooked it in a skillet, I had to rotate the tenderloin several times to make sure it cooked evenly, and it took forever to cook through. And although combining techniques was a possibility—browning the tenderloin stovetop, then finishing it in the oven—I thought there had to be a simpler way to cook this little critter.

Since the pork tenderloin was a new cut, I looked at the classic beef tenderloin—the same cut out of a cow—for comparison. They weren't even close in size. Weighing just 12 ounces, the pork tenderloin was a mere shadow of its beefy 5-pound cousin. Clearly, the pork tenderloin was much too small to roast well, regardless of oven temperature.

Although the beef and pork tenderloin were dramatically different in size, they were almost identically shaped—each long and torpedolike, thick at one end and tapering to a thin tail. Just as beef tenderloin could be cut into individual steaks or filet mignons and seared, I realized that pork tenderloin could be cut into "medallions" or little filet mignons of pork and seared as well.

Turning pork tenderloin into medallions takes just a few minutes. While the skillet is heating, remove the tenderloins (they usually travel in pairs) from the packaging and pat them dry. Starting at the thick end, cut each tenderloin, crosswise, into approximately six 1 1/2-inch-thick medallions and two tail pieces. Press each medallion, cut side up, with your fingertips until the meat is about 1 inch thick. The two thin tail pieces require no additional preparation.

After searing for three to four minutes on each side, the pork medallions have cooked to a solid medium. If you prefer pork cooked medium well, simply turn the heat to low and let the meat cook in the pan for another minute or two.

Seared Pork Tenderloin Medallions

2 pork tenderloins (about 1½ pounds total), patted dry and cut crosswise into 1½-inch medallions, each pressed with fingertips to ¾- to 1-inch thickness

2 tablespoons olive or vegetable oil

Salt and ground black pepper

A pan sauce, uncooked relish, or flavored butter

1. Set a heavy-bottomed 12-inch skillet over low heat for 5 to 10 minutes, or medium heat for 3 to 4 minutes, while preparing the meal and seasoning the medallions. Three to four minutes before searing the medallions, turn on the exhaust fan and increase heat to high.

2. Set medallions on a plate, drizzle with oil and turn to coat. Sprinkle with salt and pepper.

3. A minute or so after the residual oils in the skillet send up wisps of smoke, put the medallions in the pan. Cook over high heat until the meat develops a thick, rich brown crust, 3½ to 4 minutes. Turn the medallions and continue to cook over high heat until the remaining sides develop a thick, rich brown crust, 3 to 3½ minutes longer. (For medium-well-done medallions, turn the heat to low and cook, turning once, for a minute or two longer.) Remove to a plate.

4. Serve with an uncooked relish. Or make a pan sauce by adding ½ cup liquid to the skillet; boil until the liquid is reduced to about ¼ cup. Tilting the skillet so that the reduced liquid is at one side of the pan, whisk in butter or other enrichments until the sauce is smooth and glossy.

Uncooked Relish Possibilities (pages 171–173): All-Purpose Salsa; Parsley Relish with Capers and Cornichons; Tomato Relish with Pine Nuts, Green Olives, and Lemon Zest; Roasted Pepper Relish with Olives, Capers, and Rosemary

Flavored Butter Possibilities (pages 191–192): Parsley-Shallot-Garlic Butter; Citrus Butter

Pan Sauce Possibilities (pages 159–170): Red Wine–Dijon Pan Sauce; Marsala Wine Pan Sauce; Sauterne Sauce with Figs and Pistachios; Sweet Vermouth Pan Sauce with Prunes; Port Wine Pan Sauce with Dried Cranberries; Tomato-Rosemary Pan Sauce; Tomato-Anchovy Pan Sauce; Tomato Sauce with Black Olives and Provençal Herbs; Cooked Tomato Relish with Onion and Mint; Balsamic Vinegar Pan Sauce; Balsamic Pan Sauce with Pine Nuts and Raisins; Apple Cider Pan Sauce; Orange-Dijon Pan Sauce with Rosemary; Orange Pan Sauce with Pernod; Lemon-Caper Pan Sauce; Mustard Cream Sauce; Mushroom–Goat Cheese Pan Sauce; Green Grape–Rosemary Pan Sauce; Horseradish Pan Sauce; Black Pepper Molasses Pan Sauce; Curried Chutney Pan Sauce

SALMON

Unlike many other fish, salmon is usually farm-raised and plentiful, and, like chicken, it comes in many forms—steaks, individual fillets and whole fillets, and the whole fish, of course. When buying salmon for dinner, I always ask for the thick center-cut fillets. Thinner fillets near the tail are thin and easy to overcook, resulting in dry, chalky fish.

Salmon fillets often come skinned these days, but if searing a skin-on salmon, start it flesh side down. If you don't, the skin pulls taut as it sears, causing the fillet to bow slightly, and when turned, the flesh side tends to sear unevenly.

Like a good beefsteak, these steaklike fish are at their best when cooked medium-rare to medium-well.

Seared Salmon Fillets

4 center-cut salmon fillets (about 6 ounces each)	Salt and ground black pepper
2 tablespoons olive oil	Lemon wedges, or a pan sauce, uncooked relish, or flavored butter

1. Set a heavy-bottomed 12-inch skillet over low heat for 5 to 10 minutes, or medium heat for 3 to 4 minutes, while preparing the meal and seasoning the salmon. Three to four minutes before searing the salmon, turn on the exhaust fan and increase the heat to high.

2. Set the fillets on a plate, drizzle with oil; turn to coat. Sprinkle both sides with salt and pepper.

3. A minute or so after the residual oils in the skillet send up wisps of smoke, put the salmon fillets, flesh side down, in the pan. Cook over high heat until they develop an even, rich brown crust, 3 to 3½ minutes. Turn the fillets and continue to cook until the skin side develops an even, rich brown crust, 4 minutes longer for medium and 5 minutes longer for medium-well. Remove to a plate and let stand a few minutes or while making a sauce.

4. Serve with lemon wedges, or an uncooked relish or flavored butter. Or make a pan sauce by adding ½ cup liquid to the skillet; boil until the liquid is reduced to about ¼ cup. Tilting the skillet so that the reduced liquid is at one side of the pan, whisk in butter or other enrichments until the sauce is smooth and glossy.

Uncooked Relish Possibilities (pages 171–173): All-Purpose Salsa; Parsley Relish with Capers and Cornichons; Tomato Relish with Pine Nuts, Green Olives, and Lemon Zest; Pickled Pink Onions; Roasted Pepper Relish with Olives, Capers, and Rosemary

Flavored Butter Possibilities (pages 191–192): Parsley-Shallot-Garlic Butter; Horseradish Butter; Citrus Butter

Pan Sauce Possibilities (pages 159–170): Tomato-Tarragon Pan Sauce; Tomato-Rosemary Pan Sauce; Tomato-Anchovy Pan Sauce; Tomato Sauce with Black Olives and Provençal Herbs; Cooked Tomato Relish with Onion and Mint; White Wine Vinegar Pan Sauce; Orange Pan Sauce with Pernod; Lemon-Caper Pan Sauce; Quick Velouté; Mustard Cream Sauce; Horseradish Pan Sauce; Asian-style Sweet-and-Sour Sauce

FISH STEAKS

"You can never be too thin" doesn't apply to fish steaks. Like all the other meats in this chapter, fish steaks must be thick enough so that they don't overcook and dry out before both sides have seared. The temptation is to buy fish steaks based on portion size, but don't. Better to buy odd-sized but thick fish steaks and divvy them up after cooking, than buy four perfectly sized pieces that are too thin.

With tuna steaks, you may have a variety choice. Bluefin is dark, rich, and meaty-flavored, while yellowfin is ruby red and slightly milder. Albacore (like the stuff that's in the can) is light colored and mild flavored. While the supply of swordfish may be low along the Northeast coast at this point, the worldwide supply is actually quite strong.

Although more delicately textured than tuna and swordfish, other lighter-fleshed fish steaks such as halibut and Chilean sea bass can be seared as well.

Monkfish is another good searing candidate. Shaped like pork tenderloin, monkfish can be cut into medallions. Make sure to have the fishmonger cut the thin gray membrane from the fish before cooking it, or do it yourself.

Seared Fish Steaks

1½ pounds tuna, swordfish, or shark
steaks, cut 1 to 1¼ inches thick

2 tablespoons olive or vegetable oil

Salt and ground black pepper

Lemon wedges, or a pan sauce, uncooked
relish, or flavored butter

1. Set a heavy-bottomed 12-inch skillet over low heat for 5 to 10 minutes, or medium heat for 3 to 4 minutes, while preparing the meal and seasoning the fish steaks. Three to four minutes before searing the fish steaks, turn on the exhaust fan and increase the heat to high.

2. Set steaks on a plate, drizzle with oil; turn to coat. Sprinkle with salt and pepper.

3. A minute or so after the residual oils in the skillet send up wisps of smoke, put the fish steaks in the pan. Cook over high heat until the steaks develop a thick, rich brown crust, about 3½ to 4 minutes. Turn the steaks and continue to cook over high heat until the other sides develop a thick, rich brown crust and the fish is medium-rare to medium, 3½ to 4 minutes longer. (For medium-well-done fish, turn the heat to low and cook, turning once, for 1 to 2 minutes longer.) Remove to a plate and let stand 5 minutes.

4. Serve with lemon wedges, or an uncooked relish or flavored butter. Or make a pan sauce by adding ½ cup liquid to the skillet; boil until the liquid is reduced to about ¼ cup. Tilting the skillet so that the reduced liquid is at one side of the pan, whisk in butter or other enrichments until the sauce is smooth and glossy.

Uncooked Relish Possibilities (pages 171–173): All-Purpose Salsa; Parsley Relish with Capers and Cornichons; Tomato Relish with Pine Nuts, Green Olives, and Lemon Zest; Roasted Pepper Relish with Olives, Capers, and Rosemary

Flavored Butter Possibilities (pages 191–192): Parsley-Shallot-Garlic Butter; Horseradish Butter; Citrus Butter

Pan Sauce Possibilities (pages 159–170): Tomato-Tarragon Pan Sauce; Tomato-Rosemary Pan Sauce; Tomato-Anchovy Pan Sauce; Tomato Sauce with Black Olives and Provençal Herbs; Cooked Tomato Relish with Onion and Mint; White Wine Vinegar Pan Sauce; Orange Pan Sauce with Pernod; Lemon-Caper Pan Sauce; Quick Velouté; Mustard Cream Sauce; Horseradish Pan Sauce; Asian-style Sweet-and-Sour Sauce

SCALLOPS

Growing up on the Florida panhandle, I spent many weekends fishing with my father and mother. I was usually a good sport, but if the fish weren't biting, I was always the first to suggest we "cut bait" and head for shore.

I was a much better scalloper. Instead of sitting all day in a hot boat, I put on a bathing suit and a pair of sneakers, grabbed a long-handled net and a glass-bottomed box my dad had made, and jumped into the waist-high water. For hours I'd search for hidden scallops underwater.

When the net was full, I'd take my catch to Mom, who sat in the boat and shucked in the sun. On those days, she was the first to call it quits. One perfect day, I remember, we came home with a full gallon of shucked scallops. At night Mom would fry up a mess of the day's catch, and I ate the sweet, tender muscles like popcorn until I thought *I* would pop.

Which is why I do not like most of today's scallops. An overwhelming number of sea and bay scallops are soaked in sodium tripolyphosphate, a preservative that not only masks the scallop's delicate, sweet flavor but also causes them to gain up to 25 percent water weight.

If you've ever tried to sear and eat treated sea scallops, you know it's an unsatisfying cooking and eating experience. The moment a treated scallop hits a hot skillet, it starts to weep. The released liquid causes the scallop to steam rather than to sear, and the plump juicy muscle shrinks dramatically. The cooked scallop tastes overly salty and off. If treated sea scallops were cheaper, I might be more kind, but at $10.99 to $12.99 a pound, I expect better.

By law, treated scallops should be labeled as a "water-added scallop product," but if they aren't, ask. Buy only untreated or "dry" scallops. They're more expensive, but when you consider the added water and the off flavors of the treated ones, the choice is simple.

Although our family has been known to make a meal out of jumbo dry scallops, I don't often buy them as a main course for weeknight supper. Instead, I like to serve one or two per person as a first course. Seared about two minutes per side and served with a squeeze of lemon or a simple pan sauce, it's the ultimate fast food.

Seared Scallops

1½ pounds "dry" sea scallops (see opposite)

2 tablespoons olive or vegetable oil

Salt and ground black pepper

Lemon wedges, or a pan sauce, or flavored butter

1. Set a heavy-bottomed 12-inch skillet over low heat for 5 to 10 minutes while preparing the meal and seasoning the scallops. (To speed up the heating process, the skillet can be set over medium heat for 3 to 4 minutes.) Three to four minutes before searing the scallops, turn on the exhaust fan and increase the heat to high.

2. To season the scallops, set them on a plate and drizzle with oil; turn to coat. Sprinkle both sides with salt and pepper.

3. A minute or so after the residual oils in the skillet send up wisps of smoke, put the scallops in the pan. Cook over high heat until they develop a thick, rich brown crust, about 2 minutes. Turn them and continue to cook over high heat until the other sides develop a thick, rich brown crust, about 2 minutes longer. Remove from the pan and let stand a couple of minutes.

4. Serve with lemon wedges or flavored butter. Or make a pan sauce by adding ½ cup liquid to the skillet; boil until the liquid is reduced to about ¼ cup. Tilting the skillet so that the reduced liquid is at one side of the pan, whisk in butter or other enrichments until the sauce is smooth and glossy.

   Flavored Butter Possibilities (pages 191–192): Parsley-Shallot-Garlic Butter; Citrus Butter

   Pan Sauce Possibilities (pages 159–170): Tomato-Rosemary Pan Sauce; White Wine Vinegar Pan Sauce; Orange Pan Sauce with Pernod; Lemon-Caper Pan Sauce; Quick Velouté

HOW TO SEAR

- Choose the right size skillet, making sure the pieces of meat will have neither too much nor too little space between them.

- Make sure the skillet is heavy-bottomed. Cast iron works well unless you're making a wine sauce.

- Set the skillet over low heat for 5 to 10 minutes while preparing dinner and seasoning the meat or fish.

- Drizzle both sides of each piece of meat or fish with oil. Season both sides with salt and pepper.

- Crank up the heat under the pan and turn on the exhaust fan 3 or 4 minutes before searing.

- Cook the pieces of meat or fish over high heat until an even, rich brown crust forms, 2 to 4 minutes, depending on type and thickness of the cut. Turn and cook until the remaining side develops a crust, 2 to 4 minutes longer.

- Set a timer so that you don't lose track of time.

FLAVORED BUTTERS

I like to watch a pat of flavored butter slowly melt over a piece of seared fish or steak. Before my eyes the warm butter mingles with the juices to make a natural sauce. As much as I enjoy using flavored butters, however, I've never liked making them. The process usually starts with a whole stick of room-temperature butter into which flavorings are mashed. Once flavored, the butter is placed on plastic wrap or parchment, remolded into a long cylinder, and refrigerated or frozen. Butter discs can be sliced from the whole as needed. Making a flavored butter this way is a little too much of an ordeal for a weeknight meal. I've also known those little butter cylinders to get lost in a dark corner of my freezer for months.

I've actually come up with a less formal way of making a flavored butter that works for me on weeknights. For a flavored butter, I simply make what I need for one meal. Except for the hot summer months, I always have a chunk of butter sitting at room temperature. To the softened butter I mix in bottled horseradish, a chunk of blue cheese, or citrus zest with a squeeze of its juice. At this point, I'm done. Rather than formally shaping it, I simply smear the softened flavored butter over the cooked meat or fish. No shaping, no leftovers, just smear and serve.

Parsley-Shallot-Garlic Butter

Serves 4

For steaks, filet mignon, burgers, salmon fillets, and fish steaks.

1 garlic clove, minced

½ medium shallot, minced

1 tablespoon minced fresh parsley

4 tablespoons (½ stick) butter, at room temperature

Salt and ground black pepper

Mash garlic, shallot, and parsley into the butter; season to taste with salt and pepper. Smear flavored butter over each portion of seared meat or fish and serve immediately.

Horseradish Butter

Serves 4

For steaks, filet mignon, burgers, salmon fillets, and fish steaks.

3 tablespoons bottled pure horseradish with liquid squeezed out

3 tablespoons butter, at room temperature

½ teaspoon vinegar

Salt and ground black pepper

Mash the horseradish and butter into a paste. Add the vinegar and season to taste with salt and pepper. Smear a tablespoon of flavored butter over each portion and serve immediately.

Blue Cheese Butter

Serves 4

For steaks, filet mignon, and burgers.

2 tablespoons butter, at room temperature

2 tablespoons blue cheese

Mash the butter and blue cheese together with a fork. Smear a tablespoon of flavored butter over each steak or burger and serve immediately.

Citrus Butter

Serves 4

For fish fillets and steaks, and pork medallions if made with orange.

½ teaspoon zest and 1 teaspoon juice from a lemon or ½ teaspoon zest and 1 teaspoon juice from an orange

4 tablespoons butter, at room temperature

Mash zest and juice into the butter. Season to taste with salt and pepper. Smear a tablespoon of flavored butter over each portion and serve immediately.

The No-Hassle Roast Chicken
Dinner ... and Quick Chicken Salad

Just cut out the back—the bird flattens in a dash

For perfect roast chicken that's ready in a flash.

Whole roast chicken would be perfect supper food if it didn't take so long. Preparing even a small chicken and roasting it in a hot oven takes an hour and fifteen minutes.

However, I have discovered that butterflying, or cutting out the back and flattening a chicken, shaves nearly half an hour off the roasting time, making it a weeknight dinner possibility. Not only does removing the back save time, it also flattens out the chicken, allowing it to cook more evenly, ensuring that the breast does not overcook and dry out. If I've got forty-five minutes (forty of which is roasting time for the bird and free time for me), butterflied roast chicken with vegetables is one of the simplest meals I can get on the table.

A butterflied chicken is also easier to season. Sprinkling the skin of a whole chicken with salt and pepper does nothing for the meat, and seasoning it under its skin is difficult. But with its back cut out, the skin of a butterflied chicken is as easy to lift as a backless hospital gown, making it possible to distribute the seasonings easily directly on the meat.

First, start by preheating the oven to 450 degrees. After that, rinse the chicken, cut out its back, flatten it with your palm or fist (I don't bother with a meat pounder anymore), and pat it dry. Transfer the butterflied chicken to a foil-lined roasting pan

193

large enough to hold the chicken (and vegetables in a single layer if you are roasting them alongside the bird) and shallow enough to ensure that the chicken browns well. When roasting both chicken and vegetables, my pan of choice is a heavy-grade 18- by 12-inch pan with a 1-inch lip, but I have successfully roasted chicken and vegetables on a large jelly roll pan of similar dimensions.

With the chicken on the roasting pan, pull back the skin from each leg and thigh, sprinkling them with salt, pepper, and an herb if you like. To loosen the breast skin, cut under the skin along the breastbone, seasoning the breast as you have the legs and thighs. If preparing roast chicken for a special dinner or if you have a little more time, rub the meat with a garlic/herb paste. After pulling the skin back in place, drizzle the chicken with a little olive oil or rub it with softened butter. If you use butter, however, the chicken skin has to be thoroughly dry.

Because onions and potatoes are so easy to prepare, they are my usual choice when roasting vegetables. To prepare them for roasting alongside the chicken, halve but do not peel them, toss them in a generous amount of olive oil, sprinkle them with salt and pepper, and place them cut side down in the roasting pan. That's it.

Since the average home oven takes ten to twelve minutes to reach 450 degrees, you don't have to wait until it's fully preheated. As soon as the chicken and vegetables are prepared, put the pan in the oven. After that, you're done until dinner. You may want to make a salad or steam/sauté a vegetable (page 202), or cook up some frozen green peas, or then again you may not. With a meat, starch, and vegetable in the oven, what more do you need?

If you want to make a pan sauce to go with the chicken, do not line the roasting pan with foil. After removing the chicken and vegetables, place the roasting pan on two burners set on medium heat and pour ¼ cup each dry vermouth or white wine and chicken broth into the pan, stirring carefully to loosen the brown bits. You can roast two butterflied chickens in the 18- 12-inch pan, but you'll need a second shallow pan if roasting vegetables too. Before preheating the oven, adjust the racks to the upper and lower-middle positions, then roast the chickens on the top rack and the vegetables on the lower rack.

The chicken doesn't have to be roasted plain, and potatoes and onions aren't the only vegetables that roast well. To make barbecued chicken, deviled chicken, or lemon chicken, remove the pan from the oven after 30 minutes. Brush the chicken with barbecue sauce, squeeze on lemon juice, or season with Dijon mustard and fresh breadcrumbs. Return the pan to the oven and continue to roast until the sauce sets, the lemon permeates the meat, or the breadcrumbs brown and the chicken is fully cooked, an additional 5 to 10 minutes.

One final benefit of a butterflied chicken—it's a breeze to carve. Just one cut down the breast with kitchen shears or a chef's knife, and all that's left is a quick snip of the skin holding each leg to each breast.

Two Birds in the Oven Are . . . an Extra Meal

Instead of roasting vegetables alongside the chicken, sometimes I roast an extra chicken seasoned simply with salt and pepper. We eat roast chicken one night, and I make one of the following chicken salads later in the week.

I also buy roast chickens from the grocery store. I don't usually serve them for dinner, but use them, like canned tuna, for salads and creamed dishes. Clearly, roast turkey could be used as well.

Vegetables That Roast Well

Although many vegetables roast well, the following are a few that complement the chicken and roast in about the same amount of time. (Tomatoes are the only exception.) If using an 18- by 12-inch pan, you should be able to fit two of the following vegetables in the pan with the chicken.

- 4 yellow onions. Remove loose outer skins but it is not necessary to peel them. Halve the onions, then toss them with a generous drizzling of olive oil and season with salt and pepper.
- 4 red bliss potatoes or small russet potatoes. Scrub, halve, toss with a generous drizzling of olive oil, and season with salt and pepper.
- 8 new potatoes. Scrub, halve, toss with a generous drizzling of olive oil, and season with salt and pepper.
- 8 Italian plum tomatoes. Halve lengthwise, toss with a generous drizzling of olive oil, and season with salt and pepper. (Tomatoes are the only vegetable added to the pan partway through cooking.)
- 4 ears of corn. Shuck, brush with softened butter, and wrap in foil.
- 1 pound of cauliflower. Cut into large florets, toss with a generous drizzling of olive oil, and season with salt and pepper.

No-Hassle Roast Chicken

If your chicken is larger than the suggested size, make sure to increase roasting time.

1 chicken (3 to 3½ pounds), rinsed, patted dry, and butterflied (see page 193)

Salt and ground black pepper

2 tablespoons olive oil or softened butter

1. Adjust the oven rack to the lower-middle position and heat the oven to 450 degrees. After butterflying the chicken, place it on a foil-lined 18- by 12-inch or similar-sized shallow roasting pan. Season under the skin with salt and pepper. Pat the skin back in place and drizzle with oil or rub with butter.

2. Roast until the chicken is golden brown and its juices run clear, about 40 minutes. Let stand 5 minutes, then cut it into two breast/wing pieces and two leg/thigh pieces. Serve.

Roast Chicken with Dijon and Fresh Breadcrumbs

Follow the No-Hassle Roast Chicken recipe. After 25 minutes of roasting, remove chicken from the oven. Pour off and reserve the pan drippings. Brush the chicken with ¼ cup of Dijon mustard, then sprinkle with 1 cup of fresh breadcrumbs made from 2 slices of bread. Drizzle reserved pan drippings over the breadcrumbs. Return the chicken to the oven and continue to roast until crumbs are golden brown and juices run clear, 10 to 15 minutes longer.

Roast onions and potatoes complete this meal. Arrange prepared onions and potatoes, cut side down, in a single layer on the pan and roast alongside the chicken.

Roast Chicken with Lemon, Rosemary, and Garlic

ROSEMARY-GARLIC RUB

1 teaspoon fine-grated lemon zest	1/2 teaspoon salt
2 garlic cloves, minced	1/4 teaspoon pepper
1 1/2 teaspoons minced fresh rosemary leaves	1/2 lemon

1. Mix the first five ingredients in a small bowl.

2. Follow the No-Hassle Roast Chicken recipe, rubbing the herb paste under the loosened skin. Roast the chicken for 30 minutes. Squeeze the lemon over the chicken. Return to the oven and continue to roast until juices run clear, 5 to 10 minutes longer.

Roasted tomatoes and potatoes partner well with this chicken. Arrange prepared potatoes, cut side down, in a single layer on the pan and roast alongside the chicken. After for 20 minutes, add the prepared tomatoes, cut side up. Continue to roast until chicken is done, squeezing lemon juice on at the appropriate time, for 20 minutes longer.

Oven-Roasted Barbecued Chicken

Follow the No-Hassle Roast Chicken recipe. After 25 minutes roasting time, remove chicken from the oven and brush with 1/3 cup of prepared barbecue sauce. Return to the oven and continue to roast 10 to 15 minutes longer.

Corn on the cob and onion halves are good vegetable accompaniments to barbecued chicken. Arrange prepared onions, cut side down, and foiled corn in a single layer on the pan and roast alongside the chicken.

Tandoori-style Roast Chicken

YOGURT WITH TANDOORI SPICES

6 tablespoons plain low-fat yogurt

2 tablespoons olive oil

1 tablespoon red wine vinegar

1 tablespoon ground cumin

1 teaspoon curry powder

$\frac{1}{2}$ teaspoon garlic powder

$\frac{1}{4}$ teaspoon ground ginger

$\frac{1}{4}$ teaspoon salt

$\frac{1}{4}$ teaspoon cayenne

1. Mix all ingredients in a small bowl.

2. Follow the No-Hassle Roast Chicken recipe (page 196), pouring the yogurt mixture over the butterflied chicken before roasting.

Roast onions, cut side down, and cauliflower in a single layer alongside the chicken, tossing cauliflower with pan juices after 30 minutes of roasting.

at-a-glance

THE NO-HASSLE ROAST CHICKEN DINNER

- Adjust the oven rack to the lower-middle position and heat the oven to 450 degrees.

- Rinse the chicken, cut out its back, and flatten it.

- Place the chicken on a low-sided foil-lined roasting pan.

- Lift the chicken skin and season the meat. Pulling skin back in place, rub it with a little fat.

- Place vegetables in a single layer alongside the chicken.

- Roast until chicken is brown and the juices run clear, 35 to 40 minutes.

Quick Chicken Salad

1 No-Hassle Roast Chicken (page 196) or a store-bought roast chicken skinned and boned, meat shredded into bite-size pieces (about 4 cups)

2 medium celery ribs, cut into small dice

2 medium scallions, minced

Minced fresh herbs (see individual recipes)

Dressing (see individual recipes)

Extra ingredients (optional; see individual recipes)

Salt and ground black pepper

Mix the chicken, celery, and scallions, along with minced fresh herbs, dressing, optional extra ingredients, and salt and pepper to taste. Serve. (Can be covered and refrigerated overnight.)

Classic Chicken Salad

DRESSING:

¾ cup mayonnaise

2 tablespoons lemon juice

HERB:

2 tablespoons minced fresh parsley, basil, or tarragon

EXTRA INGREDIENTS:

None

Mix the mayonnaise and lemon juice in a small bowl, then follow the Quick Chicken Salad recipe.

Waldorf Chicken Salad

DRESSING:

¾ cup mayonnaise

2 tablespoons lemon juice

HERB:

2 tablespoons minced fresh parsley leaves

EXTRA INGREDIENTS:

1 large crisp apple, cut into small dice

6 tablespoons toasted chopped walnuts

Mix the mayonnaise and lemon juice in a small bowl, then follow the Quick Chicken Salad recipe (page 199).

Thai Chicken Salad

Serve on a bed of Bibb lettuce, if you like.

DRESSING:

2 tablespoons lime juice

2 tablespoons Asian fish sauce, such as nam pla or nuoc nam

2 tablespoons water

2 teaspoons sugar

3 tablespoons peeled and minced gingerroot

½ teaspoon hot red pepper flakes

HERBS:

2 tablespoons each: minced fresh cilantro and mint leaves

EXTRA INGREDIENTS:

¼ cup chopped dry-roasted unsalted peanuts

Mix the dressing ingredients in a small bowl, then follow the Quick Chicken Salad recipe (page 199).

Curried Chicken Salad with Raisins and Honey

DRESSING:

¾ cup mayonnaise

1½ tablespoons lemon juice

1 tablespoon honey

2 teaspoons curry powder

HERB:

2 tablespoons minced fresh parsley or cilantro

EXTRA INGREDIENTS:

6 tablespoons raisins or dried currants

Mix the mayonnaise, lemon juice, honey, and curry powder in a small bowl, then follow the Quick Chicken Salad recipe (page 199).

Chicken Salad with Hoisin Dressing

This Asian-style salad can be served on a bed of young spinach leaves with sliced cucumber and radishes. The salad can also be rolled in a flour tortilla and served as a sandwich with shredded iceberg lettuce or watercress.

DRESSING:

⅓ cup rice wine vinegar

1½ tablespoons soy sauce

3 tablespoons hoisin sauce

1 tablespoon minced fresh gingerroot

1 tablespoon toasted sesame oil

3 tablespoons vegetable oil

HERB:

2 tablespoons minced fresh cilantro

EXTRA INGREDIENTS:

6 tablespoons chopped water chestnuts

Mix the dressing ingredients in a small bowl, then follow the Quick Chicken Salad recipe (page 199).

ginger asparagus
dijon mustard flavor
butter snap peas

Steam/Sautéed Vegetables

Steam seasoned vegetables with a little fat until just done,

Remove the lid and cook until the water is all gone.

There is certainly more than one way to cook vegetables. For weeknight cooking, however, I've come to rely on a method I call the "steam/sauté." Exactly as it sounds, the vegetable is steamed, or "wet cooked," and then sautéed, or "dry cooked."

Unlike other vegetable cooking methods that often require multiple steps and pots, this dual technique is seamlessly accomplished in the same pan. No steamer contraptions, no large quantities of water to boil, no awkward vegetable draining or cooling between steps.

Similar to the method for cooking Italian sausage, the prepared vegetable is put in a large, deep skillet or Dutch oven along with a small amount of salted water to which fat and optional seasonings have been added. The pan is covered and the vegetable steams until almost tender, at which time the lid is removed, the remaining water evaporates, and the vegetable begins to sauté in the seasoned fat, intensifying the flavors.

With a few exceptions, this technique works with many of my weeknight regulars—broccoli, cauliflower, and carrots, year-round favorites; Brussels sprouts, cabbage, and squash in the fall and winter; asparagus, snow peas, and sugar snaps in the spring; and green beans in the summer. The following vegetables are ideal candidates for steam/sautéing:

- Asparagus, snapped
- Broccoli florets (stems can also be peeled and cut into $\frac{1}{2}$-inch coins)
- Brussels sprouts, trimmed
- Cabbage, quartered, cored, and cut into thick shreds
- Carrots and parsnips, peeled and sliced into $\frac{1}{2}$-inch coins
- Cauliflower florets
- Celery, trimmed and sliced $\frac{1}{2}$ inch thick
- Fennel, halved, cored, and sliced thin
- Green beans, snow peas, and sugar snap peas, trimmed
- Winter squash (such as butternut) and turnips (rutabagas and small white turnips)

Soft, high-moisture vegetables, such as bell peppers, mushrooms, onions, zucchini, and yellow squash do not need this extra steaming step before sautéing.

Onions, garlic, spices, and herbs are all optional. If you're in a hurry, just add salt and butter or oil along with the vegetable. If adding flavorings, however, remember that garlic, onions, spices, and dried herbs should be added at the beginning, along with the vegetable, while fresh herbs and other flavors like citrus zests, soy sauce, and Dijon mustard should be added once the vegetable starts to sauté.

Steam/Sautéed Vegetables

Serves 4

If you find the vegetable is not fully cooked by the time the water has evaporated, simply add a couple more tablespoons of water, cover, and continue to cook until tender. When cooking any vegetable this way, remember that all you really need is the water, fat, and salt.

⅓ cup water

1 tablespoon fat (extra-virgin olive oil, vegetable oil, butter, or bacon fat)

½ teaspoon salt

1 pound prepared vegetable

OPTIONAL AROMATICS:

½ small onion, sliced thin, or 2 medium garlic cloves, minced

Optional spices, dried/fresh herbs, and/or flavorings

Ground black pepper

1. Bring the water, fat, salt, and vegetable, along with optional aromatics, spices, dried herbs and/or other flavorings along to a boil in a Dutch oven or a large deep skillet. Cover and steam over medium-high heat until the vegetable is brightly colored and just tender, 5 to 10 minutes, depending on vegetable size.

2. Remove the lid and continue to cook until the liquid evaporates, 1 to 2 minutes longer, adding optional fresh herbs and/or other flavorings at this point. Sauté to intensify flavors, 1 to 2 minutes longer. Adjust seasonings, including pepper to taste, and serve.

Steam/Sautéed Asparagus with Garlic, Basil, and Soy

Omit salt if using soy sauce.

VEGETABLE:

1 pound asparagus, tough ends snapped off

FAT:

1 tablespoon vegetable oil

AROMATIC:

2 garlic cloves, minced

HERB AND FLAVORING:

1 tablespoon each minced fresh basil leaves

1 tablespoon soy sauce

Follow the Steam/Sautéed Vegetables recipe, adding basil and soy once the asparagus starts to sauté.

Steam/Sautéed Asparagus with Lemon and Parsley

VEGETABLE:

1 pound asparagus, tough ends snapped off

FAT:

1 tablespoon butter

HERB AND FLAVORING:

1 tablespoon minced fresh parsley

½ teaspoon fine-grated zest and 1 tablespoon juice from a small lemon

Follow the Steam/Sautéed Vegetables recipe, adding parsley, lemon zest, and juice once the asparagus starts to sauté.

Steam/Sautéed Green Beans with Butter and Tarragon

If you prefer to use dried tarragon, add ½ teaspoon at the appropriate point.

VEGETABLE:

1 pound green beans, stemmed

FAT:

1 tablespoon butter

HERB:

1½ teaspoons minced fresh tarragon

Follow the Steam/Sautéed Vegetables recipe (page 204), adding the tarragon once the beans start to sauté.

Steam/Sautéed Green Beans with Onions and Thyme

If using fresh thyme, add it to the sautéing green beans.

VEGETABLE:

1 pound green beans, stemmed

FAT:

1 tablespoon butter, olive oil, or bacon fat

AROMATIC:

½ small onion, sliced thin

HERB:

½ teaspoon dried thyme leaves (or 1½ teaspoons fresh)

Follow the Steam/Sautéed Vegetables recipe (page 204), adding onion and thyme with green beans.

Steam/Sautéed Broccoli with Garlic and Red Pepper

VEGETABLE:

1 pound broccoli florets (stems can be peeled and cut into 1-inch coins)

FAT:

1 tablespoon olive oil

AROMATIC:

1 medium garlic clove, minced

FLAVORING:

Heaping ¼ teaspoon hot red pepper flakes

Follow the Steam/Sautéed Vegetables recipe (page 204), adding the garlic and red pepper flakes with the broccoli.

Steam/Sautéed Broccoli with Ginger and Orange

Shake on a few drops of soy sauce if you like.

VEGETABLE:

1 pound broccoli florets (stems can be peeled and cut into ½-inch coins)

FAT:

1 tablespoon vegetable oil

AROMATIC:

2 garlic cloves, minced

FLAVORINGS:

½ teaspoon fine-grated orange zest

1 tablespoon minced fresh gingerroot

Follow the Steam/Sautéed Vegetables recipe (page 204), adding the garlic and ginger with the broccoli and the orange zest once the broccoli starts to sauté.

Steam/Sautéed Brussels Sprouts with Dijon Mustard

Although the technique is the same, I find Brussels sprouts need a little more water and a little more fat than other vegetables, so increase water to $1/2$ cup and increase fat up to 4 tablespoons.

VEGETABLE:

1 pound Brussels sprouts, trimmed of yellow or wilted leaves and halved lengthwise

FAT:

2–4 tablespoons butter (see note above)

FLAVORING:

2 tablespoons Dijon mustard

Follow the Steam/Sautéed Vegetables recipe (page 204), leaving a little liquid in the pan and adding mustard to form a sauce.

Steam/Sautéed Brussels Sprouts with Garlic and Pine Nuts

Like the other Brussels sprouts recipe, use $1/2$ cup water rather than $1/3$ cup to steam this vegetable, and increase the fat as necessary, up to 4 tablespoons.

VEGETABLE:

1 pound Brussels sprouts, trimmed of yellow or wilted leaves and halved lengthwise

FAT:

2–4 tablespoons butter

AROMATIC:

1 medium garlic clove, minced

FLAVORING:

2 tablespoons toasted pine nuts

Follow the Steam/Sautéed Vegetables recipe (page 204), leaving a little liquid in the pan to form a sauce. Sprinkle with pine nuts and serve.

Steam/Sautéed Cabbage with Butter and Caraway

VEGETABLE:

1 pound cabbage, cored
and shredded

FAT:

1 tablespoon butter or bacon fat

AROMATIC:

2 garlic cloves, minced

SPICE:

½ teaspoon caraway seeds

Follow the Steam/Sautéed Vegetables recipe (page 204), adding caraway with the cabbage.

Steam/Sautéed Carrots with Cumin

VEGETABLE:

1 pound carrots, peeled and cut
into ½-inch coins

FAT:

1 tablespoon butter

SPICE AND HERB:

½ teaspoon ground cumin

1 tablespoon minced fresh
parsley or cilantro leaves

Follow the Steam/Sautéed Vegetables recipe (page 204), adding the cumin with the carrots and the parsley once the carrots start to sauté.

Steam/Sautéed Carrots with Nutmeg and Butter

VEGETABLE:

1 pound carrots, peeled and cut
into ½-inch coins

FAT:

1 tablespoon butter

SPICE:

¼ teaspoon grated nutmeg

Follow the Steam/Sautéed Vegetables recipe (page 204), adding the nutmeg with the carrots.

Steam/Sautéed Cauliflower with Curry Flavorings

VEGETABLE:

1 pound cauliflower florets

FAT:

1 tablespoon vegetable oil

AROMATIC:

2 garlic cloves, minced, *or*
½ small onion, sliced thin

SPICE AND HERB:

1 teaspoon curry powder

1 tablespoon minced fresh cilantro

Follow the Steam/Sautéed Vegetables recipe (page 204), adding curry powder with the cauliflower, and cilantro once the cauliflower starts to sauté.

Steam/Sautéed Cauliflower with Oregano and Green Olives (or Capers)

VEGETABLE:

1 pound cauliflower florets from small head

FAT:

2 tablespoons olive oil

AROMATIC:

2 garlic cloves, minced

HERB AND FLAVORING:

½ teaspoon dried oregano

¼ cup pimiento-stuffed olives *or*
2 tablespoons capers

Follow the Steam/Sautéed Vegetables recipe (page 204), adding garlic and oregano with the cauliflower, and adding the olives or capers once the cauliflower starts to sauté.

Steam/Sautéed Celery with Thyme

VEGETABLE:

1 pound celery (4 large stalks),
sliced crosswise into $\frac{1}{2}$-inch pieces

FAT:

1 tablespoon butter

AROMATIC:

2 garlic cloves, minced

HERB:

$\frac{1}{2}$ teaspoon dried thyme leaves

Follow the Steam/Sautéed Vegetables recipe (page 204), adding garlic and thyme with the celery.

Steam/Sautéed Fennel

VEGETABLE:

1 pound fennel, tops trimmed
(fronds reserved), bulbs halved,
cored, and sliced thin crosswise

FAT:

1 tablespoon olive oil

FLAVORING:

1 tablespoon minced fennel fronds

Follow the Steam/Sautéed Vegetables recipe (page 204), adding the minced fennel fronds once the sliced fennel starts to sauté.

Steam/Sautéed Snow Peas with Lemon and Mint

VEGETABLE:

1 pound snow peas, strings removed

FAT:

1 tablespoon butter

AROMATIC:

2 medium garlic cloves, minced

FLAVORING AND HERB:

1/2 teaspoon fine-grated lemon zest

1 tablespoon minced fresh mint leaves

Follow the Steam/Sautéed Vegetables recipe (page 204), adding lemon zest and mint once the snow peas start to sauté.

Steam/Sautéed Sugar Snap Peas with Chives

VEGETABLE:

1 pound sugar snap peas, trimmed

FAT:

1 tablespoon butter

HERB:

1 tablespoon snipped chives

Follow the Steam/Sautéed Vegetables recipe (page 204), adding chives once sugar snaps start to sauté.

Steam/Sautéed Sugar Snap Peas with Parsley and Orange

VEGETABLE:

1 pound sugar snap peas, stems removed

FAT:

1 tablespoon butter

FLAVORING AND HERB:

½ teaspoon fine-grated orange zest

1 tablespoon minced fresh parsley leaves

Follow the Steam/Sautéed Vegetables recipe (page 204), adding the orange zest and parsley once sugar snaps start to sauté.

Steam/Sautéed Butternut Squash with Ginger and Parsley

VEGETABLE:

1 pound butternut squash, peeled and cut into 1-inch chunks

FAT:

1 tablespoon butter

AROMATIC:

2 medium garlic cloves, minced

SPICE AND HERB:

½ teaspoon powdered ginger

1 tablespoon minced fresh parsley leaves

Follow the Steam/Sautéed Vegetables recipe (page 204), adding the garlic and ginger with the squash and stirring in the parsley once the squash starts to sauté.

Steam/Sautéed Turnips with Bacon and Black Pepper

To render 1 tablespoon of bacon fat, fry 2 to 3 slices of bacon, cut into small dice, until crisp in the Dutch oven or skillet you will be using to cook the turnips. Remove the bacon with a slotted spoon, reserving it to sprinkle over the sautéing turnips, if desired. Of course, butter can be substituted for the bacon fat. Larger yellow turnips (rutabagas) can be substituted for the white turnips.

VEGETABLE:

1 pound small white turnips, peeled and cut into 1-inch chunks

FAT:

1 tablespoon bacon fat

AROMATIC:

2 garlic cloves, minced

Follow the Steam/Sautéed Vegetables recipe (page 204), adding the garlic with the turnips, seasoning with an extra grind or two of black pepper.

at-a-glance

STEAM/SAUTÉED VEGETABLES

- Bring water, fat, salt, and prepared vegetable to a boil in a Dutch oven or a large deep skillet.
- Cover and steam over medium-high heat until vegetables are brightly colored and just tender.
- Remove lid and continue to cook until liquid evaporates.
- Sauté to intensify flavors.

garlic swiss chard
beet greens zest
bright spinach

Steam/Sautéed Tender Greens

The same cooking method works for tender greens too.

Just leave out the water and steam/sauté until cooked through.

For me, there are two types of greens. Kale, turnips, collards, broccoli rabe, and mustard greens are tough, assertively flavored greens, while spinach, Swiss chard, and beet greens are mild and tender.

Unlike mild greens, which cook quickly, the more assertive greens must be shallow-blanched before sautéing to remove some of their bitterness. Unless I'm using them to make pasta with vegetables (see page 90), I usually reserve the more assertively flavored greens for weekend dinners (with pork roast there's nothing better).

Spinach, Swiss chard, and beet greens, however, are a different story. Once cleaned and stemmed, these mild, tender greens cook in just five to seven minutes. My method for cooking them? As I do with the other vegetables in this chapter, I steam/sauté them.

To steam/sauté tender greens, place two pounds of cleaned spinach, Swiss chard, or beet greens in a large deep skillet, along with a little fat (butter, olive oil, or bacon fat) and seasonings (garlic almost always). Cook the greens, covered, over medium-high heat until they wilt, three to five minutes. Uncover the skillet, and continue to cook until most of the liquid evaporates.

There are two small differences between steam/sautéing vegetables and steam/sautéing greens. First, since tender greens are so moist, there's no need to add the 1/4 cup of water to the pan. Second, use a large, deep skillet to steam/sauté the greens. You need a wide surface area so that the liquid evaporates as quickly as possible, and the skillet should be deep enough to hold two pounds of uncooked greens.

If cooking tender greens for more than four, use two skillets or cook them in batches. Twice the amount of greens in the same pan means twice the amount of liquid to evaporate, resulting in overcooked greens.

Although they cook about the same, there are different stemming techniques, depending on the variety and maturity of the green.

- For large, mature spinach and beet greens, hold each leaf between the thumb and index finger of one hand while pulling back the stem with the other.
- For young spinach and beet greens, hold a bunch by the root, leaf end down, and pinch the leaf from the stem.
- For Swiss chard, slash down both sides of each leaf with a sharp knife. Coarse-chop the washed leaves.

Steam/Sautéed Tender Greens
(Spinach, Swiss Chard, and Beet Greens)

1 tablespoon fat (extra-virgin olive oil, vegetable oil, butter, or bacon fat)

½ teaspoon salt

2 to 3 garlic cloves, minced

2 pounds fresh spinach, Swiss chard, or beet greens (or 20-ounces pack-

aged fresh spinach), stemmed and rinsed

Spices and/or dried/fresh herbs, and/or flavorings (optional)

Ground black pepper

1. Combine the fat, salt, garlic, the prepared greens, spices, or dried herbs in a large deep skillet or Dutch oven. Cover and steam over medium-high heat until the greens are wilted and brightly colored, about 5 minutes.

2. Remove the lid and continue to cook until the liquid evaporates, about 2 minutes longer. Add optional fresh herbs. Adjust the seasonings, including pepper to taste. Serve.

Steam/Sautéed Tender Greens with Bacon and Balsamic Vinegar

To render 1 tablespoon of bacon fat, fry 2 to 3 slices of bacon, cut into small dice, until crisp, in the skillet you will be using to cook the greens. Remove bacon with a slotted spoon, reserving it to sprinkle over the cooked greens, if desired.

FAT:

1 tablespoon bacon fat

FLAVORING:

1 tablespoon balsamic vinegar

Follow the Steam/Sautéed Tender Greens recipe, adding the vinegar once the liquid has evaporated.

Steam/Sautéed Tender Greens with Garlic and Red Pepper

FAT:
1 tablespoon extra-virgin olive oil

FLAVORING:
½ teaspoon hot red pepper flakes

Follow the Steam/Sautéed Tender Greens recipe (page 217), adding garlic and red pepper flakes with the greens.

Steam/Sautéed Tender Greens with Butter and Nutmeg

FAT:
1 tablespoon butter

FLAVORING:
¼ teaspoon grated nutmeg

Follow the Steam/Sautéed Tender Greens recipe (page 217), stirring in the nutmeg once the liquid has evaporated.

Steam/Sautéed Tender Greens with Lemon and Garlic

If you don't have time to grate the zest, simply serve the spinach with lemon wedges.

FAT:
1 tablespoon butter

FLAVORING:
1 teaspoon zest and 1 tablespoon juice from a small lemon

Follow the Steam/Sautéed Tender Greens recipe (page 217), adding the garlic along with the greens and lemon juice and zest once the liquid has evaporated.

Steam/Sautéed Tender Greens with Raisins and Almonds

If almonds are not already toasted, toast them over medium heat in the skillet you will be using to cook the greens, removing them from the pan before adding the greens.

FAT:

1 tablespoon butter

FLAVORINGS:

¼ cup golden raisins

3 tablespoons toasted slivered almonds

Follow the Steam/Sautéed Tender Greens recipe (page 217), adding the raisins with the garlic and greens. Stir in the almonds once the liquid has evaporated.

at-a-glance

STEAM/SAUTÉED GREENS

- Place fat, salt, and prepared greens in a large deep skillet.
- Cover and steam over medium-high heat until the vegetables are brightly colored and wilted.
- Remove the lid and continue to cook until most of the liquid evaporates.

roast mashed bake
Yukon gold butter
Idahos grate

One Potato, Two Potato, Three Potato, Four

You can roast, bake, or mash them, or make a cake of spuds.

Just remember that fat, salt, and pepper are a potato's best buds.

We've all heard we should eat like royalty at breakfast, nobility at lunch, and paupers at dinner. And from some diet gurus, we've been told that dinner should consist of either meat or starch with vegetables. Never both.

When serving dinner at our house, I ignore both bits of culinary advice. Dinner for me is not just one more fueling opportunity, it's our family meal. I like to make it special, and we eat a royal dinner as often as possible.

There are exceptions, of course, but if I make sautéed chicken cutlets, seared salmon or pork tenderloin, the plate just usually feels a little empty without starch, and potatoes are among our favorite.

I make rich, luxurious potato dishes like potato gratin or pommes Anna for special dinners, but there's no time for this during the week. My supper potato repertoire consists of four techniques—one is especially quick; all are virtually effortless.

THE CAKE

When I need quick, I think potato pancake. The ingredient list is short—grated potatoes, butter, salt, and pepper. And, since the potatoes are grated and there's no oven to preheat or large quantity of water to boil, cooking time is dramatically reduced. In fact, I can have a small crisp potato cake on a dinner plate in less than fifteen minutes.

If making a potato cake for two, reach for a small *nonstick* skillet (measuring eight inches across the top). When it's for four, grab a 10-inch nonstick skillet. For six to eight, choose a large, 12-inch nonstick skillet. Put about 1½ teaspoons of butter per potato in the cold skillet, setting it over low heat so that the butter slowly melts and turns a nutty brown. If put in a hot skillet, the butter always sputters, spits, and burns.

As the skillet heats and the butter melts, prepare the potatoes, figuring on one medium potato per person. High- and medium-starch potatoes such as Idaho and Yukon Gold make great cakes, but I've also made fine cakes out of red boiling potatoes. You can peel them or not, depending on whether you have time. If not, scrub and rinse them.

I use the food processor for big grating jobs, but for four potatoes or less I use the large holes of a box grater. So that they crisp up and brown more quickly, squeeze as much liquid as possible from the grated potatoes. For years I used either a dish towel or paper towels to accomplish the job. I never liked using a towel because the potato starch always turned it a dirty brown. Paper towels worked better until the night I served a potato cake with a paper towel running through the center. Now I use a salad spinner to remove the potato liquid. Salt and pepper the potatoes right in the spinner. Seasoning them once they're in the skillet can result in a potato cake that is heavily seasoned in one spot and bland in another. If you don't have a salad spinner, just squeeze the liquid from the potatoes by small handfuls.

When you're a minute or two from cooking, increase the heat to a strong medium. When the milk solids from the butter have turned golden brown and smell nutty, swirl the butter around the bottom and up the sides of the pan. Add the potatoes, pressing on them with a spatula to make a compact cake. When the potatoes turn golden brown on the bottom, invert the cake onto a plate and put another 1 teaspoon of butter per potato to the skillet, quickly sliding the cake back into the pan as soon as the butter melts. The cake will continue to cook through and turn golden brown on the other side. As long as it is turned occasionally, the potato cake can sit in the pan over low heat for half an hour or more.

Crisp Potato Cake for 4

You can use any size potatoes you've got as long as they add up to the approximate weight called for in each recipe.

4 small baking potatoes (or about 1 pound of potatoes), scrubbed (or peeled, if desired) and grated on the large holes of a box grater

3 tablespoons butter

1/2 teaspoon salt

Ground black pepper

1. Heat 2 tablespoons of butter over low heat in a skillet measuring 10 inches across the top. While the butter heats, grate the potatoes. Working quickly, place the grated potatoes in a salad spinner and extract as much liquid as possible. While they are still in the spinner, sprinkle potatoes with salt and pepper to taste; toss to distribute evenly. Alternatively, working with a small handful at a time, squeeze as much liquid from the potatoes as possible.

2. A minute or two before you start cooking, increase the heat to a strong medium. Put the potatoes in the pan, pressing with the fingertips or a metal spatula to form a flat cake. Cook until the bottom of the cake is golden brown and crisp, about 7 to 8 minutes. Place a small plate over the pan and invert the cake onto the plate. Add the remaining tablespoon of butter to the pan, sliding the cake back into the pan as soon as the butter melts. Continue to cook until golden brown on the remaining side, about 7 to 8 minutes longer. Reduce heat to low and continue to cook until cake bottom is crisp, about 2 minutes longer. Cut into 4 or 8 wedges and serve immediately.

Crisp Potato Cake for 2

2 small baking potatoes (or about 8 ounces of potatoes), scrubbed (or peeled, if desired) and grated on the large holes of a box grater

1 1/2 tablespoons butter

1/4 teaspoon salt

Ground black pepper

Follow the recipe for Crisp Potato Cake for 4, melting about 1 tablespoon of butter in an 8-inch skillet and decreasing cooking time on the first side of the cake to 4 minutes. Melt the remaining 1/2 tablespoon of butter in the pan once the cake has been removed and inverted on a plate. Return the cake to the pan and continue cooking 4 minutes on the second side. Cut into 4 wedges.

Crisp Potato Cake for 8

8 small baking potatoes (or about 2 pounds of potatoes) scrubbed (or peeled, if desired) and grated in the food processor or on the large holes of a box grater

6 tablespoons butter

1 teaspoon salt

Ground black pepper

Follow the recipe for Crisp Potato Cake for 4, melting 4 tablespoons of butter in a 12-inch skillet and increasing the cooking time on the first side of the cake to 10 minutes. Melt 2 tablespoons of butter in the pan once the cake has been removed to a plate; increase the cooking time to 10 minutes on the second side. Cut into 8 or 16 wedges.

at-a-glance

CRISP POTATO CAKE

- **Figuring about 1½ teaspoons for each small potato, heat butter over low heat in a skillet. Then spin or squeeze liquid from potatotes.**
- **Season potatoes with salt and pepper to taste; toss to distribute evenly.**
- **Increase the heat to a strong medium. Put the potatoes in the pan, pressing on them to form a flat cake.**
- **Cook until the cake bottom is golden brown and crisp.**
- **Invert cake onto a plate.**
- **Add a little more butter to the pan; slide the cake back in. Continue to cook until golden brown on the remaining side.**
- **Reduce the heat to low and continue to cook until the cake bottom is crisp.**

THE BAKE

When I need easy, I bake (or roast, see page 227). To bake a potato quickly, adjust the oven rack to the upper middle position and start preheating the oven to 450 degrees.

Reduce baking time by choosing small (about 6 ounces each) russets. The smaller the potato, the shorter the baking time. Don't wait for the oven to finish preheating. After rinsing the potatoes and giving each one a couple of pricks, set them directly on the oven rack. Cooked this way, small potatoes are done in about 40 minutes. Not bad for turning on the stove and lifting up the faucet lever.

Over the years I've tried cutting short the baking time, but my attempts have not been successful. Some suggest par-cooking the potatoes in the microwave, then finishing them in a hot oven. I find that brief par-cooking doesn't save significant time. Longer par-cooking results in potatoes with gummy flesh and soft, leathery skin.

Since you're heating an entire oven for just four potatoes, try to roast a chicken, or a small roast like a rib-end pork loin or the butt end of beef tenderloin. All thrive in a hot oven and should be done about the same time as the potatoes. At the very least, double the number of potatoes so that you can have home fries a few meals down the road.

at-a-glance

CARE-FREE BAKED POTATOES

- Adjust the oven rack to the upper middle position and heat the oven to 450 degrees. Scrub small baking potatoes, and prick their skins. Place them directly on the rack in the preheating oven.

- Bake until skins are crisp and potatoes are tender, about 40 minutes.

THE MASH

I'm not sure whether it's pulling out the food mill or heating up the milk, but making real mashed potatoes for a weeknight dinner is one step beyond the possible for me. I used to serve boiled potatoes, leaving the mashing, buttering, and seasoning for those at the table. Then I realized that with just a minute's more effort in the kitchen, I could have a dish almost as satisfying as real mashed potatoes.

These potatoes are nothing more than fork-mashed boiled potatoes moistened with potato cooking liquid, enriched with butter, and seasoned with salt and pepper. Because of their smooth creamy texture, red boiling potatoes are best for this dish. Choose small potatoes of similar size so that they cook quickly and evenly, rinse, then place them in a large enough saucepan so that they fit in a single layer with a little wiggle room. After adding water to cover the potatoes, put a lid on the pan and bring them to a boil and simmer them until a wooden or metal skewer inserted into the potato can be removed with no resistance. Small red boiling potatoes cook in about 25 minutes while the little new potatoes are done in 15 to 20 minutes.

Use the same testing skewer to fish the potatoes from the boiling water and transfer them to a medium bowl. Without picking up the potatoes, slash them in half with a paring knife, then add some of the potato cooking liquid, a chunk of butter, and a generous sprinkling of salt and pepper. Switch to a table fork and mash the potatoes into a lumpy mass. I like these potatoes lumpy, and I find a potato masher makes them too smooth.

If you've got time, chop a little parsley and sprinkle it over the potatoes along with another final grind of coarse black pepper. I tend to keep this potato dish simple, but any compatible ingredient could be stirred in—bacon, a mix of fresh herbs, grated cheese, roasted garlic, or pesto. I usually serve this dish as an accompaniment, but with a salad, it easily makes a meal.

The Very Simplest Mashed Potatoes

Since the potatoes are boiled whole, select small red potatoes or new red potatoes to reduce cooking time.

1½ pounds small red potatoes (8 small red potatoes or 12 new potatoes)

4 tablespoons (½ stick) room-temperature butter, cut into 4 pieces

Salt and ground black pepper

Rough-chopped fresh parsley (optional)

1. Place the potatoes in a large saucepan; cover with water. Cover and bring to a boil, then simmer until a skewer inserted into the potato can be removed with no resistance, 25 to 30 minutes for medium potatoes or 15 to 20 minutes for new potatoes.

2. Reserve ¼ cup of the cooking liquid and set aside. Use the testing skewer to transfer the cooked potatoes to a large shallow bowl. Without picking them up, slash potatoes in half with a paring knife; add the butter and reserved potato water and a generous sprinkling of salt and pepper. Roughly crush potatoes with a table fork. Adjust the seasonings, stirring in optional parsley. Serve immediately.

at-a-glance

THE VERY SIMPLEST MASHED POTATOES

- Boil potatoes until tender; drain, reserving ¼ cup cooking liquid.
- Slash the hot potatoes with a paring knife.
- Add butter, reserved potato water, and a generous sprinkling of salt and pepper.
- Roughly crush potatoes with a fork.

THE ROAST

I grew up eating a dish my mom called simply "potatoes and onions." To make it, she placed a whole sliced potato on a piece of foil, sticking a piece of onion between each potato slice. Before sealing and baking them, she nestled in three or four thin pats of butter and salted and peppered them generously. If baked long enough in a hot oven, the potatoes and onions eventually caramelized on the bottom.

I continued to make this potato dish as an adult until I came across Jacques Pépin's roasted potatoes and onions. After trying the recipe in his book *Cooking with Claudine* I haven't looked back.

His roasted potatoes and onions have all the flavor of the dish of my youth, but with even less effort. To make it, start by adjusting the oven rack to the lowest position and heating the oven to 425 degrees. Drizzle a little olive oil into an 18- by 12-inch jelly roll pan, or other shallow roasting pan, and set the pan in the preheating oven.

With the oven and pan heating, select enough potatoes and onions to fill the pan, removing the outside papery skins from the onions and scrubbing the potatoes, but peeling neither vegetable. After halving the potatoes and onions, toss them in a little olive oil, sprinkle them generously with salt, and place them cut side down on the pan.

As they roast on the oven's bottom rack, their cut sides brown while the potatoes and onions cook. No stirring, no turning. In 30 to 40 minutes, the potatoes are golden brown on the outside, soft and creamy on the inside.

Any potato roasts well, but remember to cut russets lengthwise. The larger the cut surface, the larger the area that browns.

Roasted Potatoes and Onions

I never roast less than a full roasting pan of potatoes and onions. It's so simple and the leftover vegetables are so good, why make any less? I often sprinkle the cut and salted potatoes with a dried herb—thyme or herbs de Provence—before placing them in the roasting pan. Drizzle the roasted onions with a little balsamic vinegar, if you like.

8 medium red potatoes or 12 new potatoes, scrubbed and halved

6 to 8 medium yellow onions, excess papery skin removed and onions halved (not necessary to peel)

¼ cup oil, plus extra for pan

Salt and ground black pepper

1. Adjust an oven rack to the lowest position and heat the oven to 425 degrees. Coat the bottom of an 18- by 12-inch jelly roll pan or other similar-size shallow pan with olive oil; place in the preheating oven.

2. Toss the potatoes with 2 tablespoons of oil and a generous sprinkling of salt; place, cut side down, on the roasting pan. Toss the onions with the remaining 2 tablespoons of oil and a generous sprinkling of salt; place, cut side down, on the roasting pan. Roast until potatoes and onions are tender and cut surfaces are a rich golden brown, 30 to 35 minutes. Adjust seasonings, including pepper. Serve.

at-a-glance

ROASTED POTATOES AND ONIONS

- Adjust an oven rack to the lowest position and heat the oven to 425 degrees.
- Coat a shallow roasting pan with olive oil; place in the preheating oven.
- Toss potatoes and onions with olive oil and a generous sprinkling of salt.
- Place, cut side down, on the roasting pan.
- Roast until potatoes and onions are tender and cut surfaces are a rich golden brown.

Simple Ways with Simple Sides

If you know the ratio of starch to liquid—it's often one to two or four—

And if you can tell when the starch is done, you need know nothing more.

In addition to my four potato dishes (see One Potato, Two Potato, Three Potato, Four), I rely on four quick-cooking ingredients to get me through the week—white rice, orzo, instant polenta, and couscous. Why these particular starches? They're quick. While brown and wild rice need forty-five minutes to soften, white rice cooks in just twenty minutes. Traditional polenta and risotto cook at a snail's pace and require almost constant stirring. In contrast, instant polenta cooks as quickly as its name implies, and orzo, risotto's pasta cousin, cooks to a creamy state in just eight minutes—no stirring required. Traditional couscous is a multi-stepped weekend cooking project. Instant couscous swells and softens in just five minutes.

Even bringing the cooking water to a boil, they cook in under twenty-five minutes—couscous and instant polenta in less than ten. Their shelf life is practically indefinite, so there's no reason not to have a few packages of each variety on the pantry shelf.

RICE

My mom never served rice without gravy. She always cooked it in water that was flavored with a little bit of salt and a little pat of butter. Her cooked rice was pleasantly bland and clumpy, perfect for the ladleful of rich gravy she had made from fried chicken or pot roast drippings.

I don't make pot roast or fried chicken during the week, so unless I'm making a stir-fry, bland, sticky rice isn't a very satisfying side dish. I could buy the boxes of commercially flavored rices, but I don't care much for their dehydrated vegetable flakes and artificial seasonings. I prefer to take an extra minute or two during dinner preparation to season the rice myself.

I often make a rice pilaf when I serve sautéed chicken breasts or fish, and the flavoring for my rice pilaf could be as simple as a half an onion and canned chicken broth.

To make rice pilaf, start by heating a tablespoon each of butter and olive oil in a medium saucepan over medium heat. You can use less fat, but make sure there's at least enough so that the onion is not dry as it sautés. While the butter and oil heat, chop half an onion or shallot, dropping it into the pan as soon as it's chopped.

While the onion sautés, measure the rice and open the chicken broth. When I buy rice, I pick up standard long-grain rice. I like the risotto-like way the cooked grains hold together. When my husband shops, he selects "converted" rice (the common brand is Uncle Ben's), which has undergone a steam-pressure process that causes its grains to harden and its starch to gelatinize, so that the grains of rice stay separate once cooked. Although I don't serve this treated rice with stir-fry, either style is fine for pilafs.

Once the onion has sautéed until softened, stir in the rice, adding canned chicken broth (two parts broth to one part rice). As the broth comes to a simmer, cover the pan and let the rice cook until the broth is absorbed, about twenty minutes.

If you have time, you can sauté an extra vegetable along with the onion—bell peppers, mushrooms, or garlic—but most often, I serve the rice as is or stir in simple flavorings, such as Parmesan cheese or fresh herbs once the rice is done.

My mother's rice is actually perfect for stir-fries. Like rich, flavorful gravy, stir-fry needs a simple, clean partner. My steamed rice ingredient list is short—just rice and water. I don't season or enrich the rice, knowing that the stir-fry and soy sauce will flavor it later.

To make steamed rice, start by rinsing the rice in the cooking pot, running in cold water and giving it a stir with your fingers. The water will immediately turn cloudy as the rice settles. Tilt the pot and drain out the water, being careful to keep the rice in the pot. Repeat the rinsing until the water is almost clear as the rice is stirred, five or six rinses. Drain it one final time, then add the appropriate amount of cooking water based on the quantity of rice. Since the rice has already absorbed water in the rinsing process, the standard two-to-one rice ratio does not work (see recipe for exact proportions). Cover the pot, bring the water to boil, reduce the heat, then simmer until most of the liquid is absorbed, about fifteen minutes. Turn off the heat and let the rice sit for ten minutes and up to half an hour.

I never make the exact amount of steamed rice I need for the night. I always double it so that a few days down the road, I've got a head start on a fried rice meal (see page 139).

Simple Rice Pilaf

1 tablespoon butter

1 tablespoon olive oil

½ small onion or 1 medium shallot, minced

Flavorings (optional; see below)

1 cup long-grain rice

2 cups canned low-sodium chicken broth or a mix of chicken broth and other liquids to equal 2 cups (see individual recipes)

Salt and pepper, to taste

1. Heat the butter and oil in a medium (2- to 3-quart) saucepan over medium-high heat. Add the onion and optional flavorings that need to be sautéed as soon as they are chopped; sauté until softened, 3 to 4 minutes.

2. Add the rice; stir to coat. Add broth (or a mix of broth and other liquid), bring to a simmer; reduce the heat to low and simmer until the broth is absorbed and rice is just tender, about 20 minutes. Stir in optional flavorings. Adjust seasonings, adding salt and pepper to taste. Serve.

Parmesan–Black Pepper Pilaf

LIQUID:

2 cups low-sodium chicken broth

FLAVORINGS:

6 tablespoons grated Parmesan cheese

2 teaspoons coarse-ground black pepper

Follow the Simple Rice Pilaf recipe, using all chicken broth and stirring Parmesan and pepper into the finished rice.

Lemon Rice Pilaf

LIQUID:

1¾ cups low-sodium chicken broth

¼ cup lemon juice

FLAVORINGS:

1 to 2 teaspoons lemon zest

Follow the Simple Rice Pilaf recipe, using the chicken broth and lemon juice and stirring zest into the finished rice.

Coconut Rice Pilaf

LIQUID:

1 cup coconut milk

1 cup low-sodium chicken broth

FLAVORINGS:

1 scallion, sliced thin

Follow the Simple Rice Pilaf recipe, using the coconut milk and chicken broth and stirring scallions into the finished rice.

Spanish Rice Pilaf

LIQUID:

2 cups low-sodium chicken broth

FLAVORINGS:

1 garlic clove, minced

½ medium red bell pepper, cut into ¼-inch dice

1 tablespoon minced fresh parsley leaves

Follow the Simple Rice Pilaf recipe, using all chicken broth, sautéing the garlic and bell pepper along with the onion, and stirring the minced parsley into the cooked rice.

Mushroom Rice Pilaf

LIQUID:

2 cups low-sodium chicken broth

FLAVORINGS:

8 ounces sliced mushrooms

Follow the Simple Rice Pilaf recipe (page 232), using all chicken broth and sautéing the mushrooms along with the onion until their liquid evaporates.

Saffron Rice Pilaf

LIQUID:

2 cups low-sodium chicken broth

FLAVORINGS:

2 generous pinches saffron threads

Follow the Simple Rice Pilaf recipe (page 232), using all chicken broth, and stirring saffron into the sautéing onion.

at-a-glance

SIMPLE RICE PILAF

- Heat butter and oil in a saucepan over medium-high heat.
- Sauté onions (and optional flavorings that need to be sautéed) until tender.
- Add rice; stir to coat.
- Remembering that pilaf is a 2-parts-liquid-to-1-part-rice ratio, add liquid, bring to a simmer; reduce heat to low and simmer until stock has absorbed and rice is just tender. Stir in optional flavorings.

Simple Steamed Rice for Stir-Fry and Fried Rice

When I make this rice, I usually double the recipe, using 4 cups of rice and 5½ cups of water and cooking it in a Dutch oven. I serve it with a stir-fry for one meal. A couple of days down the road, I use the leftovers to make fried rice.

> 2 cups long-grain or medium-grain white
> rice (do not use "converted" rice, such as
> Uncle Ben's, here)

1. Measure the rice into a large saucepan. Add water to cover, stirring rice with your hands until the water becomes cloudy. Carefully pour the water from the saucepan, making sure rice stays in the pan. Repeat, covering rice with water, rinsing, and pouring water from the pan, until the water is more or less clear when rice is stirred, 5 to 6 rinses.

2. Add 3 cups of water to the rinsed and drained rice; cover and bring to a boil. Reduce the heat and simmer for 15 minutes. Remove from the heat and let the rice stand, covered, 10 to 15 minutes longer.

at-a-glance

STEAMED RICE

- Rinse and drain rice several times in a saucepan until the water is more or less clear when rice is stirred.

- Add water (3 cups water for 2 cups of rice or 5½ cups water for 4 cups of rice), cover, and bring to a boil. Reduce heat and simmer for 15 minutes.

- Remove from heat and let rice stand, covered, 10 to 15 minutes longer.

ORZO

Orzo may be all pasta but it looks like the offspring of a rigatoni-rice affair. That it can be cooked like pasta or rice is one more confirmation that orzo is a wonderful hybrid of the two.

I always cooked orzo like any other pasta, boiling it in a large quantity of water and draining it when tender. I stumbled upon a better method, however, the morning one of my daughters asked if I would make orzo for her school lunch. To make a single lunch-size portion, I heated up just a quart of water.

Since I was making breakfast at the same time, I decided I'd kill two birds with one stone and serve orzo for breakfast as well. Rather than add more water to the pot to compensate for the additional orzo, I dumped half a one-pound bag of orzo into the quart of water, gave it a stir, set the lid ajar, and hoped for the best.

I half expected to return to a sticky gummy mess, but when I removed the lid, I observed that the orzo had swelled beautifully, and that the remaining liquid in the pot, thickened by the released starch, had turned saucy. When I stirred in a little butter and Parmesan cheese I got a dish akin to risotto. As we ate our breakfast that morning, we all agreed it was the best orzo we'd ever eaten.

That's how I cook orzo now. I don't have to wait for a large quantity of water to come to a boil. I don't have the extra step of draining and returning the pasta to the pot for flavoring. As soon as the orzo is done, I stir in my flavorings and serve it straight from the pot.

Making a half bag of orzo is more than I need as a side dish for four people, but there's enough left over for someone's lunch the next day. Plus, I don't end up with big boxes and bags of pasta in the pantry, only to find a quarter cup of pasta at the very bottom. Any of the following orzo recipes could be doubled and served as a main course for four to six people.

Simple Orzo

½ pound orzo (1⅓ cups)

Salt

2 tablespoons fat (olive oil or butter)

6 tablespoons grated Parmesan cheese

Ground black pepper

Flavorings (optional; see below)

Bring 1 quart of water to boil in a large saucepan. Add 1 teaspoon of salt and the orzo. Boil until orzo is tender and has absorbed the cooking liquid, 8 to 9 minutes. Stir in the fat, Parmesan, pepper to taste, and optional flavorings. Adjust seasoning. Serve.

Orzo with Lemon and Parsley

For a less rich-tasting side dish, leave out the Parmesan cheese.

FAT:

2 tablespoons butter

FLAVORINGS:

1½ teaspoons zest and ½ teaspoon juice from a lemon

2 tablespoons minced fresh parsley leaves

Follow the Simple Orzo recipe, stirring in lemon zest, juice, and parsley along with the butter and Parmesan.

Orzo with Blue Cheese and Walnuts

FAT:

2 tablespoons butter

FLAVORINGS:

¼ cup crumbled blue cheese

2 tablespoons chopped toasted walnuts

Follow the Simple Orzo recipe, stirring in blue cheese and walnuts along with the butter and Parmesan.

Orzo with Basil and Pine Nuts

This simple variation tastes like you've tossed it with fresh pesto—without all the work.

FAT:

2 tablespoons butter

FLAVORINGS:

2 tablespoons minced fresh basil leaves

2 tablespoons toasted pine nuts

Follow the Simple Orzo recipe (page 237), stirring in basil and pine nuts along with the butter and Parmesan.

Orzo with Tomatoes, Feta, and Olives

FAT:

2 tablespoons olive oil

FLAVORINGS:

3 canned tomatoes, chopped and drained

8 Kalamata olives, pitted and chopped coarse

¼ cup crumbled feta cheese

Follow the Simple Orzo recipe (page 237), stirring tomatoes, olives, and feta cheese into the orzo along with the oil and Parmesan.

Orzo with Roasted Peppers and Basil

FAT:

2 tablespoons olive oil

FLAVORINGS:

1 jarred roasted red pepper, cut into
1/4-inch dice

2 tablespoons minced fresh basil
leaves

Follow the Simple Orzo recipe (page 237), stirring in the pepper and basil along with the oil and Parmesan.

Orzo with Spinach and Parmesan

FAT:

2 tablespoons butter

FLAVORING:

2 cups packed fresh spinach, stemmed
and washed

Follow the Simple Orzo recipe (page 237), stirring in spinach with the butter and Parmesan. Cook until wilted, 2 to 3 minutes longer.

at-a-glance

SIMPLE ORZO

- Bring 1 quart water to a boil in a large saucepan.
- Remembering the ratio of 1/2 pound orzo to 1 quart of water, add 1 teaspoon salt and the orzo to boiling water.
- Boil until orzo is tender and has absorbed the cooking liquid.
- Stir in fat, Parmesan, pepper to taste, and optional flavorings.

POLENTA

We all love sausage in our family, but since my daughters don't eat red meat, I usually cook turkey sausage for them and pork sausage for my husband and me. Regardless of our different meat tastes, we all agree that we like our sausage served on a big mound of polenta and doused with a simple tomato sauce.

Unfortunately, traditional polenta is out of the question for us during the week. To make it, one must heat salted water, slowly stirring in the ground corn once the water comes to a simmer. After that, it's nonstop stirring for thirty to forty-five minutes. There are other methods that either short-cut the cooking process or eliminate much of the stirring by baking it in the oven, slow-cooking it in a double boiler, quick-cooking it in the microwave, or starting it in cold water.

For weekend cooking, I've tried and liked many of the alternative cooking methods, especially the ones that reduce stirring time. But for a quick supper, I admit to loving instant polenta.

The biggest problem with making instant polenta is trying to interpret package instructions. Many brands of instant polenta are imported from Italy, and although cooking instructions have been translated into English, measurements are still in liters. To exacerbate the problem, many polenta companies only give measurements for making the entire box. Others tell how much water to bring to a boil but fail to suggest how much polenta to add. Trying to interpret and calculate can result in polenta that is stiff, gloppy, and gummy.

When developing recipes for this book, however, I discovered that the secret of soft, creamy polenta is using a ratio of four parts water to one part instant polenta. Forget the directions on the back of the box. Instead, remember the proportions—four to one—for a pot of polenta so good you might even be tempted to serve it to guests.

Quick Polenta

You can hold polenta over very low heat for a few minutes, adding a little water if it starts to thicken.

1 cup instant polenta	**Ground black pepper**
½ teaspoon salt	**Flavorings (optional; see below)**
1 tablespoon butter	

Bring 4 cups (1 quart) of water to a boil over medium-high heat in a large saucepan or small Dutch oven. Add salt and, whisking constantly, add polenta in a thin, steady stream. Continue to whisk until the polenta thickens to a soft but not soupy consistency, about 1 to 2 minutes. Remove the pan from the heat and stir in butter, pepper to taste, and optional flavorings. Serve immediately.

Quick Polenta with Blue Cheese and Walnuts

FLAVORINGS:

¼ cup crumbled blue cheese

¼ cup toasted chopped walnuts

Follow the Quick Polenta recipe, stirring blue cheese into the cooked polenta and sprinkling 1 tablespoon of toasted chopped walnuts over each portion.

Quick Polenta with Fontina (or Baby Swiss) and Parmesan

FLAVORINGS:

1 cup coarse-grated fontina cheese

Grated Parmesan cheese

Follow the Quick Polenta recipe (page 241), stirring fontina into the cooked polenta and serving Parmesan cheese passed separately.

Quick Polenta with Corn

Since quick polenta lacks some of the real corn flavor of traditional polenta, I often boost it with frozen corn.

FLAVORINGS:

1 cup frozen corn, thawed

Grated Parmesan cheese

Follow the Quick Polenta recipe (page 241), stirring corn kernels into the cooked polenta and serving Parmesan cheese passed separately.

at-a-glance

QUICK POLENTA

- Remembering the ratio of 4 parts water to 1 part instant polenta, bring water to a boil over medium-high heat in a large saucepan or small Dutch oven.
- Add salt, then whisk in polenta in a thin, steady stream.
- Continue to whisk until polenta thickens to a soft, creamy texture.
- Stir in butter, pepper to taste, and optional flavorings. Serve immediately.

Couscous

I've made couscous the North African way. The process begins by rinsing the fine pasta in a colander, then transferring it to a large bowl to rehydrate for ten minutes. From there, the couscous is steamed a first time for ten minutes, then turned onto a large shallow pan, where the large clumps are broken up, spread, and sprinkled with additional water. Near serving time, the couscous is returned to the steamer to cook for a final twenty minutes.

This process does indeed produce the lightest, fluffiest couscous, extending a mere 2½ cups of the raw pasta into a miraculous twelve. When I want to make couscous right, I follow this technique. Unfortunately, this method does not fit into my weeknight time budget.

When making couscous for supper, follow the back-of-the-box couscous/liquid proportions. To make flavorful couscous, rehydrate the little pasta granules with chicken broth rather than water, and start, as if you were making a rice pilaf, by sautéing half an onion.

To speed up the process, heat the chicken broth in a Pyrex measuring cup in the microwave while the onion sautés. As soon as the couscous is stirred into the sautéing onion, add the hot stock, cover the pan, turn off the heat, and let it stand for a few minutes.

Fluff the couscous with a fork, stirring in a little parsley and additional flavorings if you like. Nut and dried fruit combinations are my favorite stir-ins, as evidenced in the recipes that follow. It's just that easy to make flavored couscous for supper.

Simple Couscous

1 tablespoon olive oil	¾ cup plain couscous
½ medium onion, cut into small dice	2 tablespoons minced fresh parsley leaves (optional)
1 cup low-sodium chicken broth	Flavorings (optional; see below)

1. Heat the oil in a medium saucepan over medium-high heat. Add the onion and sauté until softened, 2 to 3 minutes.

2. Meanwhile, microwave the broth on high heat in a 2-cup Pyrex measuring cup until piping hot, about 2 minutes.

3. Add couscous to the onion; stir to combine. Stir in the broth, cover, and turn off the heat. Let stand until the broth is completely absorbed, about 4 minutes. Stir in parsley with a fork and serve immediately.

Couscous with Apricots and Pistachios

FLAVORINGS:

10 dried apricots, cut into ¼-inch dice (½ cup)

2 tablespoons coarse-chopped pistachios

Follow the Simple Couscous recipe, stirring in the apricots and pistachios along with the parsley.

Couscous with Currants and Pine Nuts

FLAVORINGS:

½ cup currants or raisins

2 tablespoons toasted pine nuts

Follow the Simple Couscous recipe, stirring in currants and pine nuts along with the parsley.

Couscous with Dried Cranberries and Almonds

FLAVORINGS:

½ cup dried cranberries

2 tablespoons toasted sliced almonds

Follow the Simple Couscous recipe, stirring in cranberries and almonds along with the parsley.

at-a-glance

SIMPLE COUSCOUS

- Sauté onion in oil in a medium saucepan.
- Microwave broth until piping hot.
- Add couscous to onions; stir to combine.
- Stir in broth, cover, and turn off heat. Let stand until broth is completely absorbed.
- Stir in parsley and optional flavorings with a fork and serve immediately.

Spur-of-the-Moment Appetizers

Your appetizers can be great even if they're not planned—
Just forage through the kitchen for things you have on hand.

Whether appetizers are the main attraction or just the opener, they're important. Good hors d'oeuvres stimulate appetites, heighten senses, and generally make guests feel they're in for a good night. They don't have to be intricate, complicated, or time-consuming to be spectacular.

The evening dictates my hors d'oeuvre strategy. If I've invited friends over at the last minute (or if my husband and I have time to sit for a few minutes before dinner), I head for the refrigerator and forage for bits of cheese, cooked meats, olives, spreads, mustards, chutneys, and vegetables. I move to the pantry for nuts and breadsticks or crackers. I always keep a few loaves of French bread in the freezer, which can be sliced and baked into toast rounds in just a few minutes. Topped with a little tomato or cooked meat, fish, or cheese, they're quickly transformed into bruschetta or toasted canapés.

Vegetables such as cherry tomatoes, radishes, and celery hearts require minimal preparation and make almost instant hors d'oeuvres. Cans of chickpeas or white beans or a package of frozen green peas can be turned into a spread or dip in just a few minutes. With minimal effort and some pretty ordinary ingredients, it's not hard to quickly whet a few appetites.

The following are examples of the kinds of hors d'oeuvres I serve. Some can be made in no time; others require a little cooking time but are effortless. Most are made with kitchen staples or things I often have around. All are simple.

THE SIMPLEST

The following group of hors d'oeuvres are those I make with simple ingredients that require minimal preparation. When you shop, pick up a can of beans or a package of mixed nuts for the pantry. Keep a package of sausage or a little smoked salmon along with a loaf of bread in the freezer. Even ordinary grocery-store sharp cheddar cheese becomes special when hand-broken into small chunks, placed on a toast round or cracker, and topped with Branston pickle relish.

If you have time to doll the food up a bit, a tiny leaf of Italian parsley or a thin sliver of red onion makes the difference between a good hors d'oeuvre and a spectacular one.

When serving hors d'oeuvres to a larger, stand-up crowd, I've found that setting out a table of spreads and dips and platters of cheese doesn't work. Guests get caught up in conversation and can't get to the food. Plus balancing a drink and fiddling with food is just too much trouble. On those nights I make hors d'oeuvres that are easy to pass and easy to pick up. A sweet pea spread served with a basket of toasts for a party of six becomes sweet pea spread on toast rounds with crumbled bacon topping. A bowl of herbed yogurt cheese served with cucumber rounds becomes herbed yogurt cheese–topped cucumber rounds.

Warm White Bean Spread

*Makes about 1 1/4 cups
or enough for about
2 dozen toast rounds*

If serving this spread on toast rounds, pickled pink onions make the perfect garnish. To make the garnish, slice half a small red onion and place it in a small cup; drizzle with vinegar almost to cover. Let stand while making the bean spread, topping each finished toast round with a couple pieces of pickled onion. Even if you are serving the spread in a bowl, pickled onions can be served alongside as well.

1/4 cup olive oil

2 large garlic cloves, minced

1 tablespoon chopped fresh rosemary

1/4 teaspoon hot red pepper flakes

1 (19-ounce) can white beans, such as Great Northern or cannellini

Heat the oil along with the garlic, rosemary, and hot red pepper flakes in a large skillet. When the ingredients start to sizzle, add the beans. Coarsely mash the beans with a wooden spoon or potato masher. Transfer to a small bowl and serve with breadsticks, or serve on toast rounds (see note above).

Sweet Pea Spread with Bacon

Makes ³/₄ cup (enough for about 36 toast rounds)

If you have time, spread this green pea puree on toast rounds, garnishing each with the crumbled bacon bits. If not, simply transfer the spread to a serving bowl, sprinkle with the bacon bits, and serve with pita or bagel crisps.

3 slices bacon, cut into ¹/₄-inch pieces

2 garlic cloves, lightly crushed and peeled

1 cup frozen green peas, cooked following package instructions and drained

Fry the bacon along with the crushed garlic cloves in a medium skillet over medium heat until bacon is crisp, about 5 minutes. Transfer the bacon with a slotted spoon to a paper towel–lined plate; set aside. Combine the garlic and 2 tablespoons of bacon drippings, the cooked peas, and salt and pepper to taste in the workbowl of a food processor fitted with a steel blade. Process until puréed. With the machine still running, add 2 tablespoons of warm tap water to thin the mixture. Transfer to a small bowl and top with crumbled bacon or spread on toast rounds (see note above).

Potato Spread with Garlic, Lemon, and Olive Oil

Makes about 2 cups

This is the Greek spread skordalia (skor-dahl-YAH). I always have the ingredients for making this on hand. Baking potatoes in the microwave turns their skins leathery, but here the potato skins are removed after they are baked. The microwave cooks the potatoes in just 10 to 12 minutes, so if you prepare the other ingredients while the potatoes cook, this can be ready in about 15 minutes. Serve as a dip with toasted pita or savory bagel chips. Unlike sweet potatoes, which purée beautifully in the food processor, russets will turn gummy, so mash them with a fork, then switch to a small whisk when adding the chicken broth.

2 or 3 small to medium russet potatoes (about 12 ounces)

2 large garlic cloves, minced

1/2 teaspoon salt

Ground black pepper to taste

2 tablespoons juice from 1 lemon

1/3 cup olive oil

1/2 cup canned chicken broth

1. Cook the potatoes in the microwave on high power until soft, 10 to 12 minutes. Holding potatoes in an oven mitt, peel (or peel when cool enough to handle).

2. Mash the potatoes with the garlic, salt, pepper, lemon juice, and olive oil. Whisk in enough broth to make it a soft spread. Transfer to a serving bowl; serve at room temperature.

Spicy Sweet Potato Spread

Serve with sweet potato or root vegetable chips. Like the potatoes in the other spread, the sweet potatoes can be cooked in a microwave in just 10 to 12 minutes.

2 or 3 small to medium sweet potatoes (about 12 ounces)

2 large garlic cloves, minced

1 teaspoon hot red pepper sauce

1/2 teaspoon salt

1/4 teaspoon cayenne pepper

1/4 cup juice from 2 limes

2/3 cup olive oil

1/3 cup canned chicken broth

1. Cook the potatoes in the microwave on high power until soft, 10 to 12 minutes. Holding potatoes in an oven mitt, peel (or peel when cool enough to handle).

2. Process the potatoes, garlic, pepper sauce, salt, cayenne, and lime juice in the workbowl of the food processor fitted with the metal blade until puréed. With the machine running, gradually add oil through the feeder tube. Continue to process, adding broth through the feeder tube until the mixture is light and silky. Transfer to a serving bowl.

Hummus

For a little kick, add a pinch of cayenne pepper along with the salt. To serve, mound hummus on a large plate or platter, drizzle with a little olive oil if you like, and sprinkle with paprika. Serve with cucumber slices or pita and piquant black olives.

2 garlic cloves

¼ cup parsley leaves

1 (19-ounce) can chickpeas, drained and rinsed

2 tablespoons olive oil

2 tablespoons tahini (sesame paste)

¼ cup juice from 2 lemons

Salt and ground black pepper

Process the garlic and parsley in the workbowl of a food processor fitted with the steel blade. Add the chickpeas, olive oil, tahini, lemon juice, and salt and pepper to taste; continue to process until the mixture is completely puréed. Adjust seasoning; transfer to a bowl and serve at room temperature, or cover and refrigerate until ready to serve.

The Simplest Guacamole

Makes about 1 1/2 cups

2 medium avocados, peeled and pitted

2 tablespoons juice from a lime

Salt

Coarsely mash avocados with lime juice in a small bowl. Season to taste with salt. Serve immediately or cover with a sheet of plastic wrap pressed directly over the dip to keep it from discoloring.

Simple Cheese Quesadillas

Makes 4 dozen wedges (or serves 4 as a main course)

Served with a salad, quesadillas can move from appetizer to main course. Serve with All-Purpose Salsa (page 171) and The Simplest Guacamole.

8 (8-inch) flour tortillas

2 cups (8 ounces) grated Monterey Jack or Pepper Jack cheese

Additional ingredients such as 1/2 cup pimiento-stuffed olives, coarsely chopped; 2 scallions, sliced thin; 2 large roasted red peppers, cut into thin strips; 1/2 can refried beans

Heat the oven to 200 degrees. Place a large heavy-bottomed skillet, preferably cast iron, over high heat. When the skillet starts to smoke, reduce the heat to medium. Place a tortilla in the hot skillet and, working quickly, sprinkle on a portion of cheese (scant 1/2 cup) and optional extra ingredients. Top with another tortilla. When the tortilla bottom crisps up and turns a dark spotty brown (about 2 minutes), turn. Continue to cook until the remaining side turns a dark spotty brown, 1 to 2 minutes longer. Transfer to an oven rack while preparing the remaining quesadillas. Cut each into 12 wedges and serve immediately.

Roasted Mixed Nuts

If you can buy roasted, unsalted mixed nuts, simply heat the nuts in the oven before tossing them with the flavorings. This recipe is adapted from *The Union Square Café Cookbook* (HarperCollins, 1994).

4 cups (1¼ pounds) mixed nuts, such as cashews, pecans, almonds and Brazil nuts

2 teaspoons butter, melted

2 teaspoons brown sugar

2 teaspoons kosher salt

¼ teaspoon cayenne pepper

2 tablespoons fresh rosemary *or* 1 teaspoon chili, curry, or five-spice powder

1. Adjust an oven rack to the lower middle position and heat the oven to 350 degrees. Arrange the nuts in a single layer on a large shallow baking pan. Bake until nuts are fragrant and have deepened slightly in color, about 10 minutes.

2. Mix the butter, sugar, salt, cayenne, and optional rosemary or spice blend in a large bowl. Add the hot nuts; toss to coat with spiced butter. Turn the nuts back onto the baking pan; cool to room temperature. Serve. (Can be stored in an airtight container up to 1 month or frozen up to 3 months.)

Toast Rounds

Makes about 2 dozen

1 good-quality baguette, sliced ⅓ inch thick (and if it's the same size as my bread, you should get about 24 slices)

Adjust an oven rack to the upper middle position and heat the oven to 425 degrees. Arrange bread on a large wire rack. Set the wire rack on the oven rack and bake until toasts are crisp and golden brown on the outside and a little soft on the inside, 4 to 5 minutes.

Rare Roast Beef on Toast Rounds with Horseradish Cream

Makes about 2 dozen

Thin-sliced leftover beef tenderloin makes a great toast topping, but any thin-sliced beef, including rare roast beef from the deli, works well.

¼ cup sour cream

4 teaspoons prepared horseradish

1 recipe Toast Rounds

12 ounces thin-sliced rare roast beef

4 cornichons, sliced thin on the diagonal for garnish (optional)

Cracked black pepper

Mix the sour cream and horseradish in a small bowl; spread a portion of horseradish cream on each toast round. Arrange the toast rounds on a serving platter and mound a portion of roast beef on each round. Garnish with a cornichon slice, sprinkle with pepper, and serve.

Roast Pork on Toast Rounds with Mango Chutney

Makes about 2 dozen

Leftover pork roast is ideal for this hors d'oeuvre, but roast pork is also available at the deli section of most grocery stores. If not, sliced pork tenderloin is the perfect size for topping toasts. To cook, heat a medium (10-inch) skillet over high heat. Place a tenderloin that has been oiled, salted, and peppered in the skillet. Cook, turning occasionally, until the meat reaches an internal temperature of 140 degrees, about 20 minutes.

Dijon mustard

1 recipe Toast Rounds (page 255)

12 ounces thin-sliced roast pork

2 tablespoons prepared chutney such as Major Grey's

Small pieces of flat parsley leaves for garnish (optional)

Lightly spread mustard on each toast round. Arrange the rounds on a serving platter. Top with a portion of pork, spoon a small dollop of chutney on each piece of pork, garnish with parsley leaves if desired, and serve.

Smoked Turkey on Toast Rounds with Cranberry Chutney

Makes 2 dozen

Dijon mustard

1 recipe Toast Rounds (page 255)

12 ounces thin-sliced smoked or roast turkey

2 tablespoons prepared cranberry chutney or whole cranberry sauce

Flat-leaf parsley sprigs for garnish

Lightly spread mustard on each toast round. Arrange the rounds on a serving platter. Mound a portion of turkey on each toast round, spoon a small dollop of chutney or cranberry sauce on each piece of turkey, garnish with parsley leaves if desired, and serve.

Smoked Salmon Toasts

Makes 2 dozen

Garnish smoked salmon toasts with one of the following: capers, minced red onion, dill or parsley sprigs, chopped boiled egg, lemon zest, thin-sliced cornichons, snipped chives, or cracked black pepper.

4 tablespoons cream cheese or butter

1 tablespoon fine-grated zest from a lemon

Pepper to taste

1 recipe Toast Rounds (page 255) or 2 dozen triangles cut from black bread

4 ounces thin-sliced smoked salmon

Mix cream cheese or butter with lemon zest and pepper. Spread on toast rounds. Arrange the rounds on a serving platter and top with a portion of smoked salmon. Garnish as desired. Serve.

Smoked Trout with Horseradish Sour Cream

Makes 2 dozen

Garnish with one of the following: capers, minced red onion, dill or parsley sprigs, chopped boiled egg, lemon zest, sliced cornichons, snipped chives, or cracked black pepper.

4 tablespoons sour cream

1 tablespoon prepared horseradish, drained

Squeeze of lemon

Ground black pepper

1 recipe Toast Rounds (page 255)

4 ounces smoked trout or whitefish, broken into 2 dozen bite-size chunks

Mix sour cream, horseradish, lemon juice, and pepper to taste in a small bowl. Spread on toast rounds. Arrange the toasts on a serving platter and top with a portion of smoked trout or whitefish. Garnish as desired. Serve.

Sardine Toasts with Mustard Butter

Makes 2 dozen

Garnish with one of the following: capers, minced red onion, dill or parsley sprigs, chopped boiled egg, lemon zest, thin-sliced cornichons, snipped chives, or cracked black pepper.

4 tablespoons (½ stick) butter, at room temperature

1 tablespoon Dijon mustard

1 recipe Toast Rounds (page 255) or 2 dozen triangles cut from black bread

2 (3¾-ounce) cans boneless, skinless sardines or 4 ounces thin-sliced smoked bluefish

Mix the butter and mustard in a small bowl. Spread on toast rounds. Arrange the toasts on a serving platter and top with a portion of sardines or bluefish. Garnish as desired. Serve.

Goat Cheese Toasts

Makes 2 dozen

Goat Cheese Toasts can be garnished with any of the following: roasted red pepper strips (jarred are fine), dabs of green or black olive paste, oil-marinated sun-dried tomato pieces, a piece of black olive or green olive, snipped chives, minced fresh parsley or parsley sprigs, fresh basil leaves, tiny diced and salted tomato, or a drizzling of olive oil with a grinding of coarse-ground black pepper.

6 ounces mild goat cheese

1 recipe Toast Rounds (see page 255)

Spread a portion of goat cheese on each toast round. Arrange toasts on a serving platter. Garnish as suggested above. Serve.

Blue Cheese Toasts

Makes 2 dozen

Garnish these with toasted and chopped walnuts or hazelnuts or tiny-diced apple or pear. Or simmer ¼ cup dried cranberries in ¼ cup of port wine in a small saucepan until the port evaporates, 2 to 3 minutes. Garnish toasts with port-infused cranberries. A mild creamy cheese such as Brie, Camembert, or even cream cheese can be used.

4 ounces blue cheese, any variety   **1 recipe Toast Rounds (see page 255)**

Spread a portion of blue cheese on each toast round. Arrange toasts on a serving platter. Garnish as suggested above. Serve.

Cheddar Toasts

Makes 2 dozen

Whole-kernel rye can usually be found in the deli section of most grocery stores. Small cocktail-size rye breads can be substituted if the whole-kernel rye is unavailable.

3 slices whole-kernel rye or black rye bread, cut into 24 triangles, or 1 recipe Toast Rounds (page 255)

1 chunk (about 6 ounces) sharp cheddar cheese, broken by hand into rough-textured bite-size pieces

2 tablespoons Branston pickle relish or chopped pickled onion

Flat-leaf parsley sprigs for garnish (optional)

Set a portion of cheese on each triangle or toast round. Spoon a portion of pickle relish alongside each chunk of cheese, garnish with parsley, if desired, and serve immediately.

FRUIT AND VEGETABLE BASES

The following fruits and vegetables make sturdy, colorful bases for seafood and chicken salads, relishes, and cheeses.

Apples

To cut an apple for an appetizer base, core it whole (an apple corer is ideal), and slice it crosswise into thin circles, halving each circle. Toss with a little lemon juice to prevent discoloration. Top with bite-size pieces of goat cheese, chunks of blue cheese with toasted chopped walnuts or hazelnuts, chunks of sharp cheddar cheese, or Curried Chicken Salad with Raisins and Honey (page 201).

Pears

To cut a pear for an hors d'oeuvre base, halve, quarter, and core it, cut each quarter into 1/4-inch-thick slices, and toss with lemon juice to prevent discoloration. Top with goat cheese or blue cheese and a toasted walnut half or hazelnut, or foie gras.

Bibb Lettuce and Radicchio

After rinsing the lettuce, remove the core from each head and carefully separate the leaves. Fill with any of the Quick Chicken Salads (see pages 199–201).

Belgian Endive

To prepare an endive, trim away the base, carefully separating out the leaves. Continue to trim the base so that the spears separate easily. Split large outer leaves lengthwise; leave smaller inner leaves whole. Each head should yield about 2 dozen appetizers. Spoon one of the following fillings at the base of each spear: Quick Chicken Salad (page 199), or chunks of blue cheese sprinkled with toasted chopped walnuts or hazelnuts.

Cucumbers

With their thin skins and few seeds, seedless English cucumbers are ideal, but regular cucumbers work as well. To prepare a common cucumber, use a vegetable peeler to remove most of the cucumber peel. Slice the cucumber crosswise into 1/4-inch slices. Yields vary, depending on cucumber size, but you should get about 30 slices out of an average-size cucumber. Top each slice with any of the Quick Chicken Salads (pages 199–201) or Herbed Yogurt Cheese (page 266).

Chilled Cherry Tomatoes with Salt and Pepper Mix

Makes 1 pint

Cutting a small X in the bottom of each tomato allows a small portion of the tomato's juice to release, which, in turn, attracts the salt mixture.

1 tablespoon kosher salt

1 tablespoon coarse-ground black pepper

1 pint cherry tomatoes, each tomato's bottom X'd with the point of a paring knife

1. Mix salt and pepper in a small bowl; set aside.

2. Arrange tomatoes in a decorative bowl with the salt mixture served alongside for dipping. Serve.

Fennel Wedges with Anchovy Mayonnaise

Makes about 2 dozen

Anchovy paste adds depth of flavor and a subtle brininess to this dip without tasting fishy. If this dip does not appeal, serve these fennel wedges with the creamy Caesar-style Dip (page 263). Don't cut out the fennel core; otherwise the wedges will fall apart.

$^1/_2$ cup mayonnaise

1 tablespoon anchovy paste

2–3 tablespoons juice from 1 lemon

2 medium fennel bulbs, halved, each half cut into 6 wedges

Mix the mayonnaise, anchovy paste, and lemon juice in a small bowl. Transfer to a small serving bowl and serve with fennel wedges.

Radishes with Butter, Salt, and Pepper

Cutting a small X in the bottom of each radish creates a rough surface that readily attracts the butter, salt, and pepper. Buy radishes with attached greens, if available. Radish leaves, stripped down to even a few small sprouts, make it easy to pick them up.

2 bunches radishes, preferably with greens attached, trimmed so that only a small portion of stem remains; radish base X'd with a paring knife

4 tablespoons ($^1/_2$ stick) butter, softened

1 tablespoon kosher salt

1 tablespoon coarse-ground black pepper

1. Prepare radishes and arrange in a serving bowl or plate. Refrigerate until ready to serve.

2. Press softened butter into a small crock and set aside at room temperature.

3. Mix the salt and pepper. Set out radishes, softened butter, and salt mixture. Serve, having guests scrape radishes across the butter, then dip in the salt mixture.

Hearts of Palm with Quick Caesar-style Dip

Makes 3 to 4 dozen pieces

To turn this dip into a salad dressing, thin it with 2 to 3 tablespoons of buttermilk for a creamy Caesar-style dressing (makes about 1 cup of dressing).

$\frac{1}{2}$ cup mayonnaise

1 large garlic clove, minced

3–4 tablespoons lemon juice

$\frac{1}{4}$ teaspoon Worcestershire sauce

1 ounce (scant $\frac{1}{2}$ cup) grated Parmesan cheese

Ground black pepper to taste

2 (14.4-ounce) cans hearts of palm, drained; large hearts quartered, small ones halved

Mix the mayonnaise, garlic, lemon juice, Worcestershire, and cheese in a small bowl; add pepper to taste. Transfer to a small serving bowl. Serve with hearts of palm.

Celery Hearts with Blue Cheese Dip

Makes 1 to 2 dozen pieces

To turn this dip into a salad dressing, thin it with about $\frac{1}{4}$ cup buttermilk for a quick blue cheese dressing. (Makes about 1 cup of dressing.)

$\frac{1}{4}$ cup sour cream

$\frac{1}{4}$ cup mayonnaise

2 teaspoons red wine vinegar

$2\frac{1}{2}$ ounces ($\frac{1}{4}$ cup) crumbled blue cheese

Salt and pepper to taste

1 celery heart, separated into stalks, thin stalks left whole, larger stalk cut lengthwise into long, thin strips

1. Mix the sour cream, mayonnaise, vinegar, blue cheese, salt to taste, and a generous grinding of pepper in a small bowl; set aside or refrigerate, depending on serving time.

2. Arrange the celery hearts in a large glass or short vase; serve with dipping sauce.

A LITTLE SOMETHING MORE

The following group of appetizers is almost as effortless as the last set, but they may require a special trip to the grocery store for special herbs. They may need a little oven time, as with the chicken wings and potatoes. Or the vegetables require steaming rather than just setting out.

Parmesan Focaccia Sticks

Makes about 30 sticks

Like breadsticks, these focaccia sticks can be stored in an airtight container up to a month.

1 store-bought plain focaccia, sliced thin

2 tablespoons olive oil

3 ounces (¾ cup) grated Parmesan cheese

1. Adjust oven racks to the upper- and lower-middle positions and heat the oven to 400 degrees. Lay the focaccia slices on parchment-lined baking sheets. Brush them with oil, then sprinkle with cheese.

2. Bake until crisp and golden brown, 10 to 12 minutes. Cool to room temperature on baking sheets. Serve.

Chickpea Crisps

Served without the Cilantro-Mint Relish, a few pappadams can be fried and ready to serve in just a few minutes.

2 cups vegetable oil for frying   **1 box (4 ounces) Indian pappadams**

Heat the oil in a 9-inch skillet to 375 degrees. Line a colander or dish drainer with paper towels for draining pappadams. Working quickly and one at a time (each disk fries in about 10 seconds), drop a pappadam into the hot oil. As it unfurls and enlarges, turn it immediately with tongs, pressing it under the oil to ensure even cooking. Fry until golden, about 5 seconds longer. Transfer to colander and stand upright to drain. The pappadams can be fried several hours ahead. Serve as is or with Cilantro-Mint Relish (see below).

Cilantro-Mint Relish

Makes about ¹/₂ cup

³/₄ cup cilantro leaves

2 tablespoons mint leaves

¹/₄ cup water

1 jalapeño (pickled or fresh), halved, stemmed, seeded, and quartered

1 thin slice gingerroot

1 teaspoon red or white wine vinegar (or pickled jalapeño vinegar if using a pickled pepper)

¹/₂ teaspoon sugar

Salt to taste

Place all ingredients in a blender; blend on high power until the mixture is puréed, scraping down the sides of the jar with a spatula.

All-Purpose Yogurt Cheese

1 quart (32 ounces) plain yogurt

Pour the yogurt into a fine-mesh strainer or cheesecloth-lined colander set over a medium bowl. Drain until the yogurt reduces to 2 cups, about 2 hours. Discard the liquid and proceed with one of the recipes that follow.

Yogurt Spread with Cucumber and Garlic (Tzatziki)

Makes 1 1/2 cups

Serve this spread with a basket of warm pita bread.

1/2 recipe (1 cup) All-Purpose Yogurt Cheese

1 cucumber, peeled, halved, seeded and grated on a medium-holed grater

2 to 3 medium garlic cloves, minced to a paste

1/2 teaspoon red wine vinegar

Salt and ground black pepper

Olive oil for drizzling

Mix all ingredients except the olive oil in a medium bowl; cover and refrigerate. (Can be refrigerated overnight.) Transfer to a serving bowl, drizzle with olive oil, and serve.

Herbed Yogurt Spread

Makes 1 generous cup

Serve this spread with warm pita bread or cucumber slices.

1/2 recipe (1 cup) All-Purpose Yogurt Cheese

2 medium scallions, sliced thin

2 to 3 medium garlic cloves, minced

2 tablespoons minced fresh parsley leaves

2 tablespoons minced fresh basil leaves or 1 teaspoon dried

Mix all ingredients in a medium bowl; cover and refrigerate. (Can be refrigerated overnight.) Transfer to a serving bowl and serve.

Roasted New Potato Wedges

Makes 48 wedges

I often serve these potatoes with Sausages with Dijon Mustard.

12 new potatoes, washed and quartered

2 tablespoons extra-virgin olive oil

2 teaspoons dried rosemary

Salt and ground black pepper

1. Adjust an oven rack to the upper middle position and heat the oven to 450 degrees. In a medium bowl, toss the potatoes with olive oil, rosemary, and a generous sprinkling of salt and pepper. Arrange the potatoes cut sides up on a large jelly roll pan or baking dish, making sure not to overcrowd the pan.

2. Roast until the cut sides are a rich nutty brown, about 25 minutes. Transfer to a serving bowl and adjust seasoning, sprinkling with additional salt and pepper. Serve warm.

Sausages with Dijon Mustard

Serves 6 to 8

Don't limit yourself to the few sausages I've suggested. Any cased sausage—pork, chicken, or turkey—can be cooked, sliced, and served as an hors d'oeuvre. If sausages are low-fat, you may want to add a little oil, along with the water, so that they brown.

1 pound sausages in casing, such as Italian or chorizo

2 teaspoons mild-flavored oil, such vegetable or canola

Dijon mustard for dipping

1. Place sausages in a large skillet. Add ¼ cup of water, cover, and bring to a boil over medium-high heat. Steam until the sausages lose their raw color, about 5 minutes. Remove the lid; continue to cook until liquid evaporates and sausages start to fry. Continue to cook sausages, turning frequently, until browned, about 5 minutes longer.

2. Transfer to a cutting board. Let stand for a couple of minutes. Slice on the diagonal into bite-size pieces. Arrange sausages on a large platter with toothpicks and a bowl of mustard.

Roasted Chicken Wings

Not only do I serve these for hors d'oeuvres, I make them for dinner when I have extra preparation time. This quantity serves 4 to 6 as a main course.

3 pounds chicken wings (about 12 whole wings separated at the joint; wingtips discarded) or 24 wing halves

2 tablespoons vegetable oil

Salt and ground black pepper

Flavoring sauce (see below)

Adjust an oven rack to the upper middle position and heat the oven to 450 degrees. Set a large wire rack over a large foil-lined shallow roasting pan, such as a jelly roll pan. Toss the wings in a large bowl with oil, salt, and pepper. Arrange them in a single layer on the wire rack. Roast until golden brown, about 40 minutes. Dump the wings into one of the sauces below; toss to coat. Pour the rendered chicken fat from the pan; turn the wings directly onto the foil-lined pan and separate with a fork. Continue to cook until glaze has set, 8 to 10 minutes longer.

Buffalo Wings

If you like chicken wings super hot, increase the hot sauce to 10 tablespoons. Tabasco-brand hot sauce is hotter than many, so if using that brand, you may want to decrease the quantity of hot sauce.

FLAVORING SAUCE:

½ cup hot red pepper sauce

½ cup mayonnaise

Mix the hot sauce and mayonnaise in a large bowl; set aside until wings are ready to be tossed. Proceed with the Roasted Chicken Wings recipe.

Savannah Wings

FLAVORING SAUCE:

¼ cup ketchup

2 tablespoons light or dark
brown sugar

1 tablespoon cider or white vinegar

Mix all ingredients in a large bowl; set aside until wings are ready to be tossed. Proceed with the Roasted Chicken Wings recipe.

Bombay Wings

FLAVORING SAUCE:

1 tablespoon curry powder

¾ cup chutney, such as Major Grey's

Mix curry and chutney in a large bowl; set aside until wings are ready to be tossed. Proceed with Roasted Chicken Wings recipe.

Boston Wings

FLAVORING SAUCE:

6 tablespoons Dijon mustard

6 tablespoons maple syrup

Mix the mustard and maple syrup in a large bowl; set aside until wings are ready to be tossed. Proceed with Roasted Chicken Wings recipe.

Peking Wings

FLAVORING SAUCE:

½ cup hoisin sauce

4 teaspoons rice wine vinegar

2 teaspoons toasted sesame oil

Mix all ingredients in a large bowl; set aside until wings are ready to be tossed. Proceed with Roasted Chicken Wings recipe.

Just Desserts

There is no one technique for quick dessert, and certainly no one rhyme,

But anything is possible with a little money, work, or time.

As a rule, we don't eat dessert at our house during the week. When I entertain casually, I make naturally simple desserts. And when I have time, I make something more elaborate.

Much like a simple dinner, a simple dessert requires either a little time, a little effort, or a little money. The following selection of desserts reflects that philosophy. If you have time to let yogurt drain, a dessert like Sour Cream–Capped Yogurt (one of my favorites) is effortless. With just a few minutes' effort, desserts like chocolate turnovers or apricot tarts are possible. Money can buy pristine-quality figs and pears and good cheeses for desserts like Figs with Mascarpone and Toasted Almonds, or Blue Cheese with Pears and Honey, neither of which requires much time or effort.

PUFF PASTRY: YOUR NEW BEST FRIEND

When making desserts, I take shortcuts whenever I can. Although I haven't found a frozen pie shell or refrigerated pie dough I thought was good enough to serve to guests, there is hope for those who want to serve from-scratch pastry but don't have time to make and roll out the dough.

Commercial frozen puff pastry is decent-quality, ready-to-bake dough. With a sheet of puff pastry, I can make hassle-free tarts, turnovers, cookies, and pastry cups in minutes.

Since it's the only brand available at my grocery store, I use Pepperidge Farm. It comes two sheets of pastry to a box. If using the entire box, thaw both sheets. If using only one sheet, retape the package, close the box, and return it to the freezer. Let the frozen pastry sit for a few minutes to soften, but the dough doesn't have to thaw completely before you begin working with it.

If necessary, the dough can be rolled out before cutting it into various shapes. When making turnovers, for example, simply trim the dough and cut it into squares. For desserts where thinner pastry is preferred—tarts, for example—roll out the dough before cutting it.

Working with puff pastry over the years, I've learned a few tips. First, don't try to make one big fruit tart out of an entire sheet—the tart does not cook through. It may taste good, but the center will be gummy and limp. Instead, make either individual tarts or a long, thin rectangular one. Also, when making cookies or rounds do not twist the cutter once you've made the cut. Make clean cuts—press down and lift up. The twisting action may compress layers, causing them to rise unevenly. The same goes for cutting puff pastry. Make clean cuts with a long, sharp knife. And finally, make sure the dough stays cold.

Even with commercial puff pastry, tarts and turnovers may still take more time than you've got. If so, make cookies. They can be cut out in five minutes and they bake in ten minutes. Start by heating the oven to 425 degrees. While the oven preheats, lay a sheet of thawed but cold puff pastry on a lightly floured work surface. Sprinkle dough sheet generously with sugar. Depending on the occasion, use cookie cutters to stamp out dough shapes. Arrange them on a parchment-lined cookie sheet and bake until they are a glossy golden brown, about ten minutes. Serve these cookies with fresh or poached fruit.

Chocolate Turnovers

I often make a half batch of these and half batch of the jam variation (see recipe below), serving guests one of each. You need nothing more than a handful of fresh raspberries to complete this dessert. These turnovers can be made ahead and refrigerated or frozen. Simply pop them in the oven close to dessert time.

1 (17¼-ounce) package Pepperidge Farm puff pastry sheets

4½ ounces semi- or bittersweet eating chocolate, such as Ghirardelli, broken into ¼-ounce pieces

1 egg, beaten

Confectioners' sugar for dusting (optional)

1. Adjust oven racks to the upper and lower middle positions and heat the oven to 425 degrees.

2. Working with one sheet at a time on a lightly floured work surface, trim the puff pastry sheets to 9- by 9-inch squares, then cut each sheet into nine 3-inch squares.

3. Working with one square of dough at a time, place a portion of chocolate onto the lower corner, brush two edges of the dough with beaten egg, and fold the dough in half diagonally to form a turnover. Place each turnover on a parchment-lined cookie sheet, spacing them about 2 inches apart (about 9 per sheet). Brush the dough tops with egg wash.

4. Bake until golden brown, switching and rotating cookie sheets halfway through baking to ensure even browning, about 15 minutes. Cool the turnovers briefly. Sprinkle with confectioners' sugar, if desired, and serve immediately.

Jam Turnovers

Makes 18

Follow the Chocolate Turnovers recipe, substituting 1 teaspoon of jam for each ¼-ounce piece of chocolate in the turnovers.

Chocolate Tarts

Serve with suggested garnishes.

½ (17¼-ounce) package Pepperidge Farm puff pastry

½ cup heavy cream

4 ounces semi- or bittersweet eating chocolate, such as Ghirardelli, broken into ¼-ounce pieces

Walnut halves, chocolate-covered espresso beans, or fresh raspberries for garnish

1. Adjust an oven rack to the upper middle position and heat the oven to 400 degrees.

2. On a lightly floured work surface, roll the pastry to a 12½- by 14-inch sheet. Using a 3¼-inch biscuit cutter, cut 12 dough circles. Turn a 12-cup muffin tin (or two 6-cup muffin tins) upside down. Spray the pan bottom with vegetable oil cooking spray. Place each dough circle over a muffin cup, pressing the dough around the muffin tin so that it takes the shape of the cup. Place a jelly roll pan over the inverted muffin tin, then set a heavy skillet, such as cast iron, over the the pan to keep the pastry from puffing. Bake until golden brown, 8 to 10 minutes. Transfer to a cooling rack.

3. Meanwhile, microwave the cream and chocolate in a 2-cup Pyrex measuring cup covered with plastic wrap on high power until the cream boils, about 2 minutes; stir until melted. Pour about 1 tablespoon of the chocolate cream into each pastry shell. Let cool until just set, about 10 minutes.

Lemon Raspberry Tartlets

Follow step 1 in the recipe for Chocolate Tarts. Omit the chocolate cream and fill each tart with 1 tablespoon of store-bought lemon curd. Top each tart with a raspberry and serve.

Simple Fruit Tart

Almond paste, unlike sugar, adds sweetness to the tart without making more syrup.

1 (17¼-ounce) package Pepperidge Farm puff pastry sheets

1 egg, beaten

¼ cup sugar

4 ounces almond paste, grated on the coarse side of a box grater

Fruit of choice (see recipes that follow)

1. Adjust oven racks to the upper and lower middle positions and heat the oven to 425 degrees.

2. Working with one sheet at a time on a lightly floured work surface, cut each pastry sheet into four. Working one square of dough at a time, fold each side of the dough ½ inch, then unfold to form a crease. Brush the four corners of dough with egg wash, and then pinch each corner to form a four-cornered lipped square. Push up the edges to re-inforce lip. With a spatula, transfer dough squares to a parchment paper–lined cookie sheet, spacing them about 2 inches apart (about 4 per sheet).

3. Working with one square at a time, sprinkle the dough base with ½ teaspoon of sugar, then sprinkle with 1 tablespoon of grated almond paste. Arrange fruit of choice over the almond paste. Sprinkle the fruit with another tablespoon of almond paste, then sprinkle almond paste with another teaspoon of sugar.

4. Bake until golden brown, switching and rotating cookie sheets halfway through baking to ensure even browning, 15 to 20 minutes. Slide parchment with tarts onto a wire rack; cool briefly and serve.

Pear-Cranberry Tarts

½ cup dried cranberries

2 pears, cut lengthwise into ¼-inch thick slices, seeds and core removed from inner slices

Follow the recipe for Simple Fruit Tart, sprinkling 1 tablespoon dried cranberries, then arranging two pear slices over each dough base at the appropriate time.

Plum Tarts

16 small Italian prune plums, quartered and pitted

Follow the recipe for Simple Fruit Tart, arranging 8 plum quarters over each dough base at the appropriate time.

Fig Tarts

16 small figs, quartered (or 8–12 large figs, quartered)

Follow recipe for Simple Fruit Tart, arranging 8 fig quarters over each dough base at the appropriate time.

Apricot Tarts

If using large apricots, use only 1 to $1\frac{1}{2}$ per tart and cut them into sixths or eighths.

16 small apricots, quartered and pitted

Follow recipe for Simple Fruit Tart, arranging 8 apricot quarters over each dough base at the appropriate time.

Apple Tarts

**4 small apples, peeled, cored, and halved;
each half sliced thin, crosswise**

Follow recipe for Simple Fruit Tart, arranging slices from a half apple over each dough base at the appropriate time.

Raspberry-Blueberry Tarts

$\frac{1}{2}$ cup dried blueberries   **12 ounces ($\frac{3}{4}$ pint) fresh raspberries**

Follow recipe for Simple Fruit Tart, sprinkling 1 tablespoon dried blueberries then $\frac{1}{3}$ cup fresh raspberries over each dough base at the appropriate time.

ASSEMBLE-AND-SERVE DESSERTS

The following desserts may require a little refrigeration time before or after assembly, but essentially, they are effortless and foolproof.

Sour Cream–Capped Yogurt with Sugar and Berries

Serves 4

I was turned onto this dessert in the south of France. There, they spoon crème fraîche over fromage blanc. Since neither ingredient is common in this country, I tried this dish with sour cream and drained yogurt with excellent results.

1 quart plain yogurt, drained (see below)	1½ cups berries of choice
½ cup sour cream	8 teaspoons sugar or to taste

1. Drain the yogurt in a fine-mesh strainer until it is almost as thick as sour cream and has reduced to about 2 cups, about 2 hours. Refrigerate until ready to serve.

2. Just before serving, spoon a portion of yogurt onto each of 6 dessert plates. Stirring the sour cream to soften its texture, spoon 2 tablespoons over each portion of yogurt. Arrange berries around each mound of yogurt. Sprinkle each dessert with 2 teaspoons or more of sugar and serve.

Figs with Mascarpone and Toasted Almonds

If you don't sweeten the mascarpone, you can use these figs as a first course as well.

³/₄ cup mascarpone cheese (or two 3-ounce packages cream cheese)

1 tablespoon honey, plus ¹/₄ cup warmed for drizzling

12 large or 18 small fresh figs

¹/₄ cup toasted almonds, pistachios, walnuts, or hazelnuts

1. Mix the mascarpone and 1 tablespoon of honey in a small bowl.

2. Quarter the figs, cutting up to, but not through, the base, so that they look like an open flower.

3. Place a portion of figs on a dessert plate. Dollop each with a portion of sweetened cheese, sprinkle with nuts, and drizzle with the remaining honey. Serve.

Five-Minute Fruit Parfaits

4 cups berries (raspberries, blueberries, strawberries, blackberries), grapes, or peeled and sliced peaches

¹/₂ cup sour cream

¹/₄ cup brown sugar

Put ¹/₂ cup of fruit in each of 4 stemmed goblets. Top each with 2 tablespoons of sour cream, then sprinkle each with 2 teaspoons of brown sugar. Repeat layering of fruit, sour cream, and brown sugar. Refrigerate for at least 30 minutes and up to 2 hours. Serve.

Pizzelle with Whipped Cream and Berries

Pizzelle, or waffle cookies, can be found in the Italian cookie section of many grocery stores.

½ cup heavy cream

1 tablespoon plus 3 tablespoons sugar

½ teaspoon vanilla extract

8 pizzelle cookies, about 3½ inches in diameter

1½ cups mixed berries (pick 2 or more of the following: blueberries, raspberries, blackberries, gooseberries, red currants, or strawberries), stemmed and halved or quartered, depending on size

1. In a medium bowl, whip the cream with 1 tablespoon of sugar and the vanilla to soft peaks. Cover and refrigerate until ready to use.

2. Just before serving, place a pizzelle on each of 4 dessert plates. Dollop a portion of whipped cream on each cookie. Sprinkle a portion of berries over the whipped cream and around the cookie. Break each of the 4 remaining cookies in half and arrange with corners of each cookie set in whipped cream.

Hasty Pudding with Berries and Whipped Cream

Serves 4

3 cups mixed fresh or frozen berries, such as blueberries, raspberries, blackberries, or halved and quartered strawberries, depending on size

5 tablespoons sugar

1 cup heavy cream

1 teaspoon vanilla extract

6 slices firm white sandwich bread such as Pepperidge Farm, crusts trimmed, lightly flattened with hand and cut into approximate 1-inch squares

1. Mix the berries with 3 tablespoons of the sugar in a small bowl; set aside.

2. Whip the cream with the vanilla and remaining 2 tablespoons of sugar to soft peaks.

3. Arrange 3 or 4 bread squares in the bottom of each of 4 stemmed goblets. Spoon a portion of berries over the bread. Spoon some whipped cream over the berries. Repeat layering twice more, slightly reducing berry and whipped cream quantities with consecutive layers. Refrigerate until ready to serve. (Can be refrigerated up to two hours.)

Blue Cheese with Dates (Figs, Pears, or Peaches) and Honey

Serves 6

1 (6-ounce) wedge of blue cheese, cut into 6 wedges

18 medjool dates or fresh figs (or 3 ripe pears, halved, pitted, and cut into 6 wedges, or 3 peaches, halved, pitted, and cut into 6 pieces)

½ cup honey, warmed

Arrange the cheese and a portion of fruit on each of six dessert plates. Drizzle with warm honey and serve.

White Wine-Marinated Peaches

Serves 6

1½ cups fruity white wine

¾ cup sugar

½ teaspoon ground cinnamon

6 peaches, peeled, pitted, and cut into thick slices

1. Mix the wine, sugar, and cinnamon in a large serving bowl and let stand while peeling peaches.

2. Add the peaches to the wine and let stand at room temperature to blend flavors, about ½ hour. (Can be covered and refrigerated up to 2 hours.) Serve.

Red Wine-Marinated Pears and Raspberries

Serves 6

1½ cups light fruity red wine

¾ cup sugar

¼ teaspoon ground cloves

6 pears, peeled, cored, and cut into thick slices

1. Mix the wine, sugar, and cloves in a large serving bowl and let stand while peeling pears.

2. Add the pears to the wine and let stand at room temperature to blend flavors, about ½ hour. (Can be covered and refrigerated up to 2 hours.) Serve.

MENUS AT-A-GLANCE

Learning to put a meal together is a lot like learning to cook without a book. At first you follow other cooks' meal suggestions. But the more you meal plan, the more comfortable you are at figuring it out yourself. After all, no one knows your family's idiosyncrasies better than you do. In case you need a cheat sheet, here are sample menus to get you started. Most of the following menus can double as a weeknight or weekend supper or a casual dinner with friends. I've put in parentheses the desserts, appetizers, and/or first courses that could be added to dress up the meal.

(Parmesan Focaccia Sticks, page 264)
Steamed Asparagus with Vinaigrette, page 32
Pan-Seared Salmon with Lemon-Caper Pan Sauce, pages 185, 167
The Simplest Mashed Potatoes, page 225
(Hasty Pudding with Strawberries and Whipped Cream, page 279)

....

(Chickpea Crisps with Cilantro-Mint Relish, page 265)
(Puréed Cauliflower Soup, page 51)
Sautéed Chicken Cutlets with Curried Chutney Pan Sauce, pages 147, 170
Simple Couscous, page 244
Steam/Sautéed Green Beans, page 204
(Sour Cream-Capped Yogurt with Sugar and Berries, page 276)

(Warm White Bean Spread with Toast Rounds, page 248)
The Simple Tossed Salad with Goat Cheese and Beets, page 21
No-Hassle Roast Chicken with Roasted Potatoes and Onions, pages 196, 228
(Apple Tarts, page 275)

....

(Egg Rolls—I buy them uncooked from the local Chinese restaurant. They can be pan-fried, in a half inch of vegetable oil in a large saucepan right before dinner.)
Stir-Fried Chicken with Zucchini and Baby Corn, page 126
Simple Steamed Rice, page 235
Fresh Pineapple

Greek-style Dinner Salad, page 24
Pasta in Simple Tomato Sauce with Bacon,
    Bay Scallops, and Basil, page 89
Italian Bread
(Pizzelle with Whipped Cream and Berries,
    page 278)

. . . .

Radish-Parsley Salad with Vinaigrette, page
    33
The Big Fat Omelet with Cream Cheese and
    Caraway, page 58
(Jam Turnovers, page 272)

. . . .

(Roasted Mixed Nuts, page 254)
Braised Celery Hearts with Vinaigrette, page
    34
Pan-Seared Steak with Blue Cheese Butter,
    pages 178, 192
Potato Cake, page 222
(Chocolate Tarts, page 273)

(Quick Ravioli with Wild Mushroom Filling,
    page 111)
Pan-Seared Pork Tenderloin Medallions with
    Balsamic Vinegar Pan Sauce, pages 183, 165
Steam Sautéed Tender Greens with Raisins
    and Almonds, page 219
(Figs with Mascarpone and Toasted Almonds,
    page 277)

. . . .

The Simple Tossed Salad with Egg and
    Artichoke, page 21
Orzo with Spinach and Parmesan (recipe
    doubled for a main course), page 239
French Bread
(Five-Minute Fruit Parfaits, page 277)

. . . .

(Sweet Pea Spread with Bacon, page 249)
Sautéed Fish Fillets with Orange and
    Grapefruit Salsa, page 153, 171
Simple Rice Pilaf, page 232
Steam Sautéed Asparagus, page 203
(White Wine–Marinated Peaches, page 280)

INDEX

Roast Chicken with Dijon and
   Fresh Breadcrumbs, 196
Roast Chicken with Lemon,
   Rosemary, and Garlic, 197
Roasted Chicken Wings, 268-69
Saffron-Chicken Vegetable Soup,
   45
sautéed, 145-46
Sautéed Boneless, Skinless
   Chicken Cutlets, 147
for soups, 35-36
Stir-Fried Chicken, Snow Peas,
   and Water Chestnuts, 127
in stir-fries, 122
Tandoori-style Roast Chicken,
   198
in Tomato Sauce with Chicken
   and Red Peppers, 88
Chicken salad
   Chicken Salad with Hoisin
      Dressing, 201
   Classic Chicken Salad, 199
   Curried Chicken Salad with
      Raisins and Honey, 201
   Quick Chicken Salad, 199-201
   Thai Chicken Salad, 200
   Waldorf Chicken Salad, 200
Chickpeas
   Chickpea Crisps, 265
   in Chickpeas, Red Onion, and
      Feta Salad, 23
   in Frittata with Kale, 73
   in Sausage Soup with
      Mushrooms, Zucchini, and
      Chickpeas, 41
Chocolate Tarts, 273
Chocolate Turnovers, 272
Chutney Pan Sauce, Curried,
   170
Clams, in Tomato Sauce with Clams
   and Parsley, 86
Coleslaw, Quick, 28
Collard greens, with pasta, 93
Corn
   roasted, 195
   in Stir-Fried Chicken with Baby
      Corn and Zucchini, 126
Couscous, 229, 243-45
   Couscous with Apricots and
      Pistachios, 244
   Couscous with Currants and Pine
      Nuts, 245
   Couscous with Dried Cranberries
      and Almonds, 245
   Simple Couscous, 244-45

Crab
   in Big Fat Omelet, 63
   in Quick Lasagna with Asparagus,
      Crabmeat, Lemon Sauce, 119
Cranberry Tarts, Pear-, 274
Croutons, 18
Cucumber
   in appetizers, 260
   in Greek-style Dinner Salad, 24
   in Tomato, Cucumber Salad, 26
Curly endive, with pasta, 93
Curry
   Curried Cauliflower Soup, 51
   Curried Chicken Salad with
      Raisins and Honey, 201
   Curried Chicken Soup with
      Potatoes and Zucchini, 45
   Curried Chutney Pan Sauce, 170
   Steam/Sautéed Cauliflower with
      Curry Flavorings, 210

Dates, Blue Cheese with Honey and,
   279
Desserts, 270-80
   Apple Tarts, 275
   Apricot Tarts, 275
   Blue Cheese with Dates (Figs,
      Pears, or Peaches), Honey, 279
   Chocolate Tarts, 273
   Chocolate Turnovers, 272
   Fig Tarts, 275
   Figs with Mascarpone and
      Toasted Almonds, 277
   Five-Minute Fruit Parfaits, 277
   Hasty Pudding with Berries and
      Whipped Cream, 279
   Pear-Cranberry Tart, 274
   Pizzelle with Whipped Cream and
      Berries, 278
   Plum Tarts, 275
   Raspberry-Blueberry Tarts, 275
   Red Wine-Marinated Pears and
      Raspberries, 280
   Simple Fruit Tart, 274-75
   Sour Cream-Capped Yogurt with
      Sugar and Berries, 276
   White Wine-Marinated Peaches,
      280
Duck, Sautéed Duck Breasts, 156-57

Egg and Artichoke Salad, 21. *See also*
   Frittatas; Omelets
Eggplant
   in Pasta with Eggplant, Tomato,
      and Rosemary, 104

in Quick Eggplant Lasagna with
   Toasted Breadcrumbs, 116
in Stir-Fried Tofu with Haricots
   Verts and Eggplant, 129
in stir-fry, 123
Escarole
   with pasta, 93
   in White Bean Soup with Ham
      and Escarole, 39

Fennel
   in Fennel and Orange Salad,
      26
   Fennel Wedges with Anchovy
      Mayonnaise, 261
   in Frittata with Fennel and
      Fontina, 72
   in Pasta with Fennel, Red Onion,
      and Parsley, 103
   Steam/Sautéed Fennel, 211
Figs
   Blue Cheese with Figs, Honey,
      279
   Fig Tarts, 275
   Figs with Mascarpone and
      Toasted Almonds, 277
   in Sauterne Pan Sauce with Figs
      and Pistachios, 160
Fish. *See also* Salmon; Shellfish
   Fish Soup with Cabbage and
      Potatoes, 46
   fish steaks, 186-87
   Sardine Toasts with Mustard
      Butter, 258
   Sautéed Fish Fillets, 153
   seared, 176
   Seared Fish Steaks, 186-87
   shopping for, 9
   Smoked Trout with Horseradish
      Sour Cream, 257
   for soups, 36
Fried rice, 134-35
   Fried Rice with Celery, Peppers,
      and Mushrooms, 140
   Fried Rice with Chicken and
      Celery, 141
   Fried Rice with Pork and
      Mushrooms, 140
   Fried Rice with Shrimp and Water
      Chestnuts, 140
   Simple Fried Rice, 138-41
   Simple Steamed Rice for Stir-Fry
      and Fried Rice, 235
Frittatas, 65-75
   Big Frittata, 68

basics skillet
hearty drizzle
soothing
deglaze fresh
pan sauces
stir-fries wine
simmer roast
quick
chutney relish
vinaigrette
cutlets spreads
turnover bake